America and the automobile

America and the automobile: technology, reform and social change

Peter J. Ling

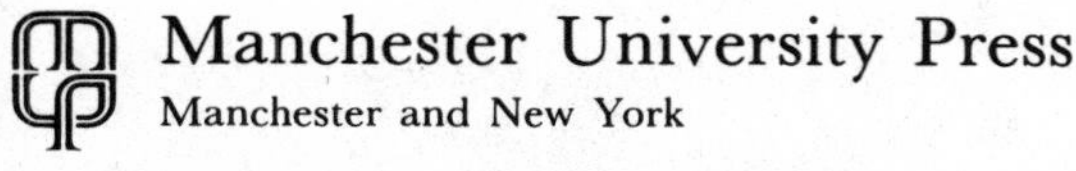

Manchester University Press
Manchester and New York

distributed exclusively in the USA and Canada by St. Martin's Press

Published by Manchester University Press
Oxford Road, Manchester M13 9PL, UK
and Room 400, 175 Fifth Avenue,
New York, NY 10010, USA

Distributed exclusively in the USA and Canada
by St. Martin's Press, Inc.,
175 Fifth Avenue, New York, NY 10010, USA

British Library cataloguing in publication data
Ling, Peter J.
America and the automobile: technology, reform and
social change, 1893–1923
1. United States. Economic growth. Role, 1893–1923 of road transport
I. Title
339.5'0973

Library of Congress cataloging in publication data
Ling, Peter J.
America and the automobile: technology, reform, and social
change, 1893–1923 / Peter J. Ling.
p. cm.
Includes bibliographical references.
ISBN 0-7190-2636-9
1. Automobile industry and trade — United States — History.
2. United States — Economic conditions — 1865–1918. 3. United States —
Economic conditions — 1918–1945. I. Title.
HD9710.U52L56 1989
338.4'76292'0973 - dc20 89-36257

ISBN 0-7190-2636-9 *hardback*

Printed in Great Britain
by Billings of Worcester

Contents

Acknowledgements

In the light of recent events, I look upon the publication of this book with understandable relief. In the wake of five house moves, three job changes, one house fire, and the addition of two children to the family, I can safely say that the book's completion depended on the generous support of others. Some of these debts I wish to acknowledge here.

As a British student of the United States, I am well aware of the extent to which I rely on the efforts of American scholars. The bibliography indicates specific contributions, but the guidance provided by the work of Paul Barrett, Michael Berger, William Bowers, David Gartman, David Hounshell, Joseph Interrante, Wayne Lewchuk, Clay McShane, Stephen Meyer, and Bruce Seely deserves mention. No work on the automobile in America can escape the influence of James Flink and John Rae and this is no exception. More generally, the work of David Harvey, Kenneth Jackson, Alan Trachtenberg and Robert Wiebe has shaped the interpretation offered here. Notwithstanding these attributions, the faults that remain are mine alone.

This study began as a doctoral thesis under the supervision of Dr. Robert Garson at Keele University and his encouragement sustained it. A Department of Education and Science research award and a small grant from the David Bruce Centre for American Studies at Keele enabled me to consult American sources. David Crippen of the Ford Archives, Dearborn and the staff of both the Detroit Public Library and the Michigan Historical Collections, Ann Arbor, were particularly helpful. Final publication was assisted by a grant from the Twenty Seven Foundation.

However, much of the research was undertaken solely with the private backing of family and friends, not least the willingness of Dr. Sheila Sheehan, M.D. of Detroit to employ an English historian as her medical secretary. In all my endeavours, my mother, Elizabeth Ling always had greater faith than I and my inlaws, the redoubtable Rubyan clan of Detroit underwrote several years of part-time research, partly, I suspect, because the Reverend R. P. Rubyan well remembered the trials of graduate work. Back in England, Mike Abramson, Anne Brownlow, and Dave Russell at Lancashire Polytechnic were supportive, while Edge Hill College provided essential clerical help during my brief time there. Judith Webster struggled with a 'user hostile' computer to prepare the typescript and Juanita Griffiths at M.U.P. proved patient when family illness interrupted the final tasks of page proofing and indexing.

Finally, an apology to my children, David, Martha and Gareth, for spending too much time behind a wall of books. Doubtless, they don't yet realize how often they brightened the gloom within my study. Their exuberance and good health was a tribute to my wife, Saronne Rubyan-Ling's willingness to take the strain of parenting while I escaped. The greatest sacrifices have been hers and so, I dedicate this book to her; a meagre accolade for one so lovely.

Peter J. Ling

Chapter 1

Introduction: Changing gear

The major contention of this study is that the automobile was the latest in a series of transport innovations designed to expedite the flow of goods and services and thus to accelerate the circulation of capital and its eventual accumulation. By linking the many constituent parts of the industrialised nation together, and particularly by incorporating hitherto self-sufficient or relatively isolated regions more fully into the cash economy, these technological innovations served to transmit the heightened pace of industrial production to other phases in the cycle of capital accumulation. The image of changing gears is intended to capture the character of this interconnectedness. Like the gears in a motor car, the transport network linked the scattered elements of production and consumption in a manner which sought to contain the stresses and inefficiencies which might otherwise retard the rate of return to capital. As in the automobile itself, these gears were designed to bring into synchronism elements which might otherwise move at such differing rates that the flow of the capital accumulation cycle would be impaired. In particular, automotive road transport could transmit the heightened pace of industrial production to more laggardly phases. This is evident when we consider the way in which the introduction of the automobile manifested the same tendencies of consolidation and centralisation in rural America as those advocated by Progressive social reformers.[1]

By incorporating the rural hinterland more effectively within industrial capitalism, the automobile and its infrastructural counterpart, highway improvement, strengthened the characteristic 'politics of accommodation' of the Progressive Era rather than the Populist 'politics of resistance'. The rural self-sufficiency remembered by the 'Wool Hat Boys' of Georgia gave way to the marketing patterns of metropolitanism in which the assumption of universal auto ownership created a new pattern for the distribution of social institutions which, in turn, made motoring essential. For Progressives, such an evolution was an inevitable passage to a new level of social efficiency at which technology compensated for social dislocation. As Robert Wiebe sensed more than twenty years ago, the Progressive mood was an ironically earnest pursuit of equilibrium in which a large and disparate set of Americans sought to check and re-balance a society which seemed on the verge of being rent asunder by the unregulated engine of capitalism.[2]

Wiebe, along with Samuel P. Hays, helped to launch an 'organisational synthesis' to explain the impetus behind the reform movements of the Progressive Era. Whereas Richard Hofstadter had characterised Populism as the revolt of the unorganised against the consequences of organisation, Hays and Wiebe saw Progressivism as an extension of organisation and of its bureaucratic spirit by members of what Wiebe termed the 'new middle class'. As we will endeavour to show, the automobile appealed quickly to this group who perceived that it could overcome both the deficiencies of a rural order weakened by isolation and the social problems of an urban society contaminated by pathological overcrowding. In both instances, the character of Progressive reform was crucially defined by its uneasiness with the collectivism of socialism and its acceptance of the institution of private property. Railroads, accordingly, were regulated rather than nationalised and mass transit was nagged to improve its services but left unsubsidised.[3]

The Progressive Era was also animated socially and politically by the recognition of the dangerous consequences of myopia among the powerful interests. As Wiebe and Kolko discovered, business, or more precisely large corporate business, perceived the dangers of *laissez-faire* and moved to contain them. This recognition that a stable market was preferable to the volatile conditions of cut-throat competition has been linked by business historians to the transition from family firm to public corporation. The latter employed the professional – managerial stratum which constituted the 'new middle class'. Less entrepreneurial and more dispassionate in their approach, these managers sought an orderly market-place in which the volatility of the trade cycle was restrained in their favour. This approach is evident in this study in such figures as Colonel Albert A. Pope, a bicycle manufacturer, eager to make roads fit for cycling, who strove to persuade railroad leaders and others that poor roads impeded the flow of goods, and thus reduced efficiency and increased the potential for financial crises caused by seasonal irregularities of distribution and consumption. A more striking example with which this study concludes is the Ford Motor Company in 1914 which introduced its celebrated Five Dollar Day as a sophisticated programme of personnel management designed to eliminate the high and costly turnover of labour at the Highland Park plant.[4]

However, the Progressive Era, although filled with examples of business attempts at self-regulation and associative initiatives, also marked a new phase in state involvement which was born of the recognition that the general interest was not readily addressed by the efforts of partisans. Clear testimony of this failure was given by the environment in which Americans lived. In the fields of both conservation and urban planning, therefore, the Progressives called for expert supervision to save the ruling order from self-destruction by regulating its activities. In their attempts to do so, they ran up against what Robert Fogelsong has defined as the 'property contradiction' and the 'capitalist – democracy contradiction' in American capitalism. The first of these contradictions inhibited rational planning in the general interest because the pursuit of any scheme for the general welfare had to be compatible with the basic premiss of American capitalism: namely, the sanctity of private property. Thus, municipal ownership of public utilities was complicated by the need to fix an equitable purchase price in the context of a judicial system usually sympathetic to the interests of private investors. Similarly, since the process of highway improvement entailed the same process of legal acquisition of property, a desire to keep condemnation and litigation costs down ensured that new widened streets were laid out through low-income neighbourhoods. The purpose of such projects was ostensibly to advance the well-being of the community in general. However, since these public plans were intended to sustain an inequitable system and benefited particular parties while adversely affecting others, this notion of impartiality and of pursuing the public interest had to be protected against challenge. This was where the planners confronted what Fogelsong terms the 'capitalist – democracy contradiction' whereby they had to protect and advance the interests of a minority ruling class within a system ostensibly committed to majority rule. Planners were therefore anxious to protect themselves from public accountability by serving on appointed boards rather than in elective office. They also strove to emphasise their technical and ostensibly objective qualifications for the task of planning and to avoid too close an association with vested interests. The examination of highway reform in Chapter 4 well-illustrates this process both in terms of the establishment of the technical authority of professionally staffed highway commissions and the careful avoidance of any direct endorsement of policies proposed by the automobile industry.[5]

In this sense, the professional and managerial groups, who also bought the first automobiles, were themselves gears in the social mechanism attempting to synchronise and harmonise, and to contain those tensions which might otherwise wreck the system entirely and require its wholesale reconstruction. This is a work, therefore, that stresses the conservative intentions of liberal reform. The introduction of the motor car and the subsequent rise of motoring as a social practice in the United States between 1893 and 1923 can be partly explained by the recurrent urge to extend the reach of the market and to secure a more rapid rate of capital accumulation inherent to a capitalist economy. Other capitalist economies exhibited similar trends and the process of motor car ownership diffusion was especially marked in those 'frontier' states – Canada, Australia, Argentina as well as the United States – where a mechanism was needed to incorporate large areas of low population density into the cash economy. However, this stark Marxian interpretation of the introduction of the automobile is too reductionist and mechanistic to be adequate on its own.[6]

Any attempt to comprehend the historical significance of the automobile's introduction must also consider its cultural as well as functional appeal. The reality of motoring both as a singular source of satisfaction to particular individuals and as a convenient expedient which surmounts the immediate daily pitfalls of poor community planning is too well-documented to be ignored. Motorists may have driven from A to B because under capitalism it was economical to build suburban homes and still enjoy economies of scale by grouping office blocks and industrial plants in specialised districts. But they also drove because the motor car allowed greater flexibility in terms of one's route than did public transit and because it ensured individual privacy which the latter did not. Encouraged by an elaborate promotional literature, motorists also found psychological satisfaction in car ownership and motoring which were not inherent to the process of transport. Motoring, ironically, became an agency of the antimodernism examined by T.J. Jackson Lears. Like other facets of this complex cultural phenomenon, motoring acted as a therapy which adjusted individuals to the strains of modern life by giving a sense of release while tying the people concerned more tightly to the existing order. To paraphrase Hofstadter's description of Populism quoted earlier, such anti-modernism represented the revolt of the organised against the strain of organisational life. In an impersonal, inter-dependent world of order, mechanised production and subordination, motoring could be embraced as an activity which relied upon personal initiative, gave a sense of independence, and permitted wilful individualism. It also rewarded personal artisanship, particularly for those who bought early automobiles and had to do their own repairs and add their own accessories. Thus, just as automotive transport provided the means by which American capitalism could gear up for a more rapid cycle of capital accumulation, so the same technology in its social and recreational use provided a therapeutic mechanism for individuals seeking to shift gears down to a slower more relaxed pace, even when that relaxation had as its preliminary the exhilaration of high speed.[7]

The signal importance of the automobile in this respect was that it was not simply a therapeutic mechanism potentially in itself but that it linked its owners to other palliatives of the new consumer culture. Capitalism is always seeking to reduce items to a cash basis and by the early twentieth century in the industrialised West, this process had added to the spectrum of goods and services a new range of commoditised experiences, notably movies but later to include that staple of contemporary life, the package holiday. For Americans in the first wave of mass car ownership up until 1923, discovering their own land's 'wide open spaces' was a key aspect of leisure which soothed discontent and so legitimised the social order.[8]

The richness of the historiography of the Progressive period reflects the complex and ambivalent character of the age itself. While some historians have seen the period as the triumph of organisational man whereby sovereign individuals, guided by reason and expertise, formed interlocking organisations to perpetuate order and increase efficiency, other historians have stressed the nostalgic impulse of leading public figures who were eager to restore the democratic Republic to its original virtuous condition as an organic community reliant upon voluntary associations and the inculcation of moral values. Industrialisation and urbanisation had produced such dramatic social changes that the former bastions of republicanism – the family business and the yeoman's farm – no longer wielded their former influence in the nation's affairs. Compounding these changes, the turn of the century witnessed the peak period of immigration to the United States inspiring once again the nativist fear that the new immigrants from southern and eastern Europe did not possess the qualities of earlier generations of transplants to the New World and so threatened to undermine the fabric of the Republic. This preoccupation with the moral character of the nation among public figures of the Progressive Era gave rise to a variety of social control efforts, ranging from Prohibition to less overt forms of hegemonic direction. Thus, the adoption of the automobile by Americans occurred in the midst of particularly earnest efforts to change people.[9]

Why, then, did the same generation that launched the 'noble experiment' of Prohibition also become the first to experience mass automobile ownership? Even setting aside the lethal possibilities of drink and driving, there were some respectable Americans who doubted whether the lower orders could cope with car ownership since in more senses than one, it took them away from their proper station in life. Bankers were among the first to express alarm at the spread of auto ownership since such expensive purchases depleted savings. The reports of traffic police in Chicago and Detroit also suggest that motoring by lower-class citizens was viewed as a distinctive social hazard. These misgivings persisted as credit sales of automobiles became the first of many consumer purchases on the instalment plan. As traffic congestion increased, transit managers, downtown businesses and middle-class motorists became disgruntled at the inconvenience of sharing road space with the low-income motorist. However, this discontent was overshadowed by the arguments against the motor car's remaining a rich man's plaything.[10]

Woodrow Wilson, as President of Princeton University, feared that the invidious distinction drawn by wealthy motorists by their conspicuous consumption of an expensive automobile was an incitement to class hatred. More widely held was the view that the mobility offered by the motor car would be beneficial to the citizen. Behind such thinking was the 'reform Darwinist' conviction that the betterment of individuals could be achieved by the improvement of their habitat. By breaking down the spatial barriers which rendered rural farm communities ignorant, economically uncompetitive, socially backward and institutionally under-resourced, Progressives sought to initiate a process whereby they would evolve in knowledge, efficiency, and social and cultural amenities. Similarly, in urban areas Progressives sought to extend middle-class standards of hygiene and morality to lower-class, frequently immigrant, Americans by dispersing the huddled masses of the densely populated wards of the great cities to detached single-family residences located further out from the city's core. In so far as auto ownership was viewed as a facilitator of these changes, Progressives were supportive of mass motoring. At the very least, it would enable individuals to escape temporarily from the confines of an inadequate home environment.[11]

In the pages that follow, we will examine the introduction of the automobile in terms of these two processes of changing the gears of an industrial capitalist economy and of changing people by changing the environment which they inhabit. Since rural Americans adopted the car as their principal means of transport earlier than did their urban compatriots, we begin our study by considering the incorporation of agrarian America at the turn of the century in which motoring as a social practice became a mechanism for the realisation of Progressive reforms intended to gear up rural life to modern industrial standards of efficiency. An essential part of this process was the reform of highway administration and a large-scale road-building programme. Illustrative of the role played by the professional–managerial strata of the middle class in securing the long-term structural needs of capitalism, the highway engineers emerged as astute political operators securing their own position and legitimising the highway improvement programme as a project in the interests of all. Next, by examining the traffic crisis in the nation's cities, we seek to show how transport innovation was linked to the objectives of decongesting the city for economic and social reasons. We consider how the inflexibility and indiscriminate nature of mass transit limited its appeal as industry relocated and as the privatism of middle-class domestic life condemned the unregulated intimacy of public transit. These, we argue, were the sources of demand for the automobile in the United States. The concluding chapters of the study seek to link these motivating forces to the means by which the automobile was made available to a large proportion of the American population by the early 1920s. We thus explore the paradox of a mode of production that restrained movement and stifled the individual worker's autonomy being set up to produce a vehicle to enhance movement and the sense of personal independence. We look at the exhibits and ethos of the Columbian Exposition of 1893 to see what it reveals about the origins of this coercive architecture of production and its counterbalancing, therapeutic culture of consumption. The internal combustion engine, it appears, was initially viewed as simply another power source for mass transit and when electricity demonstrated its effectiveness in this field, leading American capitalists sought to complement rail transit with electric road vehicles. However, the origins of mass production in the auto industry were more evident in the Fair's machine-tool, bicycle, and carriage and wagon exhibits with their emphasis on standardisation and flow production as well as in the Exposition's general plan with its stress on the subordination of individual units to create an integrated pattern. Ironically, the legacy of the Exposition for planners thus predisposed the planning profession to support mass transit as the principal means of urban commuting in the 1920s.

The study concludes with an analysis of developments in the auto industry itself, showing how the coercive architecture of production was designed by Ford managers to eliminate workers' control over production. By incorporating skill into the design of plant and machinery and eliminating wherever possible the moments of respite and choice in the worker's assigned task by a sustained flow of work, Ford engineers made the working environment itself coercive. As a recent sociological study of the assembly line explained:

> The line provides a superb form of technical and impersonal control for management. One of the latent functions of the line is that it makes it unnecessary for the foreman to act primarily as a 'pusher'. As one auto worker says: 'The average guy fighting the line has two foremen. One is the regular foreman, the other is the damn line itself'.[12]

Henry Ford himself admitted that 'we regulated the speed of men by the speed of the conveyor'. According to Ralph Epstein in his pioneering early study of the auto industry, the moving assembly lines represented managerial control over production extended to the extreme limit because 'Not only are the design, shape, size and quality of the work predetermined, but the rate at which each operation must be performed by the workers is rigidly controlled by a power machine, which even may be driven from another building.' The workers did not know when the gears might be changed to make the lines flow faster. The first moving assembly-lines at the Hudson Motor Car Company had a maximum line speed of three feet per minute. This had been achieved by a gradual acceleration, but if financial circumstances required it the pace of production could be rapidly raised. As new automobile sales slumped in the recession of 1920 – 21, Ford shut down its plant in January 1921 to ease a cash-flow crisis while it awaited an influx of coerced cash payments from Ford dealers across the country. Between 60 and 70 per cent of the workforce were shortly called back and obliged to man the lines at a pace which permitted a doubling of Model T production that year.[13]

Industrial journalist Harold W. Slauson had grasped the significance of the innovations at the Ford Motor Company shortly after their introduction in 1914. The 'human element' in the mass production system, Slauson declared, was 'in reality, the one *variable* that must be dealt with'. Accordingly, Slauson observed, the Ford plan's purpose was 'to hold this variable within as restricted limits as possible, and in fact, to reduce it to a *constant*'. Similarly, reflecting on the new methods of work introduced by American capitalists, the imprisoned Italian communist, Antonio Gramsci, declared them to be collectively 'the instrument used to select and maintain in stability a skilled labour force suited to the system of production and work'. Just as the gears in an automobile permit the smooth variation of the transmission of power, so the architecture of production and its accompanying strategies ensured that the workforce responded to managerial commands.[14]

Gramsci believed that the rationalisation of work in America was connected to the national prohibition of the sale of alcoholic beverage since the latter was intended to consolidate the efforts of industrialists to control the morality of their workers. Indeed, the sum of these initiatives constituted in his view 'the biggest collective effort to date to create, with unprecedented speed, and with a consciousness of purpose unmarked in history, a new type of worker and of man'. Observing from the vantage point of fascist Italy, Gramsci was more sensitive in this instance to the authoritarian paternalism within Progressive efforts to find a stable basis for industrial capitalism. He overlooked therefore the extent to which both the Five Dollar Day pattern of moral supervision and the imposition of Prohibition were defeated, or at least, superseded by the subtler social control methods of a culture of consumption which did not share the repressive psychology of redemptive self-denial of the earlier initiatives. Aldous Huxley's dystopian novel *Brave New World* shared Gramsci's insight that the coming of mass production, courtesy of 'Our Ford', marked an attempt to manufacture new types of man, but from Huxley's English perspective, the simple dictatorship appropriate for the lowest, genetically engineered human forms had to be supplemented with other forms of subordination for the middle ranks for whom the reality of submission was softened by the therapy of 'soma' holidays.[15]

Despite Gramsci's insistence that the appetites of labour had to be curbed by capital, the practice of American capitalism in the 1920s was inconsistent in this regard. While some capitalists complained that workers were buying cars before homes and were dissipating their energies emulating movie stars, others saw these new consumer habits as remunerative to themselves in terms of the expanded market for goods which they created, and also as potentially a hitherto ignored source of stability. Given the continued unwillingness of capitalists to share the benefits of enhanced productivity equitably with their workers in the form of generally high wages, the key to mass participation in a therapeutic culture of consumption lay in the expansion of credit. This enabled workers to secure items that were widely advertised as having an enriching effect on individual or family life and thus legitimised the strain of work, according to the traditional moral economy of pain and pleasure: namely, endure, so that you may subsequently enjoy. Furthermore, this precarious acquisition of extolled goods also served to reinforce a sense of dependence by sharpening the contrast between the lives of the employed and those of the jobless. Thus, the consumer culture of which the automobile was such a conspicuous feature in the 1920s served both to facilitate the smooth acceleration of capital accumulation in a boom and to inhibit labour's desire to challenge the hegemony of capital.[16]

The image of changing gears which I have used to convey the significance of the automobile in Progressive America has one further aspect. In American car culture, the practice of changing gears was increasingly displaced in the post-World War II period by automatic transmission. By selecting the image of changing gears, this study stresses the human intervention essential to technological development. Despite the efforts of Ford and other auto industrialists, auto workers retained the potential for resistance, and were destined to find within the rationalised workplace a new basis for class-consciousness. The automobile that brought farmers more frequently to the chain store to purchase items formerly made at home was also essential to their efforts to organise, as the Non-Partisan League showed in the Great Plains. Similarly, the automobile that allowed for suburban flight and reinforced the separation of the politics of the workplace from the politics of the home neighbourhood, also sustained the organic networks of ethnic affiliation by providing a flexible means of transport. Ultimately, what changed America between 1893 and 1923 was not the auto, as one Middletown resident of the 1920s believed, but rather Americans under capitalism.[17]

Notes

1 For the social production of the built environment, see D. Harvey, *The Urbanization of Capital*, 1985. For the notion of incorporation as a social process dominating late-nineteenth-century US history, see A. Trachtenberg, *The Incorporation of America*, 1982.

2 *See Chapter 2, below; B. C. Shaw, The Wool Hat Boys*; 1984. S. Hahn, *The Roots of Southern Populism*, 1983; J. Interrante, 'You can't go to town in a bathtub: automobile movement and the re-organization of rural urban space 1900–1930', *Radical History Review*, XXI, Fall, 1979, pp. 151–68; R. Wiebe, *The Search For Order*, 1967.

3 S. P. Hays, *The Response to Industrialism*, 1957; R. Hofstadter, *The Age of Reform*, 1955; Wiebe, op. cit.; see Chapter 5 below.

4 R. Wiebe, *Businessmen and Reform*, 1962; G. Kolko, *The Triumph of Conservatism*, 1963; A. D. Chandler, *The Visible Hand*, 1977; see Chapters 3 and 6 below.

5 R. L. McCormick, 'The discovery that business corrupts politics: a re-appraisal of the origins of progressivism', *American Historical Review*, LXXXVI, April, 1981; S. P. Hays, *Conservation and the Gospel of Efficiency*, 1959; R. Fogelsong, *Planning the Capitalist City*, 1986, pp. 24–5; see Chapter 4 below for my discussion of highway policy.

6 Bardou *et al, The Automobile Revolution*, 1982, Table 6-1, p. 112.

7 T. J. Jackson Lears, *No Place of Grace*, 1981, pp. 55, 304; cf. W. Belasco, *Americans on the Road*, 1979, p. 5.

8 Belasco, op. cit., passim; P. Schmitt, *Back to Nature: Arcadian Myth in America*, 1969; R. S. Lynd and H. M. Lynd, *Middletown*, 1929.

9 R. Crunden, *Ministers of Reform*, 1982; D. Danhom, *'The World of Hope': Progressives and the Struggle for an Ethical Public Life*, 1987; J. Higham, *Strangers in the Land*, 1955.

10 J. Flink, *The Car Culture*, 1975, pp. 29, 145; Detroit Police Department, *The Story of the Detroit Police 1916–1917*, 1917, pp. 129–62, Burton Historical Collection, Detroit Public Library; P. Barrett, 'Mass transit, the automobile and public policy in Chicago, 1900–1930', unpublished PhD, University of Illinois, Chicago, 1976, p. 155; see also Chapter 4 below.

11 See Chapters 2 and 3 below.

12 B. J. Widick, ed., *Auto Work and its Discontents*, 1976, pp. 76–7, quoted by D. Gartman, *Auto Slavery*, 1986, p. 97.

13 H. Ford, *Moving Forward*, 1931, p. 39; R. C. Epstein, *The Automobile Industry*, 1928, p. 33; Gartman, *Auto Slavery*, p. 96; S. Meyer, *The Five Dollar Day*, 1982, p. 197.

14 H. W. Slauson, 'A ten-million dollar efficiency plan', *Machinery*, Oct. 1914, p. 86, quoted by Meyer, op. cit., p. 95; Gramsci, quoted by Gartman, op. cit., p. 207.

15 Gartman, loc. cit.; A. Huxley, *Brave New World*, 1932.

16 Cf. R. W. Fox and T. J. Jackson Lears, eds, *The Culture of Consumption*, 1983; and R. W. Edsforth, 'A second industrial revolution: the transformation of class, culture and society in twentieth century Flint', PhD thesis, Michigan State University, 1982.

17 R. Lynd and H. M. Lynd, *Middletown*, 1929, p. 251.

Chapter 2

The end of the 'island' community

In 1890, 65% of the US population lived in rural areas; by 1920, the proportion had fallen to 44% and would decline further. Despite this demographic shift, rural America was crucial to the early car industry. The US automobile industry overtook its chief foreign rival, France, in 1905, when a glut of cars for the urban luxury market encouraged auto makers to design strong durable vehicles for the farmer. The celebrated Ford Model T epitomised the rugged moderately-priced motor car which appealed to an increasingly prosperous agricultural sector. By 1909, the industry acknowledged that it was relying on two great sources of demand – 'the farmer and the man with the middle-class income'.[1]

The farmers who were able to invest in cars between 1905 and 1925 represented the survivors of a traumatic process of adjustment to the rise of corporate capitalism. While there remained enclaves of subsistence farming in areas of the Midwest and more especially in Appalachia and the South, in general the market economy dominated by 1905, as it had in the West and South-West from the onset of farm settlement after the Civil War. In the West, especially in California, agri-business was a more accurate description of the pattern of land use because the stress was upon the farm as a capitalist enterprise. These capitalist relations of production were evident in the increasing concentration of land ownership, capital, and of control of vital natural resources (water supplies) and in the production of a growing agricultural surplus for a global market.[2]

Fittingly, therefore, it was the rich agri-business state of California which led the nation in its ratio of population to car registrations both in 1910 and in 1929 and over the same period the crop belts of the agricultural states of the trans-Mississippi West continued to be the next best market for cars. Even the South, which lagged behind other agricultural regions in its adoption of the automobile, increased its car registrations per capita during the decade 1910 to 1920 more rapidly than did the industrial belt of the Mid-West, New England and Middle Atlantic states. By 1927, car consumption was lowest in American cities of 100,000 population or more (54 per cent of families) while it was highest (over 60 per cent) in towns of under 1000 population.[3]

This spectacular expansion of car ownership in the countryside, and with it the use of stationary gasoline engines on the farm, occurred in a society which was still coming to terms with an earlier wave of inventions – railroads and steamships, agricultural machinery and chemicals. The opening up of Western settlement by the railroad and of world markets by steamships, the raising of farm productivity by mechanisation and chemical fertiliser strengthened a new 'social structure of accumulation' by raising the capital costs of farming, and by reducing the unit price of agricultural commodities. These trends favoured the agri-businessman at the expense of the yeoman family farmer. The credit squeeze of the early 1890s, in particular, produced many foreclosures which relegated former family farmers to tenantry. At the same time, the perils of reliance upon a single crop or a single carrier revealed to the farm community its impotence within the national corporate market-place. This sense of exasperation was one of the material foundations for Populism.[4]

Populism was a multi-faceted movement. It included, especially in the South, a radical politics of resistance to the penetration of a capitalist market economy into a society of independent producers with important communal traditions of common grazing and hunting rights. However, Populism also took the form of an electoral 'politics of inclusion' in which different factions of the bourgeoisie – industrial, agrarian and financial – competed to be included in a capitalist market-place on the best terms possible. This is especially true of non-Southern Populism. As a precondition for the diffusion of car ownership, Populism is more relevant in terms of its accommodationist strand, which with the return of prosperity was able to pursue its objectives of cultural self-assimilation into an industrial capitalist economy via the various Progressive movements. Significantly, Populism was a minor movement in a state like California whereas Progressivism under Hiram Johnson was a major force. It was the temporarily downhearted entrepreneurial farmers within Populism, who had retained their land in the desperate 1890s, who were able to buy automobiles early and to use them to modernise their local communities. These Populists had also believed that an expanded money supply would facilitate the circulation of commodities. They were seeking ways to bridge the gap between their buying in one place and selling in another. Their concern led them to chafe at the costs within the circulation process. They complained about the storage charges of grain elevator companies and the commissions of cotton factors, lawyers and bankers, and they railed most of all against the cost of transportation. Not surprisingly, therefore, they adopted the automobile once it had demonstrated its practicality in rural conditions. The motor truck and tractor were also embraced when they had been improved sufficiently during World War I. However, in the interim, motoring gave an important sense of inclusion.[5]

Rich or poor, all American farmers of the 1890s would have conceded the validity of Marx's observation that: 'The product is really finished only when it is on the market'. Any reduction in the cost of transportation was important to an agricultural sector which had become dependent upon the market-place because crops had become useful principally in terms of exchange value. In the words of one Southern farmer: 'Cash is good to eat'. This reliance upon exchange rendered the physical means of exchange – transport – a crucial cost factor. Throughout the post-Civil War period, this imperative expressed itself in frantic efforts to get rail links and, once these had been secured, in rural anger at the tariffs levied by carriers. In the industrial sector, these distribution costs were offset by a reduction in the time taken up by production. Indeed, speed of 'throughput' became a central criterion of efficiency in industry, beginning in such enterprises as flour milling, brewing and meat packing. The farmer, in contrast, was less capable of producing his commodities more quickly and so, instead, strove to produce more. The latter was a precarious strategy for success, as was demonstrated by the impact of falling prices due to increased supply in the early 1890s. Transport was especially vital for producers of fresh produce which would spoil rapidly, a factor which intensified the sense of dependence upon the carriers and also the wish for some other means of reaching the market. Appropriately, the automobile found favour quickly in dairy areas such as Wisconsin and in states producing fruit and vegetables such as California and New Jersey. Eventually, the term 'truck farming' testified to the importance of transport in this branch of agriculture.[6]

Long-distance trade, because it separates production and consumption by a relatively long time interval, provides one of the material bases of the credit system. In effect, the credit system allows money to circulate in space independently of its equivalent commodities. It also places finance capitalists in a powerful position similar to that enjoyed by railroad leaders. Significantly, agrarian protests in the 1890s pointed specifically to these two allied groups as the enemy of the independent farmer – producer and in the Omaha Platform of 1892 called upon their elected representatives to reduce the power of 'Goldbug' bankers and railroad barons by the establishment of a credit system tailored more specifically to agricultural needs and by public ownership of the railroads. As we shall see in the next chapter, Populists also called for highway improvement which would provide an alternative or a complement to the railroad network.[7]

For those farmers and small-town dwellers, anxious to be included in the capitalist system on better terms, road transport innovation, like bimetallic currency, represented a prospect of special significance. Bryan's defeat in 1896 postponed hopes of bimetallism, but the possibility of road improvement remained, provided these Progressive pursuers of rural incorporation could overcome those other members of the rural community who remained wedded to the system of local highway administration whereby largely unimproved roads were maintained by the community itself. Thus, ambitions for social mobility tended to produce a desire for enhanced physical mobility. Of the many utopian novels published in the wake of Edward Bellamy's *Looking Backward* (1888), one of the few to include the automobile was Milan C. Edson's *Solaris Farm* (1900). Dedicating his work to the 'improvement of agriculturalists as a class', Edson offered a vision of scientific farming communally organised but with industrial-style flow production in the potting shed. The use of electric cars in the novel encourages a national programme of road improvement and thus overturns the tyranny of the railroads.[8]

Edson's hopes of uplifting the agricultural community were representative of the Progressive programme of social reform. Insignificant in itself, his novel was a minor fragment of a vast literature produced by an emergent corporate liberalism which was eager to adjust the different elements within the nation in the interests of morality and efficiency in order to ensure social stability. This would require a more active and responsive state to meet communal responsibilities to individuals and underprivileged groups. The fulfilment of these moral obligations by state agencies would legitimise the existing social order and so encourage all classes to maintain and increase the efficiency of that society. However, the efficient organisation of public and private enterprises within this Progressive society depended upon the delegation of authority to experts whose special training allegedly gave them the objectivity to perceive the full scope of society's problems as well as the technical competence to solve them.[9]

The return of prosperity gave Progressive Americans the opportunity to readjust society as the support for Populism waned. The supply of agricultural produce remained fairly stable between 1897 and 1916 while the demand from the urban industrial markets increased. To farmers in the crop belts of the Midwest, this meant prosperity. Elsewhere, localities and entire regions, particularly in the South, had little share in what has been called 'the golden age of American farming'. In general, however, farmers received steadily higher prices for their products and in addition land values rose sharply. It was this plenty which provided the financial means and the confidence necessary for farmers to buy automobiles.[10]

Despite this agricultural prosperity, concern over the state of rural America remained an important feature of social and political discussion in the Progressive Era, in part because of the disproportionate electoral influence of rural areas to which politicians were responsive. Nevertheless, the rural constituency was shrinking: from 63.9 per cent of the nation in 1890 to 53.7 per cent in 1910, to roughly 44 per cent in 1920. The proportion employed in agriculture itself fell still more sharply. In the 1870s half the nation's workforce was in farm occupations, but fifty years later, less than a quarter of America's gainfully employed tended the soil. Those who remained farmers continued to accrue debts. As the Midwestern farm population dropped between 1900 and 1920, the size and the value of farms increased and so, too, did the difficulties of moving up the tenure ladder from labourer to farm owner. Farm indebtedness increased 163 per cent between 1910 and 1920. The growing demand for food from the nation's cities, the shrinking rural population and the chronic indebtedness and poverty of much of rural America indicated to Progressive leaders, such as Theodore Roosevelt, that the old order was no longer functioning in the countryside and that a systematic adjustment of rural society was required.[11]

This old order had been sustained by its isolation, a flaw alluded to repeatedly in Progressives' discussions of American rural life. In their view, the balanced stable progress of the nation required that this isolation be ended, and by the time the United States became the world's first true car culture, it had been ended. By 1927, a study of the automobile's impact on retail centres declared that the isolated frontier community in the agricultural states had passed away and concluded that while there were other factors, 'the motor car has been not only the most important single factor but also an agency facilitating the action of other forces working to this end'. This echoed the comment of a Muncie, Indiana, resident who believed that the social changes of the three decades prior to 1924 could all be attributed to the 'A-U-T-O', thus exemplifying the popular tendency to grant technology an autonomy of action it does not possess. In the pages that follow, I will argue that the changes associated with the onset of rural motoring were abetted by the cumulative weakness of rural institutions by that time and by the active concurrent desire of a 'Progressive' middle class who were eager to rebuild rural American society according to ideals of efficiency derived from industrial capitalism.[12]

Central to Marx's analysis of capitalism was its need for a constantly expanding market, and equally vital to his consideration of the United States was the belief that the process of capitalism was given greater latitude there by the potential for geographical expansion which acted as a temporary safety-valve. The rapid settlement of the West and the associated construction of a national rail network in the period between 1865 and 1925 testified to the force of this impulse to form a larger market: a larger arena for investment, accumulation and labour recruitment. In the countryside, the logic of agricultural mechanisation under capitalism encouraged the sparse settlement, the social consequences of which the Progressives deplored. It was as much the pursuit of agri-business by the American farmer as bad roads and the limited range of horse transport which left the average farm family in 1920 three miles from the local church, five miles from the nearest market, six miles from the high school and the family doctor, and fourteen miles from the nearest hospital. Moreover, the quality of most of the service institutions within the daily travel radius of the farm family was increasingly adjudged to be substandard.[13]

The Progressives were convinced that isolation eroded rural institutions. Government surveys noted the psychological distress of farm wives. Other commentators pondered the roots and consequences of a steady exodus of rural youths to the city. Social institutions such as the rural school and the rural church, were subject to study by social reformers. Perceived as potential anchors for the community, both school and church were commonly deemed inadequate to modern needs by the Progressives. Noting the 'complete and fundamental change in our whole economic system within the past century', the Country Life Commission of 1908 observed that the adjustment to 'progress', by which they meant industrial capitalism, in all farm occupations 'has been tardy, because the whole structure of a traditional and fundamental system has been involved'. In particular, the individualism of the American farmer which reduced his capital resources and market leverage, had handicapped the agricultural sector by slowing the development of corporate institutions. The commission called for efforts to stimulate 'effective co-operation' among farmers, to put them on a level with the organised interest with which they had to do business. In doing so, it implied that the injustices endured by rural Americans were partly the inevitable penalties inflicted upon laggards in the evolutionary struggle.[14]

In a typical expression of the Progressive impulse to reconcile old and new values, Theodore Roosevelt introduced the Country Life Commission's report by declaring that the farm population stood 'for what is fundamentally best and most needed in our life', yet endorsed the commission's demand for 'nothing more nor less than the gradual rebuilding of a new agriculture and a new rural life'. What was best and most needed, it transpired, was the transformation of rural American society so that it conformed to industrial standards. The envisaged agrarian society would require new leadership. The commission stressed that existing farmers were ignorant and hence contributed to such problems as soil erosion, poor highways, inadequate credit and generally unsatisfactory business arrangements. The new farm leadership would not be drawn from this tradition of inefficiency but would be trained by outside experts and guided by their example. The county extension service had begun in 1903 with the US Department of Agriculture's organisation of 'demonstration' farms. By 1909, the colleges of agriculture, state experimental stations, the national farmers' associations and other professionally staffed agencies had joined in the process of instruction. Indicative of the underlying goal of social legitimation behind these efforts, in 1911 the American Bankers' Association established its own 'Committee on Agricultural Development and Education' in an attempt to improve banker–farmer relations and make farmers 'more successful producers, a better credit risk, and a more contented and prosperous people'. It would then be appropriate for such successful and prosperous farmers to buy automobiles on credit whereas currently it was viewed by rural bankers as imprudent.[15]

These efforts to modernise the agricultural sector have tended to be neglected in favour of the more enduring efforts to regulate 'Big Business' and establish standards for consumer protection in the industrial sphere. It is true that Progressive social reform efforts began in the cities where the problems of adjustment to rapid change were most conspicuous. Indeed, Progressives drew upon the nostalgic image of the intimate farm community with its extended family structure in their condemnations of the alienation and anonymity of urban life. However, by the time the automobile was introduced, these features of American rural culture had already been undermined by the demographic attrition stemming from rapid speculative settlement and mechanised cash-crop farming. The more widely scattered the general rural population, the more attenuated became the ties of kinship. One of the 'big' events of Edward Eastman's boyhood, he recalled, was the annual visit to 'grandpa's house' which was less than an hour's distance away by car in 1928, but which had previously taken a full day of discomfort in a buggy pulled by a worn-out farm-horse. The significance of such a visit, however, lay not simply in the barrier of distance to be overcome, but in the paucity of competing social attractions. One rural sociologist remembered that in the days before motoring: 'it was almost impossible to find a group of rural boys of approximately the same age who got together often enough to make organized games possible'. Turn-of-the-century Tom Sawyers were lucky to find a Huck Finn.[16]

Even before car ownership extended the spatial perimeter of the rural community, its intimacy and neighbourliness had faltered. Traditional neighbourly ties, rooted in a shared sense of place and a common way of life, as well as family ties were already giving way to new relationships. The motor-car merely reinforced an incipient pattern, whose failings were confirmed by the psychological distress found among farm wives and the steady flow of rural youth to the towns and cities. In this sense, the automobile fulfilled a demand for a social alternative to the dysfunctional communal life of the open countryside by 1910. For, as one observer noted, 'Today, the automobile enables farmers to pick their associates much as do the people in the cities. The intimate friends may be miles away.' To an extent these new friendships became more specific as the rural inhabitant's geographical breadth of acquaintance increased: there were different friends for different occasions: friends to shop with, friends from church, 'drinking buddies' and 'work mates', rather than simply family and neighbours: a specialisation more urban and industrial in character than the enforced intimacy of the agrarian tradition.[17]

Social reformers, worried especially by the loss of rural population to the cities, attributed the migration to the failure of rural social institutions. For reformers, the rural school epitomised these deficiencies resulting from rural isolation. With acutely limited resources, it typically served eight to thirty pupils whose ages spanned all eight primary grades. Housed in a single-room building, which was commonly poorly heated in winter and badly ventilated in summer, the school was poorly equipped in all other respects too, depending for its educational success upon a solitary teacher, who was usually female and always underpaid. In the circumstances, technical training in agricultural science was virtually unknown, but perhaps the gravest defect of this elementary school was that it led nowhere. Rural areas possessed neither the youth nor the revenue within their school districts to support their own high schools. Town high schools were located at too great a distance in horse-and-buggy terms to permit a farm child to commute. As well as the cost of boarding in town during term-time, the rural student was subject to non-resident tuition fees. Moreover, the instruction received was likely to be geared to non-agricultural careers. Thus, the Progressive goal of stabilising the farm population at a new level of efficiency was undermined by the high-school curriculum. It is less clear whether the majority of farm families resented a pattern of schooling that offered their children a potentially wider choice of career than simply farming.[18]

Indeed, even before the motor car, the weaknesses of the rural school were encouraging a townward drift among families which was then reinforced in the children by the nature of the town school's curriculum. Moreover, Progressive efforts to improve the quality of education as measured by the standards of an industrial society tended to accelerate the out-migration from rural areas. The educational reform movement in the New South illustrates this process. In 1900, 82 per cent of the Southern population was classified as living in rural areas. Despite several bold ventures, the South's industrial growth had failed to keep pace with that of the North or West. Indeed, it held a smaller portion of the nation's investment in terms of capital and plant in 1900 than it had before the Civil War. Its inhabitants were poor, having a per capita income of $509; less than half of the US average of $1165. If any section of the United States epitomised what the Country Life Commission referred to as 'the results of the unequal development of our contemporary civilization', it was the South.[19]

The Country Life Commission urged its supporters to picture for themselves 'a new rural social structure, developed from the strong resident forces of the open country' and then, to 'set at work all the agencies that will tend to bring this about'. The New Southerners gave themselves the same objectives, though they were less certain of the strength of the residents of the open country. They believed blacks to be inherently restricted in their social potential while the rural whites were enervated by what Walter Hines Page termed a 'smothering atmosphere' of 'old thoughts'. Like the immigrant workers at Ford's Highland Park plant, these rural Americans in the Progressives' view would have to be instructed in the 'right' way to work and the 'right' way to live.[20]

Leaders of the New South movement used school reform as a primary step in their efforts to reshape the habits of Southern working people. Backed by John D. Rockefeller, Jnr., who also funded the agricultural extension services in other regions, the Southern Education Board (SEB) began its work in North Carolina in 1901. Its overriding goal was typically Progressive in tone: 'to raise the masses to a higher plane of life'. As part of this work of uplift, an auxiliary organisation, the Women's Association for the Betterment of Public School-Houses (WABPS), devised ways of making the buildings themselves more attractive, sanitary and comfortable places. In pursuit of their goal, both the SEB and the WABPS sought to persuade individual counties to consolidate small school districts. This would provide the fiscal and administrative basis for schools well-equipped to train Southern children 'to fill the position defined by circumstances' without going 'so far as to make [them] discontented with their lot or [to] fill their minds with vain ambition'. The latter dangers were particularly feared by Southern Progressives in the case of blacks. However, one considerable obstacle to school consolidation was the range of limited transport on poor roads. A US government bulletin of 1914 explained that for pedestrians the feasible school catchment area was within a 3-mile radius. Horse-drawn vehicles extended the limit to 6 or 7 miles, but a motor bus could convey pupils from 15 to 20 miles away, multiplying the possible area served by a single school by as much as sixty-four times. Automotive technology could thus fulfil Progressive policy.[21]

In general, the teaching profession, as members of the professional – managerial stratum that comprised the 'new middle class', advocated consolidation on the grounds of efficiency. Like the nation's business leaders, school administrators characterised efficiency as the maximum use of fixed capital investment. Thus, a large school, like a large factory, was more efficient because it commanded greater fiscal resources and utilised the educational materials provided to best advantage by organising instruction in an integrated building with specialist teachers steadily at work on the product, the pupils themselves. By 1923, advocates of school consolidation also pointed to studies indicating that children at consolidated schools had better test scores than their counterparts in single-teacher schoolrooms. Like the integrated factory, the consolidated school produced a better standard product. The only remaining defence of the local school was the barrier of distance and this was demolished by the increased use of the automobile. However, one must stress that the Progressive wish for school consolidation preceded the onset of rural motoring. It was already a well-defined professional objective whose achievement motoring served to justify. Even though a significant portion of the population was still without automobiles at the start of the Twenties, rural sociologist Walter Burr argued that car-enhanced mobility made the original communal boundaries irrelevant. The 'district school begins to fail', he wrote in 1921, 'because, although its development was a recognition that education is a community function, it does not have a community scope in the new order of things'. Thus, progress, as exemplified by the new automobile age, justified the consolidation of schools, and an adjustment once sought by Progressives was now declared by them to have been inevitable.[22]

The 1907 Country Life Commission had noted that some farm families moved to the town in order to secure a high school education for their children. The consolidation of schools in the 1920s reinforced this trend by removing elementary schools from the open countryside. Car ownership, and eventually school buses, gave access to the new consolidated schools, but access was not the same as communal sympathy. Under school consolidation, communities of different social types were united for educational purposes. Leadership in the enlarged school districts remained with the middle classes who tended to see public education as designed to instruct the labouring population for their future role. Teachers were to mould young minds and where possible influence their parents. Given the low population density of the open country under mechanised cash-crop agriculture, the people of the hinterland were consistently outnumbered and outvoted, and so the elementary curriculum, like the high school's before it, reflected town rather than country concerns. Parental influence was expressed through parent – teacher associations, direct successors to middle-class reform groups like the WABPS, which usually met at the school, the location of which was based on the assumption of car ownership. Consolidation coincided with the establishment of an effective pattern of supervision of teachers by their professional superiors, the county superintendents for the first time.Prior to the 1920s, the wide geographical scope of the superintendency precluded regular visitation. Thereafter, the consolidation of schools long urged by the superintendents and the purchase of automobiles for their use facilitated regular inspection. Thus, the hierarchical unity of the profession was strengthened during this period while the localised influence of the hinterland was weakened. As we shall see in the next chapter, there is a clear parallel between these developments in education and those taking place concurrently in the field of highway administration. In both cases, local influence was superseded by professional discipline within larger bureaucratic organizations. The new middle class was riding to power in the automobile.[23]

Like the rural schoolma'am, the country clergyman experienced status anxiety as he fell from grace under the scrutiny of Progressive reformers. The old-style rural preacher fulfilled neither his traditional spiritual nor his expanding social role satisfactorily in the opinion of Progressives. Roosevelt's Country Life Commission foresaw the need to replace him with the kind of 'Social Gospel' minister who had responded so earnestly to the challenge of change in the cities. Well before car ownership became widespread, surveys of rural churches highlighted a story of inefficient use of resources. The country town had too many churches: Belleville, Ohio, for example, had five Protestant churches with a total seating capacity of 1675 for the town's 913 people, only 513 of whom were regular churchgoers. In contrast, open-country residents relied for their Christian comfort upon passing circuit riders. Walter Burr, whose father had been a circuit rider, recalled that the circuit rides from the town-based church to outlying settlements 'came alarmingly near to being an exploitation of a group of farmers by the town churches in order to obtain the money for the support of a city preacher'.[24]

Although it was common for each generation to lament a decline in religious values, the evidence suggests that, even before the advent of motoring or other secular pleasures, late-nineteenth-century rural church attendance never rose above 40 per cent of the total population, though there were considerable regional variations. Sectarian rivalry ensured that town ministers had to compete for their respective share in this poor harvest of souls; hence, the need for an eloquent 'city' preacher. The latter also commonly possessed an ulterior motive; namely, to secure the attention of his ecclesiastical superiors and thus gain promotion to a more prestigious, urban pastorate. As early as the 1870s, Washington Gladden had attacked the denominational rivalry that led to over-churching. By the early twentieth century, Gladden was convinced that the traditional rural church was a dying institution which was being artificially sustained 'by the vigorous working of the denominational bellows'. The reality of competing with one another made the task of making church services interesting a major preoccupation for ministers. By basing its appeal on entertainment as much as piety, however, the rural church left itself vulnerable to competition from secular entertainment, which was made more accessible to car-owning parishioners with the advent of motoring.[25]

The greater mobility of a car-owning congregation intensified ecclesiastical competition by bringing more churches as well as secular enticements into the contest for souls. The affluent and aspiring portion of the congregation was the object of particularly fierce struggles since its allegiance was profitable and prestigious, if expensive. One religious commentator explained:

> The families that are ambitious enough to covet better education for their children also covet better advantages in church and religious instruction. The town church, with its resident pastor, graded Sunday school and young people's organizations, invites attendance by offering more adequate religious training. As a result the more advanced and abler farm families are steadily being drawn off from the rural community and the rural church loses leadership.

The writer associated this migration of the 'Progressive' middle class with 'the coming of hard-surfaced roads and the automobile', but in practice the depletion of congregations which justified consolidation of facilities pre-dated the widespread diffusion of car ownership in the same way that the call for school consolidation preceded mass motoring. Leading churchmen, like their professional counterparts in education, welcomed consolidation. In their view, the competitiveness and overabundance of churches impeded the work of the 'Social Gospel'. As the Board of Home Missions of the US Presbyterian Church declared in true Progressive style: 'The old efficiency which was reckoned in new converts and new congregations must be replaced by a new efficiency reckoned in social service'.[26]

In practice, such efficiency could mean the closure of small rural churches. It is one of the many ironies of the automobile's cultural application that the use of a vehicle which enhanced mobility should be accompanied by a concentration of rural social institutions. Rural sociologist Warren Wilson pointed out in 1923 that the automobile enabled ministers in Montana to reach remote ranches. Similarly, the car-driving preacher was vital to some black sects in the rural South because they could afford neither a permanent pastor nor a church building. Despite these examples, the mobility offered by car ownership instilled an assumption of accessibility in ministers as well as teachers. By overcoming the barrier of distance, car ownership was believed to have eliminated the only obstacle between the professional man and his clients. Given this assumption, it is important to recall that, despite the falling price of American motor cars, not every rural inhabitant could afford one. As rural institutions were adjusted according to the middle-class assumption of universal car ownership those without cars lost the limited facilities which had formerly served a less mobile population. The deficiencies of the old rural order in its late, attenuated stage – its poverty, relative deprivation, loneliness, dwindling population, poor schools and sporadic religious life – certainly encouraged rural Americans to annihilate the barrier of space that separated their faltering agrarian culture from the industrial market-place. They did so either by permanent migration cityward or by buying motor cars. The more prosperous members of the rural community could most readily afford the expense of car ownership. They were also most likely to be 'Progressive' in outlook. They used their new mobility to express their own preference for a more urban-like distribution of services. By patronising the schools and churches of nearby towns, they accelerated the decline of open-country schools and chapels. In a similar way, they encouraged a redistribution of retail outlets as they shopped around for the widest selection and the best deal. Moreover they were the first to take advantage of the unprecedented progress in health care as the medical profession splintered into hundreds of specialisms. The middle classes in the countryside were no longer loyal to the nearest general practitioner and he, in turn, was no longer dependent upon them.[27]

Physicians were among the first professional groups to adopt the automobile as a business vehicle. In a special 'automobile issue' of the *Journal of the American Medical Association* in 1906, various physicians discussed the car's advantages. One AMA member declared: 'The auto enables the physician to spend more time in his office, that can be profitably employed in studying or recreation, the value of which cannot be computed in dollars and cents.' Others were readier to place a price on the time saved. One physician candidly admitted that he 'saw visions of a $20,000 practice annually in consequence of purchasing an automobile' because he could visit his patients 'with more speed, and oftener', and would race his professional rivals to the scene of an accident. Such comments reveal that, despite its ethical restrictions, medical practice remained a small business enterprise, and like other businesses, it desired increased trade. Distance had restricted trade. A study of the distribution of US physicians observed that 'in the era of the horse and buggy, a distance of even five miles rendered the competition of the town doctor in ordinary practice a negligible factor'.[28]

Such inaccessibility, of course, also had its tragic side. The simple fact of distance, aggravated by bad roads, made the uncomfortable journey of the chronically sick to the hospital a common prelude to the grave. A doctor told the auto trade journal *Horseless Age* in 1901 that the two days' journey to and from the hospital by horse could now be covered by car in ninety minutes. No amount of nostalgia can obscure the needless suffering and fatalities in rural America prior to the motor car. However, the redistribution of health facilities which occurred with the diffusion of car ownership was shaped by other considerations also, which the assumed universality of car ownership served to justify. Not least was the increasingly technocratic character of the medical profession as the success of scientific research compounded the dominance of urban physicians in the medical schools, on hospital staffs, and within professional associations. The very real technical inadequacies of rural medical practice were magnified by the tendency of 'progressive' physicians to insist upon the objectivity of technical procedures rather than trust a clinical interpretation of the patient's history and physical condition. Lacking the technical resources of his urban colleagues, the rural physician faced their professional criticism and his own financial decline. His expenses increased because even when he bought a car, bad roads in the winter often obliged him to keep his horse and buggy also. He had fewer patients, or more precisely, fewer affluent ones since the latter were among the first to purchase an automobile. They 'could now patronize the town physician without extra expense as an incident to the occasional visit to town'. The larger towns offered an array of specialists whose credentials commonly outshone those of the country doctor. Moreover, the urban physician was usually on the hospital staff and so admission to hospital involved transferring the patient to the care of an urban physician. As a result of these professional changes, there was a marked exodus of doctors from country villages in the years following the First World War. A third of those towns of 1000 population or less which had resident physicians in 1914 had none by 1927. Such changes were commonly attributed to the impact of the automobile but it was more a matter of the internal politics of the medical profession than of technological determinism.[29]

As a member of the Progressive new middle class, a physician was likely to see himself and to be identified by others as part of the community's social 'establishment'. He was likely to be ambitious enough to desire better educational facilities for his children and to feel more comfortable in a community that could afford a more active church, a high school, a library and a better selection of shops. The fiscal realities of a depopulated or impoverished rural landscape under capitalism meant that, as rural sociologist John H. Kolb explained, 'not every town and country community can expect to have its own social institutions'. While acknowledging the rural denizens' need for 'their own neighborhood life and organization', Kolb concluded that they couldn't 'hope to maintain such social institutions as the high school, library, or hospital without taking into account the neighboring town or city'. Medical services, too, established themselves according to these calculations. Moreover, the relocated doctors reorganised their practices along more businesslike lines. To offset increased costs, the small-town doctor raised his fees and demanded immediate payment. Justified initially by reference to 'his time-consuming and expensive drives into the country', rising fees in practice reflected the expansion of the physician's market beyond 'a severely limited area and clientele'.[30]

Motor-borne patients also enjoyed greater choice of physician, but the essential nature of the doctor–patient relationship remained in the doctor's favour. This was demonstrated by the physicians' decision to cut back and in some cases eliminate house-calls. Dr Frank Billings reported in 1924 that many doctors who had depended upon house-calls until recently now refused 'to give this real obligation to the public and compel their patients who are too ill to visit the office to go to the hospital'. Thus, like the teacher and the clergyman, the rural physician adapted his practice on the assumption of universal access to automotive transport. In this way, the automobile became a necessity for rural Americans, an essential purchase which even the impoverished tenant or farm labourer did without at his peril.[31]

For the small-scale farmer reliant upon his own labour, restrictions on his mobility remained. Writing in 1923, minister and sociologist Warren Wilson noted that the 'claims of domesticated animals upon the farmer are such as to chain his foot to the homestead'. Paid labour could tend to the animals whilst the wealthier farmer travelled far afield, and so the mobility provided by the automobile was determined by economic status. Nevertheless, car ownership did allow more travel for all rural motorists than the former Saturday buggy-ride into town. Without exhausting the farm's horse power one could go for an evening drive. In this new pattern of traffic, speed did not dictate shopping at the nearest crossroads and so the general trade and service functions of numerous small retail centres were lost to neighbouring towns. In the latter, speciality shops attracted customers from a wider radius by their larger selection of goods, while the giant corporate retailers extended their influence by the construction of chain stores or even department stores in suburban communities and industrial satellite towns. Intended to take advantage principally of the greater surplus income of the middle-class market, such stores were also accessible to farm families by car for those 'special' purchases. Studies of car travel in the Twenties indicated that most motor journeys measured under twenty miles, a distance within the range of horse and wagon but covered more quickly by car. Car ownership thus promoted more frequent trips rather than longer ones.[32]

Frequent travel undermined self-sufficiency. Robert and Helen Lynd observed that the 'great bulk of the things consumed by American families is no longer made in the home and the efforts of the family members are focused instead on buying a living'. A 1930 study of bread consumption showed that 66 per cent of farm households, 75 per cent of village homes, and 90 per cent of urban households bought their daily bread rather than baking it themselves. Once accustomed to the convenience of store-bought goods, Americans became reliant upon them and as a corollary, dependent upon car ownership because it provided access to the store. Thus, when the Lynds discovered that car ownership was valued more highly than clothes, food and adequate sanitation, what they uncovered was the role of motoring as the essential facilitator in a culture of consumption. Without a car, the rural family had less access to clothes, food, or to the jobs which paid for internal plumbing.[33]

As agricultural production became more industrial in character – that is, more mechanised, capital-intensive and specialised – farm tenancy increased. A growing number of the roughly 38 per cent of farmers classed as tenants between 1910 and 1925 became sharecroppers with little or no capital. Nevertheless, these farmers bought cars to get access to the market. By 1926, 93 per cent of Iowan farm owner-occupiers had automobiles and so did 89 per cent of the state's tenant farmers. Both used their cars to get to town but the purpose of their visits was a function of their disposable income. One could go to the Patrons of Husbandry's (commonly called the National Grange) ball and frequent the movie theatre, while the other was less able to do so, but still needed an automobile in order to go to town to buy essentials, like bread and clothes.[34]

Rural motor-car ownership even among the poorly paid was pointed to as a sign of progress. As a champion of automobiles for the rural American, Henry Ford believed that:

> a very decided drift away from the farms was checked by three elements – the cheap automobile, the good roads over which the farmer might travel to market, [and] the moving picture theatre in the community where the farmer and his family might enjoy an evening's entertainment.

Ford's comment reflected the Progressive conviction that it was isolation which was driving rural Americans from the land, but as Roy Holmes pointed out in 1912, the drift cityward was most rapid 'in those communities best provided with modern conveniences ... The more closely men are drawn together the more surely does the old order pass.' Thus, the technological innovations that Ford celebrated were unlikely to stem the migration from the land. Another car manufacturer, John Willys, was more perceptive. 'It didn't keep the boy and girl on the farm', he observed of the car, 'but it provided the farmer with the means for getting people from the towns to take their places.' Farm families displaced by the onslaught of agri-business could be recruited as labour, during the sowing and harvesting in particular. Nevertheless, the belief that auto ownership gave equal freedom to all persisted. One commentator, observing that the automobile was becoming 'as much a part of the farm laborer's equipment as the bag of tools is the carpenter's', went on to say that the car made the labourer 'independent'. 'If he can get out any time he likes, he doesn't want to. He's contented. That's the moral value of it.' In the eyes of capital, such docility of labour was a great asset. However, one needs to make it clear that the car did not alter basically the type of work the labourer was skilled to do nor significantly did it enable him to produce independently. He still sold his labour to buy a living. Indeed, far from enhancing the position of farm labour, the automobile may be said to have devalued it by making a migratory labour force more accessible to the agricultural employer. Independence for a working man would require more than a car, but this is not to deny that the automobile provided him with a feeling of independence.[35]

Around the same time as the Country Life Commission contemplated the need to reform rural America, the automobile began to be advertised in the rural community as a sensible purchase. In 1909, the low-priced Maxwell became the first car to be advertised in farm journals and country weeklies. The initial two-month advertising campaign was so successful that the Maxwell Company extended it. Other car producers in the low-price range followed suit, stressing that the motor car would put the rural inhabitant on a par with urban Americans and would improve its owner's efficiency. It is revealing to note the functions to which advertisers referred in their efforts to sell motoring. For example, a rival of the Ford Model T, the Brush Runabout was advertised in 1911 in terms of 'going to town, "getting around" the farm, taking the produce to market and bringing back supplies. The women folk can use the car for visiting or shopping, or the children for going to school.' Significantly 'going to town' took precedence over inspecting crops and distributing produce, an unconscious indication of the car's role as a means of incorporating the rural consumer within the corporate industrial economy.[36]

The acceptance of the automobile by rural Americans during the prosperous first decade of this century reflected the transition away from the Populist politics of resisting the extension of the capitalist market-place with its inherent inequalities. Progressive spokesmen addressed themselves to those rural inhabitants who desired to be included in the capitalist economy. While Progressive rhetoric invoked agrarian virtues of self-reliance and individualism, Progressive leaders acknowledged less noisily that, by 1900, the pattern of commercial relations and the concentration of capital had made these traditional traits sources of weakness not strength. The geographical isolation, which had fostered self-reliance, had also blocked effective interest-group organisation, preventing the farmer from forming the typical coalitions used to compete within the narrowing field of a corporate economy. Progressive reformers wanted to end the isolation, to annihilate the space which prevented not only the free exchange of goods and services, but also what they regarded as 'fair competition': a basic tenet of economic liberalism. The end of isolation would also enable rural social institutions to fulfil their obligations more effectively and so permit some form of conservation of the agrarian Republic whose myth still resounded in the corporate liberal mind.[37]

In practice, as an attempt at preserving the material basis of American republicanism, Progressive reform in its rural aspect, as in others, was inadequate to the giant task before it. Moreover, it was infused with a profound ambivalence towards industrial capitalism, and susceptible to emotional mystification. Appalled by the human casualties of the pursuit of capital accumulation, Progressives remained, none the less, infatuated by its energy. Incensed by the corruptness of the political economy, Progressives still retained a faith in honest experts as great individual saviours. The automobile, as a symbol, thus became infused with a volatile mixture of a reverence for the past and a fascination with the future, of a simultaneous yearning for stability and for dramatic change, of an acknowledgement of the collective, interdependent character of modern life alongside the wish for individual control. These conflicting feelings came to rest upon the motor car, enshrouding it in a complex imagery.

Nor was the car's appeal illusory. It would be foolish to minimise the material benefits arising from rural car use, and this account should not be interpreted as an attempt to do so. At the same time, it is valuable to note how the assumption that accessibility was the same as communal solidarity allowed new deficiencies to develop in place of the old constraints of isolation. The rural America into which the automobile was introduced was already weakened by its 'colonial' status within an increasingly industrial capitalist economy, and this weakness greatly influenced the pattern of car use and its impact. There was nothing inevitable about this pattern. The motor car could have remained an option offering certain specific advantages: either for recreation or for cross-movement between mass-transit lines; instead it became a prerequisite for survival. Car ownership did not ease social inequality; rather, it gave it a new medium of expression by making the cost of such ownership a burden calibrated to overall economic status. To the Babbitts of Main Street, the automobile was a versatile vehicle for both work and play, but to the migrant worker it was a means of precarious survival. To corporate America in the 1920s the motor car was the vital engine of consumption whose purchase and use, often on credit, facilitated the accumulation of capital by incorporating the nation into a single market. The inherent urge within capitalism to expand the market whilst simultaneously reducing the period required for the circulation of capital was neatly squared by the motor car. By incorporating hitherto isolated places, automobility extended the market, yet at the same time it quickened the pace of distribution and sales.[38]

The rural society into which the car came was already weakened by an imcomplete adjustment to industrial capitalism. This weakness greatly influenced the way in which the automobile came to be used and hence its impact. The inadequacies of rural social arrangements were already sufficiently acute to encourage outward migration. This depopulation of the countryside eroded still further vital social institutions such as the school and the church. Simultaneously, the Progressive middle class called for reform and the volleys of criticism within the professions compelled the rural teacher, minister and doctor to assume the role of reformer. Progressive reform sought to readjust the rural order according to the precepts of industrial efficiency. This entailed the gradual removal of power from the local level and the establishment of bureaucratic organisations arranged according to a professional hierarchy of expertise. The traditional Madisonian method of social regulation, namely expanding the constituency beyond the power base of parochial groups, tried first in the federal Constitution, was applied again. We will look more closely at the surrendering of local control in the next chapter. The shift from a 'horse culture' to a 'car culture' was a momentous step, which appeared to place more power at the disposal of the individual, whilst simultaneously enmeshing the formerly self-sufficient in a metropolitan web of interdependence. The evolution of a car-owning consumer culture was not the automatic consequence of motoring, as contemporaries argued. Instead, it reflected the process of capitalism and the American response to it. Technology did not determine the symmetry between Progressive goals of institutional rationalisation in the countryside and the impact of the motor car. Rather, Americans made the new geographical configuration of metropolitanism and they did so according to the logic of capitalism.[39]

Notes

1 US Bureau of the Census, *Historical Statistics of the United States, Colonial Times to 1957*, 1961, p. 14; James J. Flink, *The Car Culture*, 1975, p. 28.

2 A. Eugene Havens *et al.*, eds, *Studies in the Transformation of US Agriculture*, 1986, pp. 27–8.

3 Flink, op. cit., pp. 141–2; cf. Joseph Interrante, 'The road to autopia: the automobile and the spatial transformation of American culture', *Michigan Quarterly Review*, Special Double Issue: The Automobile and American Culture, XIX–XX, Fall 1980 – Winter 1981, p. 508.

4 For 'social structure of accumulation', see Richard Edward *et al.*, *Segmented Work, Divided Workers: the Historical Transformation of Labor in the United States*, 1982, pp. 22–6.

5 Steven Hahn, *The Roots of Southern Populism: Yeoman Farmers and the Transformation of the Georgia Upcountry, 1850–1890*, 1983, *passim*; Stanley B. Parsons, *The Populist Context: Rural versus Urban Power on a Great Plains Frontier*, 1973, *passim*; Havens, op. cit., p. 35; David Harvey, *The Urbanization of Capital*, 1985, p. 35.

6 Bruce Palmer, *Man Over Money: Southern Populist Critique of American Capitalism*, 1980, *passim*; Alfred D. Chandler, *The Visible Hand: the Managerial Revolution in American Business*, 1977, *passim*; Gilbert Fite, *The Farmer's Frontier, 1865–1900*, 1966, *passim*.

7 Harvey, loc cit.; John D. Hicks, *The Populist Revolt: a History of the Farmers' Alliance and the People's Party, 1931, passim*.

8 Milan C. Edson, *Solaris Farm*, 1971, preface; p. 106.

9 Havens *et al.*, op. cit., pp. 38–9.

10 William L. Bowers, *The Country Life Movement in America 1900–1920*, 1974, p. 11.

11 For the relative position of agriculture, see Simon Kuznets, *National Income: a Summary of Findings*, 1946, p. 41; Carolyn Howe, 'Farmers' movements and the changing structure of agriculture', in Havens *et al.*, op. cit., p. 126.

12 Committee on Business Research of College of Business Administration, *The Influence of Automobiles and Good Roads on Retail Trade Centres*, Nebraska Studies in Business, No. 18, University of Nebraska Press, Lincoln, 1927, p. 18, as cited by Michael Berger, *The Devil's Wagon in God's Country: the Automobile and Social Change in Rural America*, 1979, p. 113. Taken with Bowers's study, Berger's work provides a valuable introduction to the literature of social change in the countryside, and I have been guided by them. However, neither work connects the social changes attributed to the automobile to the Progressive reform agenda. Robert S. and Helen M. Lynd, *Middletown: a Study in Modern American Culture*, 1929, p. 251.

13 David Harvey, op. cit., pp. 52–3; US Department of Agriculture, *The Farm Woman's Problems*, Circular No. 148, 1920, p. 12.

14 For the Country Life Commission, see *Report of the Country Life Commission*, (hereafter, *CLC Report*), Senate Doc. 705, 60th Cong., 2nd sess., 1909; quotation, p. 21. The CLC, established by President Roosevelt, consisted of Liberty Hyde Bailey, Kenyon Butterfield, Gifford Pinchot, Walter H. Page, Henry Wallace, Charles S. Barrett and William A. Beard, see Bowers, op. cit., p. 25.

15 *CLC Report*, pp. 9, 17, 6–7, 15–16; US Department of Agriculture, *History of Agricultural Education in the United States, 1785–1925*, Miscellaneous Publication No. 36, 1929; Howe, 'Farmers' Movements', Havens *et al.*, op. cit., p. 132.

16 Edward R. Eastman, *These Changing Times: a Story of Farm Progress During the First Quarter of the Twentieth Century*, 1927, p. 8; Carl C. Taylor, *Rural Sociology in its Economic, Historical and Psychological Aspects*, revised ed., 1933, p. 507. For concern over rural depopulation, see Liberty H. Bailey, 'Why do boys leave the farm?, *Century*, LXXII, July 1906, pp. 410–16; Truman S. Vance, 'Why young people leave the farms', *Independent*, LXX, 16 March 1911, pp. 553–60.

17 James M. Williams, *The Expansion of Rural Life: the Social Psychology of Rural Development*, 1931, p. 154.

18 Eastman, op. cit., pp. 140–41; cf. Liberty H. Bailey, 'The common schools and the farm youth', *Century*, LXXIV, October 1907, pp. 960–67.

19 James L. Leloudis II, 'School reform in the New South: the Woman's Association for the Betterment of Public Schoolhouses in North Carolina, 1902–1919', *Journal of American History*, LXIX, March 1983, pp. 886–909. Despite the prominence of men like Walter H. Page in both the CLC and the New South movement, Leloudis does not link school reform to the Country Life movement. Quotation from *CLC Report*, p. 21; Leloudis, op. cit., p. 897.

20 *CLC Report*, p. 19; Leloudis, op. cit., p. 897.

21 Leloudis, op. cit., pp. 899, 888; US Department of the Interior, Bureau of Education, *Consolidation of Rural Schools and Transportation of Pupils at the Public Expense*, Bulletin No. 30, 1914, p. 44.

22 For the school as a factory, see Herbert Betts, *New Ideals in Rural Schools*, 1913, p. 25; John M. Foote, 'A comparative study of instruction in consolidated and one-teacher schools', *Journal of Rural Education*, II, April 1923, pp. 350–7; Walter Burr, *Rural Organizations*, 1921, pp. 144–5.

23 *CLC Report*, p. 9; C. W. Stone, 'Do we want the county as the school district?', *Journal of Rural Education*, II, March 1923, p. 311; US Department of the Interior, Bureau of Education, *Rural School Supervision*, Bulletin No. 48, 1917, pp. 31–2.

24 *CLC Report*, p. 19; Lewis Atherton, *Main Street on the Middle Border*, 1966, p. 257; Walter Burr, *Small Towns: an Estimate of their Trade and Culture*, 1929, pp. 250–51.

25 Atherton, op. cit., pp. 379, 170; James H. Madison, 'Reformers and the rural church, 1900–1950', *Journal of American History*, LXXIII, December 1986, p. 651.

26 Alva W. Taylor, 'Moving the country up to town', *Christian Century*, XL, 1923, p. 178; O. R. Geyer, 'Motorizing the rural church', *Scientific American*, 14 May 1921, pp. 386–7; Madison, op. cit., p. 650.

27 Warren H. Wilson, 'What the automobile has done to and for the country church', *Annals of the American Academy of Political and Social Science*, CXVI, November 1914, p. 83; David L. Cohn, *Combustion on Wheels: an Informal History of the Automobile*, 1944 p. 19. James Flink cites a 1920 survey which ranked those who gained most from car ownership as real estate and insurance agents, then medical doctors, salesmen, clergymen and school supervisors before farmers; op. cit., p. 160. The car was most easily secured and most profitably used by the middle classes.

28 Ralph C. Epstein, *The Automobile Industry: its Economic and Commercial Development*, 1928, p. 96; *Journal of the American Medical Association*, XLVI, 21 April 1906, pp. 1203, 1172; Dr H. L. S. 'The automobile is my business', *Horseless Age*, VII, 1901, p. 21; Lewis Mayers and Leonard V. Harrison, *The Distribution of Physicians in the United States*, 1924, pp. 12–13.

29 Dr H. L. S., op. cit., p. 23; Harry H. Moore, *American Medicine and the People's Health: an Outline with Statistical Data on the Organization of Medicine in the United States with Special Reference to the Adjustment of the Medical Services to Social and Economic Change*, 1927, pp. 515–16; Mayers and Harrison, op. cit., pp. 12–13, 35; W. S. Rankin, 'Rural medical and hospital services', *American Journal of Public Health*, 17 January 1927, p. 18.

30 John H. Kolb, *Service Institutions for Town and Country*, Research Bulletin No. 66, University of Wisconsin Agricultural Experimental Station, Madison, 1925, p. 54; A. W. Taylor, 'Moving the country up to town', loc. cit.; Mayers and Harrison, op. cit., pp. 87–8.

31 Samuel H. Adams, 'Medically helpless', *Ladies' Home Journal*, February 1924, p. 150.

32 Warren H. Wilson, *The Evolution of the Country Community*, 1923, p. 117; H. Van Norman, 'Rural conveniences', *Annals of the American Academy of Political and Social Science*, XL, March 1912, p. 166; Interrante, op. cit., pp. 509–11; Lynd and Lynd, *Middletown*, pp. 30, 177, 497–8.

33 Lynd and Lynd, op. cit., pp. 30, 177, 497–8, 254–6; Interrante, op. cit., pp. 509–11, 515–16.

34 Interrante, loc. cit.; Ernest Groves, *The Rural Mind and Social Welfare*, 1922, p. 149.

35 Ford and Willys cited by Samuel R. McKelvie, 'What the movies mean to the farmer', *Annals of the American Academy of Political and Social Science*, CXXVIII, November 1926, pp. 132, 124; Henry I. Dodge, 'Transportation and the cost of living', *Country Gentleman*, 27 February 1919, p. 26.

36 Berger, op. cit., pp. 15–35; for the shift in rural attitudes, see 'Farmers' coming around', *Motor Age*, VIII, 30 November 1905, p. 11; 'Farmers' and not foes', *Motor Age*, XI, 1 October 1908, p. 14; 'Farmers taking to automobiles', *Motor World*, XX, 8 April 1909, p. 68. For Maxwell, see Frank Presbrey, *The History and Development of Advertising*, 1929, p. 560; Brush advertisement, see Floyd Clymer, *Treasury of Early American Automobiles, 1877–1925*, 1950, p. 104.

37 Howe, 'Farmers' movements', *passim; CLC Report*, pp. 9, 5–6; E. K. Eyerley, 'Co-operative movements among farmers', *Annals of the American Academy of Political and Social Science*, XL, March 1912, pp. 58–68.

38 Havens, op. cit., *passim*; David Harvey, op. cit., p. 37.

39 Lynd and Lynd, op. cit., p. 251; Roderick D. McKenzie, *The Metropolitan Community*, Recent Social Trends Monograph, 1933, p. 6.

Chapter 3

The politics of highway engineering

David Harvey has recently reminded us of Marx's observation that under capitalism, 'even spatial distance reduces itself to time: the important thing is not the market's distance in space, but the speed ... with which it can be reached'. We have already noted how the automobile served a dual need within capitalism: first, by breaking down spatial barriers to exchange it expanded the scope of the market; and secondly, by increasing the speed of travel, it increased what Marx termed the 'annihilation of space by time'. This phrase does not mean that the spatial aspect becomes irrelevant, instead, it implies a process by which space is organised to meet the time-discipline of capitalism. This process did not begin with the automobile. One needs only to recall the role that the railroads had played in the standardisation of time, and in the twentieth century, this process of reducing distance to units of time has become an ingrained habit of speech: a three-hour flight, a twenty-minute drive, and so on. Yet this emphasis upon the automobile's systemic role runs contrary to the dominant images of the automobile and of motoring which stress its individualistic, libertarian character. Omitted from this powerful traditional imagery is any recognition of the massive process of infrastructural investment which underpins American automobility. This includes not only the construction and maintenance of the highway system which is our principal concern here but also the establishment of an elaborate apparatus for traffic control. The introduction of the automobile to Progressive America cannot be properly understood without an examination of the highway reforms which facilitated motoring by the establishment of roads suited to the speed of auto traffic since this was what the Progressive middle classes demanded.[1]

Such an examination confirms the interpretation presented earlier, that the impact of the automobile is more accurately understood as part of a process of adjustment to the rise of corporate capitalism in America rather than as a prime example of the deterministic nature of autonomous technological developments. In his classic study of the Progressive Era, Robert Wiebe has argued that Americans were confronted by a struggle between the forces of a waning locally oriented society and those of a rising historical bloc which he terms 'the new middle class'. The latter, according to Wiebe, favoured centralised, bureaucratic decision-making as the most efficient way of organising a national industrial economy. We hope to place the introduction of the automobile in the context of this clash by examining the way in which road reform produced a highway system not only geared to the commuting habits of this middle class and to the long-haul traffic needs of a corporate economy, but also one which was administered by professional bureaucrats to whom power was surrendered on the basis of technical expertise.[2]

Prior to 1900, the call for highway improvement had come principally from cycling enthusiasts through such bodies as the League of American Wheelmen, whose President, Colonel Albert A. Pope, lobbied extensively for state and federal appropriations for road construction. During the mid-1890s, highway improvement had also been a key element in the proposals of the Ohio Populist, Jacob Coxey, who had called for a Congressional appropriation of $500 million for the purpose of providing work for the unemployed during the depression of 1893 to 1896. A prosperous quarry owner in Masillon, Ohio, Coxey was a firm believer in the need to expand the money supply by issuing banknotes; he named his son, Legal Tender, as a token of his commitment. It was whilst driving home over a road of endless ruts and potholes in December 1891 that Coxey became convinced that the nation needed a systematic highway construction programme. The severe economic downturn of 1893 led Coxey to link his highway plans to his calls for currency reform. The unemployed should be supported by public works projects funded by deficit spending in the form of non-interest-paying bonds issued by the federal government. This proto-Keynesian plan for ending a depression was introduced to Congress by Coxey's local congressman but was defeated. However, the promise of employment and currency reform attracted favourable Populist attention. Most Populists favoured anything that might reduce the power of the railroads. As one Virginian editor wrote: 'Why not go to work on the muddy, deep-rutted, abominable turnpikes and country roads of the state and let the railroads alone?'[3]

This call for Good Roads among the Populists was yet another aspect of what we have termed 'the politics of inclusion' within the movement. While some Populists, especially in the South were intent upon resisting the incorporation of their communities within the impersonal cash nexus of a national corporate market-place and looked to political action to restore agrarian producer republicanism, others, notably in the Midwest, wanted an easing of credit to enable them to compete more effectively in the market-place. Highway improvement could easily be presented as a measure against the hated railroads, but in practice it could equally prove beneficial to the railroad companies and other businesses dealing with rural communities. Accordingly, the Good Roads cause was backed financially by urban business interests, notably railroads and mail-order houses, which regarded poor rural roads as a restraint on their trade. The nation's leading bicycle manufacturer, Albert Pope, rallied early business support. In a letter to railroad leaders, he pointed out that wagon roads acted as 'feeders' for the railroads. 'When highways are impassable', he explained:

> freight and passenger earnings are necessarily diminished, and the price of railroad securities lowered; when roads are in good condition, merchandise is accumulated at the depots, and in moving it trains are delayed and accidents increased. A uniform good condition of roads would enable railroads to handle freight more expeditiously and advantageously.

In a sense, Pope was transferring to the nation's transport system the insight he had gained within his own bicycle factories where the productivity of the machining departments was balked by bottlenecks in the laborious final assembling and finishing operations. He thus recognised what was fast becoming a fundamental tenet of Big Business, namely, that the speed of flow through the industrial process from raw materials to final sale was a crucial determinant of profit since it measured the optimum use of fixed capital investment. Marx had similarly stressed the need for capitalism to renew and improve transport and communications systems in order to guarantee regular delivery as well as to maximise speed and minimise costs.[4]

Highway improvement, from this perspective, becomes part of the process of changing what I term the 'architecture of production' of corporate capitalism. Good roads regularised the pace at which finished goods flowed out to the consumers. Railroad leaders appreciated this tendency. They encouraged road improvement by offering reduced rates for shipping road construction materials and, after 1900, sponsoring Good Roads Trains to publicise the issue in rural communities. Equally mindful of the benefits of infrastructural improvements which speeded up the circuit of production and sale, the mail-order houses sponsored the campaign for Rural Free Delivery (RFD) which was first tried around Charleston, West Virginia, in 1896. RFD prepared the way for federal aid for road construction by circumventing constitutional constraints via its linking of highway improvement to a federal function, delivering the mail. The involvement of the state provided the favourable circumstances necessary to encourage the heavy fixed-capital investment required by offering immediate rewards to road construction and materials companies. Jacob Coxey's company would presumably have benefited from a federal highway programme, and once built, the roads would not only encourage the sale of Pope bicycles, but expedite the transport of crops to the rail depot and of mail-order items to the rural consumer. Thus, highway improvement was a logical part of the politics of inclusion.[5]

However, while highway construction would improve the performance of American capitalism and would potentially benefit several interested parties, its very profitability made it a contentious 'pork-barrel' measure. Farmers, in particular, were deeply suspicious since they felt that they would bear the tax burden more surely than they would reap the benefits. The latter, they feared, would be dealt out by corrupt politicians to their cronies. The Gilded Age had provided enough revelations of the corrupt character of American politicians to make hard-pressed citizens hesitant to hand over such a vast public works' project to the disreputable politicians at local, state and national level. Boss Tweed of New York City and Pennsylvania state boss, Matthew Quay, were two notorious examples of public figures who had profited from road improvement schemes. Consequently, before appropriations for road improvement could gain approval, ordinary citizens had to be convinced that there was some chance that the money would be used honestly and wisely. This was typical of that important strand within Progressive reform which advocated a more professional approach to public administration. Often linked to fiscal conservatism, this campaign for efficiency often urged the application of the nation's business expertise to government. Albert Pope reminded fellow members of the Hartford Board of Trade 'that it must be you who shall shoulder the responsibility of starting a legislative movement ... [and] shall see it through to a right and proper determination'.[6]

To business leaders, like Pope, it seemed that they alone had the intelligence to ensure the nation's progress. This was clear when they considered what they regarded as the illogical reluctance of the farming community to support road improvement. Railroad leaders believed that the farmer was 'the greatest sufferer from the poor country roads', yet he appeared willing to 'wallow in mud all the days of his life rather than pay for good roads'. The deplorable state of American roads served to indict the system of local highway administration. The practice of working out one's road taxes by a few days of statute labour each year under the unchiding supervision of a neighbour, who had been elected road overseer often for reasons other than his knowledge of highway engineering, infuriated business interests, cyclists, and eventually motorists. One railroad official complained to Pope that 'the average road supervisor or overseer in the country districts of the Western states has about as little idea of how to make a good road as a Sioux Indian'.[7]

Like the Country Life Movement, the Good Roads campaign represented an attempt to adjust American rural society so that it might be more effectively incorporated within industrial capitalism. The leaders of this endeavour were either businessmen seeking to cultivate the rural market or cash-crop farmers and small-town tradesmen anxious to be included in the larger market-place. By 1905, the wealthier farmers of the National Grange were willing to endorse proposals for highway improvement at their annual conference. When investigators from the Roosevelt Commission on Country Life held town meetings to hear the complaints of rural America in 1907, road improvement was one of the two most often mentioned needs of rural people. However, the minutes of these meetings also indicate that most of those who spoke were non-farmers. This has led William Bowers to conclude that the movement for reform in the countryside was instigated by essentially urban business interests and subsequently received agricultural support according to the degree to which the farmer was 'market-conscious'.[8]

Good Roads leaders, like their counterparts in the broader Country Life Movement, held out the promise of better living conditions and greater business opportunities to farmers. In an often-repeated address, Michigan's principal Good Roads campaigner, Horatio Earle declared that good roads:

> save a portion of the cost and facilitate transportation; they make centralized and better schools possible, they make it easier to get to

> church, library, club, grange, lodge; and, far from the least, they socialize the countryside; practically, with the help of the automobile, turning the country into one big village and bringing every farmhouse within a few minutes' ride of all the desirable attractions.

Thus, the benefits promised by good roads and the automobile were precisely those counted upon by the Country Life Commission to create a new agriculture and a new rural life, synchronised to the faster pace of urban industrial capitalism.[9]

Men like Earle were typical of the Progressive middle class that backed leaders like Theodore Roosevelt in their efforts to accommodate industrial capitalism as the engine behind a strong nation-state. Other Good Roads advocates, like Archer B. Hulbert, employed the equally characteristic Progressive tactic of the jeremiad, warning that the American paradise would be lost without reform but adding that paradise might yet be restored if the people backed Progressive efforts to revitalise the grand old Republic. Hulbert, for example, pleaded that:

> the farm has been too much to the American nation, its product of boys and girls has been too eternally precious to the cause of liberty for which our nation stands, to permit a system of highways on this continent, which will make it a place where now in the twentieth century, foreigners only, can be happy.

Expressing the nativist strand within Progressive thought, Hulbert depicts America as a place where bad roads prevent effective Americanisation.[10]

In the event, the new transport system of car and highway advocated by Good Roads leaders did not restore the agrarian Republic but it did facilitate the operation of a deeply incorporated civilisation. The specialisation of function within industrialism led to the spatial transformation of American capitalism, particularly when the organisational innovations associated with the rise of corporate management produced a bureaucracy capable of supervising widely dispersed operations. A key aspect of these bureaucracies was that they concentrated authority while dispersing responsibility. The technology employed by such organisations tended to be capital-intensive and the decision-making positions within them tended to be gained by professional technicians trained to pursue a capitalist standard of efficiency. The two trends – specialisation of knowledge and concentration of authority – resulted in a wresting of power away from the immediate locality since only large-scale units could command the capital resources needed to perform efficiently by corporate standards.[11]

In the case of road improvement, only the state, or at the very least, the county, possessed the tax-base or credit to buy costly road equipment. Moreover, only highly trained engineers could estimate the technical requirements for construction and maintenance of a major highway and only they could ensure that expensive machinery was efficiently used. By background and training, this new class of highway official was similar to the new corporate business elite. Initially, energetic businessmen, like agricultural machinery salesman Horatio Earle in Michigan or Coleman DuPont in Delaware, took the lead in establishing state highway departments, and even at the national level, it was left to ebullient figures such as Colonel Roy Stone and Martin Dodge to expand the work of the Office of Public Roads. Such Good Roads advocates were primarily salesmen, eager to convince local inhabitants that they needed and wanted improved roads. Such flamboyant efforts attracted public attention to the issue but after 1905, they began to excite suspicion because they were perceived to be representative of private business interests trying to sway public policy in their own favour.[12]

Despite this recognition that business had corrupted politics, many Progressives continued to regard the application of modern managerial techniques as the remedy for the failings of public administration. To escape the unholy alliance of venal politicians and ambitious businessmen, Progressives turned to experts, believing, as Robert Wiebe has explained, that 'the process of becoming an expert, of immersing oneself in the scientific method, eradicated petty passions and narrow ambitions, just as it removed faults in reasoning'. Reverence for the expert was evident across the diverse canon of Progressive reform and Good Roads advocates regularly invoked it. The rationale behind the redistribution of power to technical experts was that the technical knowledge needed for wise policy decisions was not accessible to the masses, nor even to their elected representatives. Logan Page, Head of the Office of Public Roads (OPR), declared in 1909:

> In this age of specialists, it almost surpasses belief that the American people, so practical in all other lines of endeavor, should permit their golden millions to be frittered away by men who for the most part know little or nothing about either the science or the art of road building.[13]

While earlier historians stressed the popular accountability secured by the political victories of the Progressive Era – direct election of senators, primaries, referendum and recall, and female suffrage – more recently, historians have taken note of a contrary trend of reforms designed to restrict office-holding to a particular group, drawn almost invariably from the middle class. Thus, whilst trying to open up the political process, Progressives simultaneously sought to reserve positions for 'well-educated' men, hoping to replace the established political machines by the predominance of middle-class influences within government. To Progressive Americans, meritocracy seemed safer for America than unguided democracy largely because they saw themselves as exemplars of merit. An article on road reform published in *Country Life in America* in 1913 presented these doubts about democracy in a particularly acute form. The author decried the influence of 'George', the average citizen, in matters he did not understand. 'We let "George"', he complained,

> elect our city governments and then froth at the mouth because of graft. We let 'George' control the trusts, and then write letters to the newspapers denouncing high prices. And we let 'George' in the person of an inefficient highway engineer, an unscientific roadbuilder, or a well-meaning but utterly ignorant town council, dictate the form, kind, and construction of our highways.[14]

The solution was to train the people like 'George' to place their trust resolutely in the objective expertise of professional men. Arthur Blanchard, Professor of Highway Engineering at Columbia University, also called for a campaign to increase public respect for highway engineers by convincing the people that 'engineers are broadminded, well-educated men, capable of holding with credit the highest administrative office, and do not constitute a tribe of human beings capable only of running a transit, turning a lathe, or wiring a house'. Blanchard also complained that the pressure on engineers from elected officials, eager to hasten the highly visible process of public works, such as street paving, made it difficult for engineers to be as painstaking as they would wish in preparing for construction. At the same time, engineers were highly susceptible to the force of commercial argument and strove to run their projects along business lines. This was understandable because in the face of pressures to cut costs the newly established professionals needed to consolidate their positions by long tenure. This required political astuteness. Frank B. King, City Engineer for Lawton, Oklahoma, complained to a municipal reform journal about the practice of appointing new engineers with each change of administration 'for the simple reason that some friend wanted the place'. Thus, expertise was tempered by the need for political sycophancy.[15]

The early history of the Wayne County Road Commission provides an early example of the interaction of experts and local political and economic interests. Wayne County, home of Detroit, was already recognised by 1905 as a major auto producing centre. As the wealthiest county in Michigan, it had the most motorists and its car makers and dealers were eager to sponsor highway improvement. Wayne County was also Horatio Earle's political base. Earle campaigned successfully for a referendum on the establishment of a county board system which endorsed his proposals by a margin of nearly six to one. He had already secured state legislation stipulating that any future Wayne Country highway system should be centrally controlled by a board of three appointed commissioners. Under the terms of this Act of 1905, one board member was selected by Mayor Codd of Detroit, who chose Edward Hines at Earle's behest. The other two members were chosen by the Wayne County Clerk, who selected Henry Ford and Cassius Benton on Earle's recommendation. Hines was the most devoted Good Roads supporter of the three appointees, having been a member of the Michigan Wheelmen when Earle joined them in 1896. Benton was a Republican stalwart chosen to improve Earle's chances in the gubernatorial race of 1908. The choice of Ford as the representative of the Detroit car interest is less readily explained as he was just one of many Detroit car producers at this stage.[16]

Earle's choice of Ford would be less noteworthy were it not for certain parallels between the policies pursued by the newly established commission and those developed concurrently at the Ford Motor Company. As we shall see, in 1906, Henry Ford and the company secretary, James Couzens, initiated a strategy of reducing the company's reliance on outside contractors by manufacturing many key components. In pursuit of efficient production of these parts, they took a special interest in the development of new machinery which permitted the specialisation of the worker's task. To facilitate the rapid assembling of components, they pursued strict interchangeability of parts and moved the company towards a smoother, more sequential arrangement of production. The Road Commission's construction operations did not reach the same systematic level. However, the degree to which it strove to attain these same objectives is remarkable.[17]

However, the parallels did not stem from Ford's involvement

since he, along with Benton, resigned after only a few months when the board's work was stalled by politically inspired litigation concerning the constitutionality of its appointment. Only Edward Hines of the original commissioners survived the subsequent reorganisation, and so the policies pursued thereafter, in so far as they constituted one man's vision, were probably his. More significantly, the parallels between auto maker and road-building agency in Detroit suggest a common view among its business class of what constituted a Progressive pattern of organisation. Reviewing his experience as a Wayne County Road Commissioner in 1911, Hines told fellow members of the Detroit Chamber of Commerce that the first few years of actual road building had vindicated the board's decision not to rely on outside contractors. This had given the board an opportunity to operate efficiently according to its own systematic plans. The entire enterprise was said to be operated 'along factory lines', a contention confirmed by the board's annual reports which alluded to a complex system of daily reports, cost sheets and specialised job categories. The commissioners boasted that their procedures 'could be effectively used in any large business enterprise'.[18]

The board was particularly proud of its refinement of the division of labour in road construction. The annual report for 1907–8 spoke of 'using one crew to do all the tile and ditching, another crew to do the tarring: another crew for gradework, etc.'. The same report declared that the commissioners had eliminated 'so far as lay in their power, all manual and horse labor where the same or better results could be secured by machinery'. Over the next two years, the board spent around $45,000 on road equipment, including steam traction engines used to pull 7–ton wagons to the construction site and to haul other equipment, such as ploughs, once there. A self-propelled concrete mixer with a boom attachment for loading and pouring was another purchase which, the board reported, displaced between twelve and sixteen labourers. Steam-powered graders displaced a similar number of horses. By 1914 a portable single-track industrial railway which could be laid along the side of the road had eased the problems of hauling materials to the site. Its train of thirty cars required a crew of only three instead of many teamsters. Similarly a gasoline-powered pump and temporary pipeline replaced the eight teams formerly needed just to bring water.[19]

Since most road work was unskilled, mechanisation tended to displace unskilled labourers. At the same time, however, the board was also anxious to reduce the level of skill required. It closely supervised the construction of concrete crock (drainage tile) and culverts to achieve uniformity and so eliminate fitting at the site. By 1914, the commissioners had purchased an experimental mechanical road finisher to complete the concrete laying process. This displaced hand finishers. The board not only pursued similar strategies of technological application but also experienced labour problems comparable to those found in Detroit's auto plants. The preponderance of unskilled work and the seasonal nature of the job helped to ensure that the vast majority of workers were new immigrants. The board complained that this contributed to problems of high labour turnover rates and absenteeism, which worsened as the wages available to unskilled workers in the local auto industry increased and the supply of labour tightened during World War I. Thus, the commissioners repudiated the common practice of subcontracting road construction in order to pursue a systematic strategy of road improvement which strove to save money by extensive mechanisation, subdivision of labour, and standardised concrete construction. While it is not suggested that the board achieved anything like the level of systematic control, mechanisation, standardisation and de-skilling attained at the Ford Motor Company during the course of 1914, it belonged, none the less, to the same cult of efficiency, the assumptions of which permeated the Progressive Era and vitally shaped the process of technological innovation.[20]

It may be argued that Wayne County represents a special case because the road commissioners had the almost guaranteed support of the expanding local car industry. Despite this support, the board, like road authorities elsewhere, had to win over other business interests and cultivate the rural and working class vote for electoral purposes. The board acknowledged that there were two broad categories of traffic: the farm-to-urban-market vehicles, which were usually horse-drawn prior to 1920, and the suburbanite recreational and commuter traffic, which was increasingly automotive. For political purposes, the board astutely recognised that the former class provided a more acceptable rationale for its work. Accordingly, it argued that 'a system of good roads is a good investment not only for active road users but for buyers of the daily necessities of life'.[21]

Seeking popular support, highway authorities proclaimed that the vital road users were 'those who carry to the city the produce for the sustenance of the workers'. The argument drew strength from the Progressive Era's anxiety over the demographic shift of America's population from the country, which raised fears of a food shortage. It also reflected the persistent physiocratic belief, embodied in Bryan's celebrated 'Cross of Gold' speech of 1896, that agriculture was the eternal corner-stone of American prosperity, but more importantly it gave road improvement a material significance for the masses of non-vehicle owning citizens. Good Roads advocates publicised the cost of American road haulage. A *Scientific American* article of 1908 reported that it cost the American farmer more to haul his wheat to the rail depot (an average distance of 9 miles) than it did to ship the same wheat from New York to Liverpool. The head of the Office of Public Roads, Logan Page, cited a Bureau of Statistics survey which showed that average American road haulage cost 23 cents per ton per mile compared to a European average of only 10 cents. The difference, he told readers of *World's Work* in 1909, was caused by bad roads.[22]

By emphasising the benefits of highway improvement for the farmer and the hungry urban worker, road reformers depicted the advantages for the touring motorist and commuter as a 'secondary consideration' which could be 'promoted without disregarding the more important matter of local traffic'. Yet it was the middle-class motorist who benefited most immediately from the highway construction programme in Wayne County. The commissioners began by improving the main highways from the Detroit city limit to the county line. Suburban commuters could therefore enjoy these good county roads before passing on to the streets of Detroit. While agricultural produce could also be hauled more quickly on these improved roads, agricultural carriers first had to reach them by traversing unchanged secondary tracks. If the board's claim that priority would be given to speeding the delivery of produce had been sincere, it should have improved the secondary highways on which most farms were located in order to improve access to the nearest main road or better still, the nearest rail freight or inter-urban transit depot.[23]

Given the relatively high and rapidly increasing level of auto ownership in Wayne County, it may be argued, none the less, that the board showed exceptional foresight since not only did it develop Detroit's radial streets in anticipation of the suburban expansion of future decades but it also pioneered by its use of concrete which proved the most durable surface under the stress of mass motoring. But this ignores the fact that the improvements were proposed by the board as principally beneficial to the local farmers seeking to supply the urban workforce. At that time, the motor truck was a rarity; there were 10,000 trucks in the United States in 1910. Consequently, most farm produce was hauled by wagon and team. Such horse-drawn transport did not require concrete roads. Indeed, hard-surface roads were more treacherous for horses, particularly after a light rain. The concrete surface was therefore provided for motorists and once constructed, the board acknowledged, it attracted motorists from neighbouring routes, thus creating a level of car traffic which disturbed horse-drawn wagons. The need to switch to automotive vehicles in order to secure a safe place in the onward rush of cars on improved highways contributed to the expansion of trucking after 1914.[24]

Not only did the construction of auto highways have a deterrent effect on horse-drawn traffic but the auto traffic itself destroyed the less expensive types of roads that had sufficed to carry horse-drawn vehicles. Early accounts of motor touring referred to the dust clouds thrown up by the cars. Motorists responded by wearing elaborate protective clothing, the provision of which became an industry in itself. The dust was a visible sign of the car's erosion of the road surface. Nevertheless, even in 1906, it was unthinkable for Progressive members of the middle class to propose restrictions on motoring by a minority to protect the existing roads of the entire nation. As *Scientific American* declared:

> As matters now stand, the only way in which to avoid dust-raising is to reduce speed to a point considerably below the present speed limit; and this is out of the question. The automobile has come to stay. It is an industry too vast, a sport too noble to be subjected to any restriction which would ultimately kill its popularity.

The author concluded that 'if the automobile may not be brought down to the road, the road must be brought up to the automobile and some way found by which the dust horror may be mitigated, if not entirely removed'.[25]

Thus, at a time when the majority of Americans were not motorists, it was unthinkable to restrain motoring on grounds of social costs. Rather, traditional social practices which aggravated the car's detrimental impact, such as local road administration, had to be eliminated to allow further technological innovation – concrete roads. By 1912, the increase in automobile traffic was forcing France and Great Britain to replace their previously acclaimed macadamised roads because they now required expensive annual maintenance. Logan Page pointed out in 1913 that there were more cars registered in New York State alone than in France and Germany combined. The estimated tolerance of macadamised roads in terms of traffic was 75 motor cars per mile. Yet the United States had 113 cars per mile of improved highway. Suitable surfaces for motorists, such as those tried in Wayne County, were therefore urgently needed if the potential of the automobile as a means of accelerating the flow of goods and services in the economy was to be realised.[26]

The Ford Times boasted that: 'Every *Ford* that is sold produces a voter for good roads'. It continued: 'Fords are sold to the great, producing, industrious and serious middle classes, the class whose voters greatly outnumber all others in the ballot box.' Owning a Ford thus signified that one belonged to the great industrious, productive and serious middle class. Such propaganda was designed to challenge the image of motoring as a pastime of the idle rich, whose lives were not spent productively but frivolously. More revealingly still, the declaration that the votes of this solid middle class always outnumber all others expressed the cherished hope of Progressive America; namely, that democracy could be so organised that it always voted the middle-class way. Progressives liked to believe that the great middle class was motivated by a concern for the commonweal that transcended any narrow interest and, as paragons of the middle class, experts and engineers, 'broad-minded, well-educated men', enjoyed the confidence of Progressive reformers in a way in which politicians and businessmen *per se* did not. As Bruce Seely has pointed out, this left a large area of discretion in policy making to the technicians chosen to administer it.[27]

Just as technology does not develop autonomously outside of other historical trends, so technicians cannot be regarded as a purely disinterested group, free from the ambitions and needs evident in other social groups. Rivalry and self-interest can be seen behind the actions of highway administrators at every level from county road board to the Office of Public Roads. When Horatio Earle proposed an immediate $2 million bond issue to finance construction of a 200-mile integrated trunk-line system of concrete roads in Wayne County in June 1910, the road commissioners objected. While they naturally favoured more money for highway improvement they were opposed to the idea of issuing all the bonds at once to permit construction in a single year. Edward Hines was anxious to retain control of road building in Wayne County and this would be lost to subcontractors under Earle's plan. Hines's fellow commissioner, John Haggerty, had a small road material business that would potentially profit most if the scheme was spread over several years, while the third member of the board, William Murdock, a prosperous farmer, was alarmed by the prospect of the county's bonded indebtedness increasing by $2 million at a stroke. For his part, Earle, as a leading figure in the American Road Builders' Association (ARBA), was anxious to secure a large short-term project that would provide work for numerous contractors. The compromise was to secure public approval for the full bond issue but to leave the speed of issuing itself to the road commissioners' discretion. The latter thus retained control of road construction and with $2 million in bonds at its disposal, they were less dependent on the County Board of Supervisors for revenue. The commissioners did not seek approval of a road tax from the board for five years after 1912.[28]

At the state level, also, highway administrators strove first to consolidate their own position. Prior to his unsuccessful bid for the governorship in 1908, Horatio Earle sought to disguise his own objective of a centralised system of highway administration in order not to alarm the rural electorate. Thus, the Cash Tax Act of 1907, while it replaced statute labour by a cash tax and established the township as the smallest highway administrative unit did not abolish the office of overseer (of whom there were 25,000 in Michigan), allowing these local figures to retain the prestige of their title. Earle's successor, Townsend Ely, continued to reinforce the highway commission's political position by countering the pressure from urban motoring interests for the construction of durable trunk-line routes by publicly insisting that short-haul, farm-to-market roads were his department's priority. This led national figures, like C. H. Claudy, to complain that Michigan suffered from 'road smallpox' because the sharing of power with the local road authorities had resulted in 'hundreds of miles of roads, beginning nowhere, going nowhere, ending nowhere'. Nevertheless, despite Ely's public stance, his department was actively preparing plans for a change of priorities which came with the passage of the state Trunk Line Highway Law of 1913.[29]

By 1912, demand for road improvement was widespread. Car sales did indeed seem to produce votes for good roads. Motorists organised themselves into clubs and then state associations affiliated to the American Automobile Association which emerged as a powerful proxy for the auto industry in the political lobbying process. There was also a proliferation of Good Roads groups, each calling for the furtherance of its own scheme. This combination of a large industrial lobby and many disparate highway improvement schemes produced growing pressure on governments to invest in roads, but also left room for an arbiter between these uncoordinated interests. The Progressive assumption that engineers did not play politics, a view reinforced by the disciplined approach of the highway engineering profession, ensured that these professionals played a crucial role in policy making. In reality, such engineers had their own preferences and ambitions, and their own hierarchy based upon recognised standards of professional competence and the prestige and influence of the appointment held. Highway officials at the state level influenced county officials by setting down the specifications required to receive state aid. State officials also tended to be more active in the professional organisations, one of whose aims was to establish the credentials of the profession as a source of expertise. At the apex of this professional hierarchy by 1908 stood the engineers of the federal Office of Public Roads under Logan Page.[30]

As a national highway expert, Page felt himself well qualified to supervise the framing of a national policy on highway development. With his blessing, such a policy would appear before Congress not as a piece of pork-barrel legislation to benefit the automobile industry but as the considered proposal of a scientific road builder. However, Page also knew the weaknesses of his own position. As a federal official, he had to be sensitive to the states' rights sensibilities of individual states. As a scientist, he had to endure the disheartening ignorance of public opinion and be prepared to welcome any permanent, even if minor, improvements. As a neutral administrator, he had to avoid the appearance of advocating specific policy proposals. Thus, Page only gave advice when states requested it. He responded favourably to proposals to build earth and sand-clay roads in order to encourage local communities to begin the task of road improvement, and he formed the American Association for Highway Improvement (AAHI) to speak with scientific authority on matters of highway policy.[31]

Whereas the auto manufacturers and other business interests wanted a highway policy which would accelerate the diffusion of motoring as a means of shifting the economy into a higher gear, Page, as the nation's leading highway engineer, was principally interested in establishing his profession within government at all levels. As early as 1909 Page had proposed an organisation of professional road engineers to pursue his conviction that 'reform in systems of road legislation and administration are (sic) essential to the success of the road builder, and in order that these may be brought about, public sentiment must be aroused and given proper direction'. The AAHI, with Page as its president, was founded in November 1911 to provide this direction. Like the auto clubs and the road builders, the AAHI believed that the level of highway development needed in the United States required federal funding. However, whereas the AAA wanted a federally funded national trunk-line system and the ARBA wanted a similarly funded capitol-to-capitol highway network, Page refused to advocate lavish projects requiring extensive federal intervention since they would arouse opposition. Commenting on the many calls for federal aid in 1911, *Engineering News* remarked:

> It needs but the slightest knowledge of Congressional methods and precedents to perceive that the first grant of Federal aid to highway work will be the opening of a drain out of the Treasury which may easily menace national solvency.[32]

This fear of the corrupt instincts of politicians blocked more than sixty attempts to open the floodgates of the federal Treasury between December 1911 and June 1912. Eventually, however, Progressive faith in expert counsel overcame these anxieties. The fiscal 1913 Post Office Appropriation Bill included a grant of $500,000 in federal aid for the improvement of rural post roads, provided each federal dollar was matched two for one by the states. A further $25,000 was assigned for a joint Congressional investigation of the federal aid for road improvement issue. This eased the anxieties of the editors of *Engineering News* and gave Logan Page an opportunity to establish control over the policy. Using his position as an expert witness before Congressional committees, Page supported farm-to-market over trunk-line or primary highway schemes because the former were more consistent with his official position within the Department of Agriculture. Moreover, he recognised that rural road improvement would ease the way for the establishment of powerful state highway departments in each state by calming the fears of farmers that distant legislatures would tax them for projects from which they received no visible benefit.[33]

The establishment of professionally staffed state highway departments in each state was Page's first objective in his campaign for an efficient national highway system. He accepted that such departments might have politically appointed heads but he insisted that their actual work be under the control of trained engineers. The AAHI distributed an OPR model state road bill drawn up in 1911 to guide states along the right lines. The subsequent recruitment of professional highway engineers to staff these new agencies strengthened Page's own influence as the profession's leading spokesman. State highway commissions funded road improvement on the basis of state matching funds to the counties and this partnership prepared the way for the federal aid idea advocated by Page and accepted by Congress in 1916. The Federal Aid Road Act provided funds in $5 million increments for five years rising to $25 million by 1921, marking the beginning of significant federal funding of road construction.[34]

The coming of federal aid reinforced the influence of federal highway officials which was based on their reputation for expertise. The OPR's eminence in highway research acquired a further importance as road construction struggled to respond to the unprecedented strain of motor traffic. The OPR's engineers both shared and profited from the conviction that a large proportion of road appropriations was wasted because of graft and ignorance. Their research was intended to eradicate this waste by establishing standard material requirements and construction techniques. Standardisation was also a great convenience to harried local officials under political pressure to complete projects. It was of equal help to the renamed Bureau of Public Roads' own engineers who were required after 1921 to inspect and approve local highway projects seeking federal aid. Conditions varied too widely for rigid national standards, yet state officials voluntarily adopted BPR standards 'not only for Federal-Aid work but largely for State work also'. Thus, deference within the highway engineering profession ensured that BPR standards set the framework of public policy.[35]

For automobile interests, the gradual development of a national highway network as pursued by Logan Page was too slow. However, they themselves were too tainted by charges of self-interest to challenge expert opinion. What the auto lobby required was an advocate from within the supposedly objective highway engineering profession. Despite its public image of scientific objectivity, the highway engineering profession already had sectional divisions which reflected the differing levels of urban industrial and indeed professional development. Dissatisfied highway officials from the Eastern Seaboard states organised the American Association of State Highway Officials (AASHO), which limited its membership to senior state highway officials and OPR employees. Despite a scrupulously maintained public posture of unbiased expertise, the AASHO was much more sympathetic to the objective of a national trunk-line highway system advocated by AAA and the National Highway Association than was the AAHI. Since most Eastern states had the foundation of a state highway system by 1914, leading AASHO officials such as H.G. Shirley from Maryland and G.P. Coleman from Virginia welcomed the prospect of integrating these roads into a national interstate system whereas AAHI wanted first to establish the rudiments of professional highway administration in the remaining states.[36]

The correspondence of President A.G. Batchelder of the AAA and President Roy Chapin of the National Automobile Chamber of Commerce indicates that the co-operation of Shirley and Coleman, as leaders of the new professional organisation, provided the motoring interests with a potentially powerful proxy for the advocacy of federal legislation. However, Page and his chief ally, Thomas MacDonald, Iowa's state highway commissioner and a key figure in the Mississippi Valley Conference of State Highway Departments, opposed Shirley and Coleman's position. In their view the proposed inter-urban highway network would antagonise rural and sectional constituencies and lay the profession open to charges of pandering to the automobile interests. It was too early to switch to a policy of overtly favouring trunk-line highways since professional highway administration was just establishing itself in the South and West where rural support was still needed to secure constitutional reform as well as state funding. As a result of Page and MacDonald's efforts, the Federal Aid Road Act of 1916 advanced the interests of the highway engineering profession without unduly provoking the anxieties of local elites.[37]

Like other federal programmes based on the principle of matching funds, the Road Act countered the effects potentially created by the need to recognise states' rights by placing authority with a professional group eager to achieve the national standards set by the profession. The unity provided by the hierarchically structured engineering profession allowed for a more coherent approach within an apparently decentralised administrative framework. Logan Page insisted that the 1916 Act did not 'disturb in the slightest degree the present powers and duties of the States'. Nevertheless, it compelled three states to pass constitutional amendments in order to establish the necessary highway departments. Fifteen states established highway departments at this time while eighteen others reorganised existing departments to meet federal requirements. Representatives of OPR helped to set up the highway departments in Texas, Missouri, Indiana and South Carolina, while nineteen other states consulted the federal agency. For states eager to claim their share of federal aid, the need to secure OPR approval bred an attitude of subordination. The same tendency was evident among counties applying for state aid. A dramatic centripetal movement had taken place in the name of Good Roads. The shape of the road outside one's gateway was no longer determined directly by oneself in consultation with neighbours but was decided by experts who spoke a language only their colleagues could understand, and who shared increasingly a national corporate perspective on the role of highways.[38]

The *Engineering News-Record* observed that 'the United States Office of Public Roads and Rural Engineering will have a dominating influence in all work for which application for federal aid is made'. To obtain this influence in a Congress whose committees were still dominated disproportionately by politicians from agricultural states, the Page – MacDonald faction had allied itself to the Progressive cause of ending rural isolation which meant giving priority to rural postal routes to the dismay of the Eastern faction within the AASHO and its powerful associate, the motoring lobby. The latter would endeavour to change these priorities by challenging both the administrative competence and even the professional judgement of the OPR. The 1916 Act itself provided an opportunity for such criticism since it entrusted the close supervision of approved projects to the OPR under hastily devised administrative procedures which proved clumsy and inefficient. Between 1916 and 1919, the OPR approved 1316 federal aid projects totalling 16,673 miles, yet only twelve and a half miles of road were actually constructed. One major excuse for this shortfall – the impact of international warfare on the US economy – ironically bolstered the major highway advocates by illustrating the strategic value of an interstate highway system and diminishing – albeit temporarily – opposition to federal interference. The nation's railroads could not carry the traffic produced by wartime mobilisation and the motor truck emerged as a significant freight-carrier for the first time. The sharp increase in the number of such commercial vehicles devastated the existing road network, which had been intended for lighter traffic. The war effort also stressed the need to link the nation's industrial heartland with its Eastern ports and thus drew attention away from rural road improvement. Moreover, the war also rapidly inflated the costs of highway construction in terms of labour and

and materials, making it impossible to meet the specifications of the 1916 Act in terms of types of road surface within the prescribed ceiling of $10,000 per mile.[39]

Well aware of the deficiencies of the existing scheme, Page was proposing an extension of the federal aid scheme at the time of his death in 1918. Given the threat of high unemployment after demobilisation, this was an attractive proposition to Congress, and the motoring lobby had already prepared a scheme to take advantage of these sentiments. In February 1919, Senator Charles Townsend of Michigan introduced a bill to establish a national highway commission to construct a national road system and in April a new 'umbrella' organisation, the Federal Highway Council, was organised to promote the measure. The high point of the propaganda campaign for a national highway network was the US Army's transcontinental truck convey tour of the Lincoln Highway from Washington DC to San Francisco in July 1919. 'The Army publicity', remarked car-maker Roy Chapin jubilantly, 'states that this is to demonstrate to Congress the need for a national system of highways for military purposes. What more could we want?' However, despite such public demonstrations in favour of a centralised system, proponents of the existing bilateral federal aid approach had already regrouped behind Thomas MacDonald who had been appointed as Page's successor at the renamed Bureau of Public Roads (BPR).[40]

At the time of Page's death, the AASHO had been evenly split on the issue of federal aid or national highway commission. However, by speeding the flow of aid to the states, MacDonald strengthened the position of federal aid sufficiently to secure a resolution in its favour at the AASHO 1919 convention. As a consequence, the highway engineering profession was once again able to present itself as the guardian of the public interest against the selfish forces, both of Wilsonian Big Government and of automotive Big Business, even though its members' sympathies were largely with the corporate state. By 1920, it appeared as if the motoring lobby would once again fail to secure the highway legislation it desired. However, by the start of the 1920s, middle-class motoring was already producing a traffic pattern which could be used to justify a shift in priorities to trunk-line highways between population centres. The removal of such social institutions as schools, churches and general stores from the open country was, we have argued, the result of pre-existing weaknesses rather than simply motoring but these weaknesses were rendered critical by the willingness of the middle classes to compensate for these local deficiencies by auto commuting. The ensuing relocation of rural services included a revision of the postal routes which had been the initial grounds for federal highway aid. Since the mail no longer took the back road to an outlying farm but stayed instead on the main road to town, the latter was improved so that the farmer could collect his mail presumably by car.[41]

Individual states were also better able to countenance the prospect of sharing the cost of highway improvement. The successful introduction of the gasoline tax in many states, beginning in the Pacific North-West, and the equally important earmarking of this user tax for highway purposes, provided a growing source of revenue for the construction and maintenance of a road network. Thus, by 1921, the goal of both federal aid and national highway commission supporters had become the same: an integrated trunk-line system. The Federal Highway Act of 9 November 1921 perpetuated the control of highway officials over the federal aid distribution process. The BPR requested state highway officials to prepare a classification scheme to identify national, state and local roads as a basis for establishing a national system. It permitted each state to designate up to 7 per cent of its total mileage as eligible for federal aid but required that priority be given to primary inter-city routes within this group. All federal-aid roads were to be maintained subsequently by the states, which ended the practice of delegating maintenance to the counties. Important operational details of the federal aid programme, notably the classification of roads, required BPR approval. Just as in 1916 a centripetal trend drew power from the local to the state level, obliging several states to amend their constitution in order to escape the notions of local self-government originally embodied in them. At the apex of an increasingly complex bureaucracy remained the officials of the BPR, sustained by their mastery of the politics of professionalism.[42]

The first census of US public roads in 1904 had reported that only 7 per cent of the nation's 2,151,570 miles of highway could be classed as 'improved' and much of this consisted of gravel roads, with a few miles of brick and asphalt concentrated in Coxey's Ohio. By 1924, 1,527,000 miles were classed as surfaced roads and each state had designated 7 per cent of its mileage for improvement using federal aid. To Progressive Americans, such a transformation represented a great leap forward, particularly since the standard of construction and frequency of travel in all parts of the nation had risen dramatically.

Proposed as a means of reviving the agrarian well-springs of democracy, road reform had served the Progressive purpose of reorganising the rural community so that it functioned more efficiently within a corporate economy. Advocated by Jacob Coxey as a mechanism for promoting economic recovery, highway construction was indeed a vital ingredient in the booming economy of the 1920s, demonstrating how state intervention could accelerate capital accumulation more readily than it could renew the basis for independent producer republicanism. Defended as a means of bringing the farmer's produce to market more efficiently and thus lowering the price of the worker's bread, Good Roads encouraged the practice of auto commuting and so produced such traffic congestion that the farmer had to buy a truck to deliver his goods, even if it meant the worry of another debt to the banker.[43]

The motor car, Ford or not, did not automatically produce a national auto highway system. Rather the impulse to acquire a car prior to 1920 served to identify those individuals who already favoured improved links with the world beyond their own community. Objectively, this impulse stemmed from the essential imperative towards exchange within a capitalist economy, which sought to shorten the time it took to trade. It was for this reason that mail-order houses backed Progressive rural reform whether it took the form of agricultural experimental stations and school consolidation or Rural Free Delivery and Good Roads trains; the first two measures would hopefully enable the farm community to secure some cash while the second would facilitate the circulation of capital back to the mail-order corporations. Since a practical motor truck was not available prior to the 1920s, motoring was largely a means of delivering customers rather than freight and so, despite the rhetoric of road reformers, the car served those interests desiring the incorporation of rural Americans in a consumer culture far more effectively than it served as a mechanism for moving agricultural commodities to the market.

Road reform epitomised the delegation of authority to experts, and the preceding pages have tried to show the illusory character of the idea of unbiased expertise. By entrusting highway policy to the engineers, Progressive America elevated a special interest as self-interested as the motoring lobby or road construction industry. The way in which the massive investment in highways was made reflected the need of the highway engineering profession to establish itself. Although the early history of the Wayne County Road Commission suggests that a consensus existed between public officials and business leaders as to what constituted efficiency, the larger national campaign for a systematic highway policy suggests that public officials were more sensitive to the need to legitimise their proposals than were private capitalists whose desire for immediate action in their favour threatened to arouse opposition unnecessarily. Thus, the process of eliminating traditional highway administration was a gradual one which never kept pace with the desire of corporate business to speed up the process of exchange. However, ultimately, the apparent neutrality of the highway engineers and the propaganda of general improvement with which the highway officials surrounded the issue of Good Roads facilitated a dramatic change in governmental practices as well as the nation's roads, which signalled a new phase in the incorporation of America.[44]

Notes

1 David Harvey, *The Urbanization of Capital*, 1985, p. 37.

2 Robert Wiebe, *The Search for Order, 1877–1920*, 1967, preface, pp. xiii–xiv; what follows is especially indebted to Bruce Seely, 'Highway engineers as policy makers: the Bureau of Public Roads, 1893–1944', 2 vols., unpublished PhD, University of Delaware, 1982. I would also like to thank the staff of the Wayne County Road Commission and of the Michigan Historical Collections, Ann Arbor, for their assistance.

3 Carlos A. Schwantes, *Coxey's Army: an American Odyssey*, 1985, pp. 32–7; W. D. B. Sheldon, *Populism in the Old Dominion: Virginia Farm Politics, 1885–1900*, 1967, p. 18.

4 Albert A. Pope, *Wagon Roads as Feeders to Railways*, 1892, p. 7; Alfred D. Chandler, *The Visible Hand: the Managerial Revolution in American Business*, 1977, *passim*; Harvey, loc. cit.

5 Pope, op. cit., pp. 10, 22; Wayne E. Fuller, *RFD: the Changing Face of Rural America*, 1964, *passim*.

6 Pope, *The Movement for Better Roads: an Address ... before the Board of Trade, Hartford*, 11 February 1890, pamphlet in the Burton Historical Collection, Detroit, p. 23; cf. Seely, op. cit., p. 105, note 101.

7 Pope, *Wagon Roads*, pp. 5, 11.

8 Frank Rogers, *A History of the Michigan State Highway Department, 1905–1933*, 1933, pp. 11–14; Horatio S. Earle, *The Autobiography of 'By Gum' Earle*, 1929, pp. 75, 77, 116.

9 'Farmers' wise words', *Motor Age*, VIII, 23 November 1905, p. 33; cf. the hostility of resolutions passed by the Michigan Grange in 1896: Michigan, State Board of Agriculture, *Thirty-Sixth Annual Report of the Secretary of the State Board of Agriculture, July 1, 1896–June 30, 1897*, 1898, pp. 488, 501; William Bowers, *The Country Life Movement in America, 1900-1920*, 1974, pp. 77, 26.

10 Earle, op. cit., p. 102.

11 Archer B. Hulbert, ed., *The Future of Road Making in America: a Symposium*, 1905, p. 25.

12 Alan Trachtenberg, *The Incorporation of America*, 1982. For engineers as social leaders, see Edwin T. Layton, Jr., *Revolt of the Engineers: Special Responsibility and the American Engineering Profession*, 1971; for engineers as the servants of capital, see David F. Noble, *America by Design: Science, Technology and the Rise of Corporate Capitalism*, 1979.

13 Wiebe, op. cit., pp. 111–13, 129–32; John B. Rae, 'Coleman duPont and his Road', *Delaware History*, XVI, Spring–Summer, 1975, pp. 171–83; Seely, op. cit., pp. 36–8, 47–50. Richard L. McCormick, 'The discovery that business corrupts politics', *American Historical Review*, LXXXVI, April 1981.

14 Wiebe, op. cit., p. 161; cf. J. Dalton, 'Take highways out of politics: demand of engineers', *Automotive Industries*, XLVIII, 29 March 1913, pp. 708–13; Logan W. Page, 'Good Roads: the way to progress', *World's Work*, XVIII, July 1909, p. 11815.

15 Noble, op. cit.; Gabriel Kolko, *The Truimph of Conservatism: a Re-Interpretation of American History, 1900–1916*, 1967, *passim*; C. H. Claudy, 'Don't let "George" build your roads', *Country Life in America*, XXV, December 1913, pp. 112–16.

16 Frank B. King, 'Importance of street plans and grades for towns that expect to be cities', *The American City*, IV, January 1911, pp. 233–5; Arthur Blanchard, 'Chambers of commerce and public highways', op. cit., p. 13, September 1915, pp. 217–20; Noble, op. cit., *passim*.

17 Kenneth E. Peters, 'The Good Roads movement and the Michigan State Highway Department, 1905–1917', unpublished PhD, University of Michigan, 1972, p. 94; Diaries of Horatio S. Earle, Michigan Historical Collections, entries for 8 June 1905; 6 July 1906; 6 August 1906; 28 August 1906; 2 October 1906; the only reference to the Ford Motor Company comes in the entry for 18 August 1906.

18 See Chapter 7, below.

19 Edward N Hines, 'Two million dollars for Good Roads in Wayne County', *The Detroiter*, II, October 1911, pp. 7–12; Fourth Annual Report of the Board of County Road Commissioners of Wayne County to the Board of Supervisors, Wayne County, 20 September 1910, p. 6.

20 Board of County Road Commissioners, *Ninth Annual Report*, 30 September 1915, pp. 13–17. The seasonal and immigrant character of the workforce is reflected in the commission's paybook which records Anglo-Saxon names for skilled employees and predominantly Polish and Italian names for labourers.

21 Board of County Road Commissioners, *Fourth Annual Report*, 30 September 1910, pp. 18, 20.

22 Ibid., p. 4; Peters, 'Good Roads Movement', p. 99.

23 'The political economy of Good Roads', *Scientific American*, XCIX, 19 December 1908, p. 451; Page, 'Good Roads, the way to progress', pp. 11808–9.

24 Board of Wayne County Road Commissioners, *Seventh Annual Report*, 1913, forward; idem., *Tenth Annual Report*, 1916, p. 5, cites an increase in suburban property values of 117 per cent compared to 57 per cent in Detroit as a benefit from highway improvement, locally high wages caused a rise in food prices and other necessities even prior to the wartime inflation.

25 'Concrete roads in Wayne County, Michigan', *Engineering Record*, LXIII, 7 January 1911, pp. 6–7; 'Concrete roads: methods of construction in Wayne County, Michigan', *Engineering Magazine*, XLV, June 1913, pp. 415–17; Automobile Manufacturers Association, *Automobiles of America*, 1970, p. 259, lists 1,108,000 trucks in the USA by 1920; John Harwhite, 'The motor truck and the road', *Scientific American*, CXIII, 17 July 1915, p. 66; Rollin W. Hutchinson, Jr., 'The motor truck in peace and war', *Collier's*, LVI, 8 January 1916, p. 43.

26 'Roads for automobiles', *Scientific American*, XCV, 3 November 1906, p. 318; Seely, 'Highway engineers', pp. 418–73.

27 A. W. Marks, 'Foreign road making lessons – European experience in meeting the many problems created by the automobile', *Collier's*, XLVIII, 6 January 1912, p. 56; Logan W. Page, 'Automobiles and improved roads', *Scientific American*, CIX, 6 September 1913, pp. 178, 200.

28 *Ford Times*, April 1913, p. 290.

29 Horatio Earle, 'Good Roads – will Detroit set the pace?' *The Detroiter*, I, September 1910, pp. 3–5; Peters, op. cit., pp. 124–7; Wayne County Road Commissioners, *Sixth Annual Report*, 1912, p. 8; idem., *Seventh Annual Report*, 1913, p. 8; idem., *Ninth Annual Report*, 1915, p. 6.

30 Peters, op. cit., pp. 69–72, 76–7, 83–4, 86–8, 90–1, 152–3, 157–9, 163–70.

31 Logan Page, 'Our highways and the motor car', *Collier's*, XLVIII, 6 January 1912, p. 38. For Page's early work and style of leadership at the OPR, see Seely, op. cit., pp. 38–40, 53–8.

32 Seely, op. cit., pp. 115–21.

33 Ibid., p. 66: 'American Road Builders' Association Convention', *Engineering News*, LXVIII, 12 December 1912, p. 114; Roy D. Chapin, 'The automobile manufacturer in relation to Good Roads', pp. 3–4, Miscellaneous Correspondence File, 1914, Box 1, Roy D. Chapin Papers, Bentley Library, Ann Arbor (hereafter cited as Chapin Papers); 'Federal aid for highway improvements', *Engineering News*, LXVI, 28 December 1911, p. 775.

34 Seely, op. cit., pp. 124–30, 137–9, 609; W. Stull Holt, *The Bureau of Public Roads: its History, Activities and Organization*, 1923, pp. 14–15.

35 Seely, op. cit., pp. 69–72.

36 Ibid., pp. 55–62, 73–85, 390–8. Among leading engineers who assisted the OPR in its research were Prof. Blanchard of Columbia University (see note 16, above) and New York's leading municipal engineer, Nelson P. Lewis, in Jeffrey K. Stine, *Nelson P. Lewis and the City Efficient: the Municipal Engineer in City Planning during the Progressive Era*, April 1981, *passim*.

37 Seely, op. cit., pp. 129, 140–3; A. E. Johnson, 'History of the origin, development and operation of the American Association of State Highway Officials', in the Association's *AASHO: the First Fifty Years, 1914–1964*, 1964, pp. 49–53.

38 Batchelder to Chapin, 14 March 1916, 12 April 1916, Correspondence File, Chapin Papers; Seely, op. cit., pp. 143–9.

39 Seely, op. cit., pp. 150–2, 156–8. Other applications of federal aid included agricultural experimental stations, land-grant colleges, agricultural extension services and the Forest Fire Protection Service, all, like the OPR, within the Department of Agriculture.

40 'Rules for applying Federal Aid Road Improvement Act', *Engineering News-Record*, LXXVI, 14 September 1916, p. 521; Seely, op. cit., pp. 160–4, 423–5. The switch to motor trucks was further encouraged by the 1920 rail strike. Sales of trucks and buses rose from 24,900 in 1914 to 321,789 in 1920, but dropped dramatically to 148,052 in 1921, Automobile Manufacturers Association, op. cit., p. 263.

41 Seely, op. cit., pp. 165–7, 169–70, 175–7; for auto industry's role, see Chapin to Townsend, 7 January 1919, 17 January 1919; Chapin to Batchelder, 22 January 1919; Correspondence File, Box 6, Chapin Papers.

42 Seely, op. cit., pp. 183–90, 207; 'State highway officials support federal-aid Bill', *Engineering News Record*, 14 October 1920, p. 768.

43 John C. Burnham, 'The gasoline tax and the automobile revolution', *Mississippi Valley Historical Review*, XLVIII, December 1961, pp. 435–59; Seely, op. cit., pp. 199–202; Holt, *The Bureau of Public Roads*, pp. 30–7. The limitations of federal supervision were made evident by corrupt highway administrations in states like Texas, see John D. Huddleston, 'Good Roads for Texas: a history of the Texas Highway Department', unpublished PhD, Texas A. & M. University, 1981, pp. 39–77.

44 John B. Rae, *The Road and the Car in American Life*, 1971, pp. 32–3.

Chapter 4

The suburban solution

> Humanity demands that men should have sunlight, fresh air, the sight of grass and trees. It demands these things for the man himself, and it demands them still more urgently for his wife and children. No child has a fair chance in the world who is condemned to grow up in the dirt and confinement, the dreariness, ugliness and vice of the poorer quarters of a great city ... There is then, a permanent conflict between the needs of industry and the needs of humanity. Industry says men must aggregate. Humanity says they must not, or if they must, let it be only during working hours and let the necessity not extend to their wives and children. It is the office of the city railways to reconcile these conflicting requirements.[1]

The vision of pioneer sociologist Charles Horton Cooley in 1891 usefully summarises an important aspect of Progressive attitudes to transport innovation in the urban context. Whereas the countryside was seen as debilitated by its spatial attenuation, so in the eyes of middle-class reformers, the metropolis was contaminated by its industrial congestion. In rural America, the processes of capitalism were hampered by the incomplete nature of market influence. Observing rural inefficiencies, Progressive reformers urged farmers to adopt the organisational structures of industry to enhance their pursuit of capital accumulation, and as a vital corollary to this adjustment, the reformers also advocated infrastructural investment to complete the incorporation of rural hinterland areas into the industrial economy. In this way, the circulation of capital would be expedited, and the process of capital accumulation would be legitimised by the same cultural goals of consumption which justified it to urban Americans. Applying industrial standards to the problems of the countryside, Progressive spokesmen none the less applied their prejudices to the social problems of the burgeoning American metropolises. Housing reformers like Lawrence Veiller, Jane Addams and Jacob Riis attributed the degraded quality of life of 'the other half' in large measure to overcrowding. For them and for a rapidly growing middle class, the normative standard of housing was increasingly the single-family suburban home situated in a neighbourhood where low density of population and larger building lots permitted the cultivation of private yards and the presence of grass and trees. From the arrival of the horse-car onwards, each successive transport innovation inflamed Progressive hopes that this standard could be extended to all.[2]

Henry Ford, among others, regarded cities as the product of inefficient forms of transport, and was convinced that urban life and its associated pathologies would be eliminated by the introduction of rapid transport. However, when Charles Cooley reflected on the social potential of electric rapid transit in 1891, it was commonly accepted that the agglomeration of people required under the factory system would continue to fuel urban population growth. Manufacturing remained relatively labour-intensive at this stage and so the expropriation of surplus value within the labour process still required the physical presence of large numbers of labourers each day. As early as 1860, the population density of New York City was 135.6 persons per acre, placing its inhabitants in the midst of a ubiquitous throng which ebbed and flowed in colliding currents most conspicuously at the start and end of the working day. Without co-ordination, these flows of labour and other commodities jammed, thereby offsetting the advantages of aggregated settlement to industrial production.[3]

Each city had its crowds and all city fathers shared a common desire to disperse them. Such masses did not merely impede the flow of commodities within the urban industrial system but also heightened the risk of contagious disease and social disorder. Transport was regarded as the key method of dealing with this multi-faceted problem. However, the problem was perceived in a particularistic way by different social groups and so the response was unsystematic. More importantly, the concern over congestion varied according to the level of specialisation in a given district and the power of its residents. Around the middle of the nineteenth century, major American cities developed what became known as central business districts (CBD). The specialised administrative and financial functions of the CBD required office space and this form of construction displaced older low-income residences whose occupants crowded into the small two- or three-storey houses in adjoining neighbourhoods. In the absence of any public provision for low-income housing, such neighbourhoods degenerated into slums as overcrowding increased. The ensuing exodus of those who could afford to leave produced a favourable climate for transit entrepreneurs in which municipalities sought to encourage infrastructural investment by construing their supervisory obligations in a limited fashion. By 1860, the New York city council had granted eight 99- or 999-year franchises to horse-railways with no co-ordination of routes and little provision for payment to the city.[4]

While these developments may seem peripheral to the history of the automobile, they were actually of great consequence. The emergence of the CBD as a powerful lobby for transport innovation was compounded by the acceptance of the CBD as a 'natural' nucleus by American urban planners. 'The more a social organism grows, and the higher its evolution', observed Adna Weber in 1898, 'so much the greater will the commercial centers become.' This rationalised the priority given to the social and economic interests of the CBD over those of the other metropolitan areas. In the late nineteenth century, the expansion of production in the United States required changes in the forms of industrial organisation, communication, exchange and distribution which gave added impetus to the quest for a mechanism to integrate these elements into an efficient system, synchronising all activity at a rapid pace. Simultaneously, these changes generated forces of class structuralisation via the increasing division of labour within the work process and these, too, were embodied in the changing social geography of the metropolis. The growing social distinction between blue-collar and white-collar workers was rendered more conspicuous in the United States at the turn of the century by the preponderance of new immigrants in blue-collar occupations. Overlying the social manifestation of the distinction between skilled and unskilled, there were residual ethnic resentments derived from previous social experiences, which served to subdivide and stratify the urban population even further.[5]

Moreover, the intricacies of economic life under capitalism ensured that such social differentiation within classes was not confined to the working classes. The capitalist class also was riddled with divisions, some of them arising from or being aggravated by the functional frictions between individuals within and between different sectors of the economy. While the rise of corporations and holding companies reflected a perception that long-term profits from a stabilised sector were more certain than short-term success in an open market, antagonism between financiers and industrialists and between the powerful and the aspiring in both professions ensured that the capitalist class was fragmented and neither spoke nor acted with a single mind. Thus, for our purposes, the complexity of social stratification warns against any simple attribution of residential location choices to class antipathies.

Nevertheless, income and mode of life did colour the character of suburban expansion. Those who could afford to buy a suburban home and commute to work daily were thus able to segregate themselves from those who could not. However, the desire to separate oneself from undesirable elements did not, as Kenneth Jackson points out, require suburbanisation. The latter was also a product of certain compelling Anglo-American cultural values. We have already alluded to the disquiet articulated by middle-class Americans when they considered the crowded life of the industrial cities. However, it was not simply a matter of applying the perspective of an anti-urban tradition to the material faults of the metropolis. There was also a powerful combination between the nineteenth century's 'cult of domesticity' and the economics of the real-estate market at work on the mind of the emergent middle classes.[6]

Catherine Beecher's *Treatise on Domestic Economy for the Use of Young Ladies at Home and at School*, published in 1841, was reprinted dozens of times over the next thirty years. Its recommendations implanted a vision of home in a generation of middle-class Americans. Central to Beecher's thought was the desirability of the physical and social separation of the population into the female-dominated sphere of home life, preferably suburban, and the male-dominated sphere of the business world, usually urban. By the time Charles Cooley reflected upon the social role of the street railways in 1891, this ideology of separate spheres was so deeply fixed as to appear 'natural'.[7]

Moreover, as Mary Corbin Sies has recently pointed out, the professional and managerial stratum of the middle class between 1877 and 1917 undertook to build not merely homes but entire communities embodying this ideal. The existing residential areas were unable to exclude the intrusive pressures of the masculine spheres of commerce, industry and labouring masses, and so new homes were located in suburban subdivisions. These suburbs provided the essentials for a wholesome domestic life, as this stratum of society conceived of it: a detached single-family dwelling, neighbours of a similar social background; first-rate schools; sanitary and moral surroundings, providing in particular healthy recreational opportunities for children.

In such an environment, the moral education and character-building believed to be essential for the social stability of the Republic could take place in conducive surroundings. Indeed, as the environmental determinism within Darwinism became more influential in the thinking of American social commentators, there emerged the possibility of engineering the environment in such a way as to induce its inhabitants to conform to prescribed behavioural patterns without the imposition of coercive laws and prohibitions. By changing their habitat, one might ultimately change people.[8]

Alongside this 'cult of domesticity' operated the real-estate market. In urban areas, but especially in developing suburban sections, American land was cheap by international standards. Moreover, incomes, even the often meagre wages of the working man, were almost invariably higher than those for the same job elsewhere in the world. Consequently, home ownership was relatively easily obtained in the United States. Stephen Thernstrom reported that 'real estate was strikingly available to working class men who remained in Newburyport for any length of time'. However, such ownership often required all the family to work, thus securing property at the expense of the children's education. In Detroit, Olivier Zunz has shown that in 1890 fully 55 per cent of the Germans, 46 per cent of the Irish, and 44 per cent of the Poles owned their own homes; a strikingly high level of home ownership partly facilitated by the geographical distribution of Detroit's industrial plants. However, this accessibility of industrial work simply served to provide the opportunity for long-term settlement, a factor which Thernstrom highlighted. Of equal significance in Detroit's case was a dual housing market consisting of a formal housing market operated by professional realtors and providing relatively expensive homes ($2000 upwards) for middle-class Americans, and an informal communal system of house construction in ethnic neighbourhoods in which families built their own homes on small lots. In order to reduce costs, the latter pattern of housing was characterised by an absence of public services at the time of construction as the new residents delayed the imposition of special assessments by the municipality. The laying of sewers and pavements was thus commonly postponed. Financial pressures also encouraged home owners to take in lodgers, a practice which further separated the lower-class domestic experience from the professional – managerial stratum's ideal.[9]

For the middle classes, their pursuit of this more decorous ideal depended, just as in the working man's case, upon ready access to work, and hence upon commuting speed. A simple law of geometry meant that the area of potentially residential land was increased by the square of the radius from the centre of the city. A doubling of the radius produced a quadrupling of the area available for development. Moreover, between 1865 and 1896, a sustained agricultural depression meant that the value of land was falling for farming purposes. On the edges of large communities, this encouraged farmers to sell their land. Increasingly, the least expensive housing option acceptable to those middle-class families who could afford to commute was to move outward.[10]

It proved a popular choice. By 1900, commuting was part of the common experience for inhabitants of all thirty-eight US cities whose population exceeded 100,000. As the nation's premier industrial city, its largest seaport and chief immigration entry-point, New York confronted the problems of traffic on a metropolitan scale earlier than any other American city. One historian of the city has described its transit pattern thus:

> In 1890, nearly one and a half million people were living on Manhattan Island, and nearly ninety thousand had moved into the Annexed District beyond the Harlem River. Every morning, almost as many more poured into the city for the day's work. At night, they overflowed into suburban regions to sleep. They herded on cars that crossed Brooklyn Bridge, on ferries that plowed across the East and Hudson Rivers, and down the bay to Staten Island, on trains that thundered in and out of Grand Central Station. The evening tide out of New York washed over a vast area.[11]

Despite this daily exodus stimulated by the infrastructural investment in commuter links during the 1880s, New York still had the most congested housing in the nation. Beside the inspiring span of Brooklyn Bridge on the Lower East Side the immigrant masses still huddled in squalor. Unredeemed by environmental forces, these crowds tainted local politics in the eyes of the upstate Republican machine to such an extent that only the huge annexation of hitherto suburban Brooklyn, Queens, Staten Island and the Bronx in 1898 could dilute the Tammany poison by adding middle-class voters from the outlying boroughs to the metropolitan electorate. With this municipal boundary adjustment New York City's area reached 229 square miles. Only mechanised transport could unite such a huge area.[12]

State governments, like that in Albany in 1898, might be able to perceive a need to unify the metropolis. However, while the benefits of annexation to the city continued to be listed throughout the twentieth century, the advantages of absorption to suburban communities became steadily less persuasive. Special service districts provided an alternative means for individual suburbs to enjoy a standard of water, sewerage, education, or policing provision equal, if not superior in some cases, to that provided within city limits. Most importantly, the civic pride which members of the professional and managerial elites took in the great city outside of which they increasingly chose to reside was tempered by a growing apprehension of its myriad problems. The vast influx of largely impoverished immigrants from southern and eastern Europe at the turn of the century was followed by the great migration of Southern blacks to Northern cities in the First World War period. The ensuing social problems, as John D. Buenker has observed, were attributed all too often according to firmly rooted, nativist, racist assumptions, which blamed the newcomers who were the principal victims of the social dislocation produced by rapid urban growth. Consequently, transport technology came to be used for social segregation as much as economic integration.[13]

Intemperance, vice, urban bosses, crime, and political activities deemed subversive to the existing order were held to stem from the predilections of ethnic and racial minorities. Accordingly, as the number of white native-born commuters rose markedly, the middle-class character of suburban settlement was interpreted as evidence of intrinsic ethnic differences. Even a perceptive student of urban development such as Adna Weber, who realised that working conditions and a lack of credit facilities limited the ability of lower-income groups to move to suburban housing, could none the less declare in 1898: 'To the Anglo-Saxon race, life in great cities cannot be made to seem a healthy and natural mode of existence. The fresh air and clear sunlight, the green foliage and God's clear blue sky are dear to the heart of this people.'[14] Transit was therefore essential for the 'Anglo-Saxon race' in America to enjoy a decent life. It not only allowed the middle classes communion with Nature but also allowed them to relocate away from undesirables and amongst neighbours of a similar social background to themselves. Thus, for these middle-class commuters, one essential aspect of a successful transit service was segregation. The entrepreneurs who launched the street railways were eager to serve the suburban commuter within certain limits.

Their principal aim was to make money rather than transport people and so the transit system reflected the opportunities for real-estate speculation and the existing concentration of traffic. As a result, the typical transit pattern radiated out from the city centre along busy streets towards the nearest suburban development. The higher cost of mechanised transit made its promoters in the 1880s even more concerned than their horse-car predecessors with the profits of real-estate speculation and securing control of major downtown traffic arteries.[15]

Such a transit pattern favoured cities with a concentration of administrative and service occupations downtown, such as San Francisco, Washington DC, New York, or Los Angeles. It reflected the speculative schemes of landowners who targeted the middle-class would-be suburbanites in the 1890s. F.M. Smith bought a controlling interest in Oakland's electric railways in 1893 and continued to add and consolidate transit lines until he had seventy-five miles of tracks by 1903. Along with several other local businessmen, he formed the Realty Syndicate which purchased 13,000 acres of undeveloped land between Mills College and Berkeley. The syndicate would arrange for a trolley line to extend to its subdivisions while bypassing the real-estate holdings of others. By laying streets, sidewalks and sewers, and providing home loans, the Realty Syndicate became the first choice for middle-class commuters in the Oakland area. Like Smith, Henry E. Huntington of the Pacific Electric Railway Company was more interested in speculating in southern Californian land than in transit *per se*. He put down tracks throughout the Los Angeles basin, from Santa Monica to San Bernandino and from Pasadena to Baltoa. Indeed, as early as 1910 the essential parameters of the Los Angeles metropolitan area had been defined in a sprawling horizontal pattern strikingly different to the skyscrapers and slums of New York or Chicago.[16]

Huntington spelt out the essence of his strategy in 1904. 'Railway lines', he explained:

> have to keep ahead of the procession [of settlement]. It would never do for an electric line to wait until demand for it came. It must anticipate the growth of communities and be there when the homebuilders arrive – or they are likely not to arrive at all, but to go to some section already provided with arteries of traffic.

Thus, the fundamental fact initiating transit was the profit to be made from the development of peripheral low-density residential areas. Unfortunately, the subsequent profitability of urban transit rested upon the entirely contrary principle of maximum passenger loads, and these could be most readily reached in areas of high population density, like Manhattan. Upon this contradiction, urban rapid transit in the United States would ultimately founder and the private automobile would take its place. At the turn of the century, however, this irreconcilability of objectives was obscured by traction magnates as they consolidated the old horse-car lines to form electric traction systems in the major American cities.[17]

This process of modernisation was a politically charged one. Transit promoters required municipal grants to secure their rights of way via franchises. Moreover, as railroads, street railways were obliged to secure state charters. This political dependence provided notorious occasions for bribery and graft. Despite the importance of private deals in the success of traction barons like Charles T. Yerkes, this political involvement obliged such entrepreneurs to nurture alliances between different sections of the city, particularly between central business district (CBD) interests and those of suburbia. Indeed, a significant factor in transit's eventual decline after 1920 was the disintegration of effective CBD–suburb co-operation. However, during the 1890s, the debate over mass transit saw issues such as universal transfers, through routes and flat-rate fares, gain prominence as popular rallying cries for reformers like Hazen Pingree of Detroit. The beneficiaries of such concessions included a growing number of working-class commuters. The high price of land had begun to preclude the location of large industrial plants in the vicinity of the CBD and so manufacturers began to congregate at outlying railway junctions and on waterfronts. Each day thousands of workers hurried across the city to and from the new factory districts. Frequently, however, the city-to-suburb radial pattern of the transit lines obliged workers to go downtown first in order to transfer. The increase in this practice became evident in the growing number of transfers issued which comprised around 20 per cent of total ownership on average by 1907, but in the case of the Chicago Southern constituted nearly 41 per cent of passengers.[18]

The flat-rate 'nickel' fare and universal transfers became the foundations for genuine 'mass' transit, and as such, became politically non-negotiable, a fact which severely damaged the prospects of transit modernisation in the face of competition from the automobile. The speculative excesses of the early entrepreneurs, widely publicised by the contemporary press, instilled the conviction that the public declarations of later transit officials concerning mounting liabilities and declining profits were disingenuous and that the trolley companies had hidden profits with which they could afford to preserve the flat-rate 'nickel' fare while still improving service by the construction of new lines and the purchase of new equipment.[19]

This suspicion of the traction companies was aggravated by a declining standard of comfort for transit users. Once the windfall profits from real-estate speculation had been enjoyed, company officials seemed to accept Charles T. Yerkes's dictum that: 'It is the people who hang to the strap who pay you big dividends'. Offered by way of explanation to his stockholders in the wake of newspaper criticism of overcrowding on rush-hour trains, Yerkes's declaration provided no solace for the commuting public. Overcrowding topped their list of grievances which retain a familiar ring for any public transit user. It was overcrowding that produced delayed services, breakdowns and dirty carriages and engendered a tension between occupants that provoked verbal and sometimes physical confrontations. In all these ways, the inconveniences of public transit whetted the appetite of commuters for a mechanised vehicle of their own, the automobile.[20]

Politicians of all stripes, whether reformers or bosses, cultivated this animosity for their own ends and periodically forced the transit lines to extend services or purchase new equipment, but to no avail. In the wake of a three-year rehabilitation programme by Chicago's transit companies, a survey of the ten major surface lines in January 1915 revealed that loads during the peak evening rush-hour period exceeded eighty-five passengers per forty-seat carriage. This meant less than three square feet per passenger on average. The worst crowding occurred just north and south of The Loop in light industrial and sweat-shop districts. Space per passenger in these zones diminished to just over one square foot. However, outside of these narrow sections of the trolley line, streetcar loads declined precipitously. Hence, adding streetcars to cut the congestion in these peak areas meant lowering the load per car over the entire line and thus reducing the earnings per car-hour by which transit's efficiency was gauged. A rational solution to this problem was available in the form of limited routes whereby services would turn back just beyond the peak zones and so spend most of their time in the heavy-load districts. A vociferous opposition to such services came from the traditional transit favourite, the suburban commuter, who would be inconvenienced by a reduction in what was currently a relatively frequent 'door-to-door' service.

Anxious to retain suburban patrons, downtown businesses supported this insistence that all cars run to the end of the line, even though demand there was numerically insignificant and this terminus moved further away from the crowed inner-city zones with each annual extension of the line. The same insistence on personal convenience on the part of inner-city dwellers obliged the companies to stop their streetcars on each side of an intersection and in the middle of long blocks regardless of the delays and traffic congestion thus caused.[21]

To the individual passenger, the failings of mass transit seemed to represent a broken promise since the companies had assiduously publicised the benefits which citizens would enjoy in return for the granting of a franchise and the payment of a fixed fare. The dependence of commuters upon transit made the quality of service received a particularly controversial aspect of local politics. Thus, Chicagoans rejected the purchase of the transit lines by the city in 1907 in favour of ordinances under which the private companies agreed to immediate measures to improve services. Discontent in southern California prompted Angelenos to call for lower fares for standing passengers in 1911 and to petition the state Railroad Commission for a reduction in fares on the inter-urban routes of the Pacific Electric in 1913, despite the fact that the operational costs of transit were increasing. By 1910 the majority of US transit companies had debts totalling over half of their assets and the interest payments inflated operational costs and deterred additional investment. World War I destroyed the remains of the transit industry's credit. Between 1914 and 1918 the cost of new equipment more than doubled and the general wartime inflation incited transit workers to strike for pay increases. The traditional five-cents fare could no longer support the transit industry as it stood, let alone fund its expansion and improvement.[22]

The difficulties of transit as a private enterprise in the immediate post-war years served to sustain the long-standing but usually unsuccessful campaign for municipal ownership. In Detroit's case, however, the campaign to purchase the city's street railways launched by Hazen Pingree, the celebrated reform mayor, in 1890 culminated in their purchase by Mayor James Couzens in April 1922. As in Chicago in 1907, the public decision reflected a pragmatic rather than ideological commitment, and Detroiters were prompt to transfer their resentment of inadequate transit service to the new municipal management. In September 1922, Couzens received a letter from a very disgruntled downtown worker. 'If you were a working girl', it began,

> and had to stand on your feet the greater part of the time from 9.00 a.m. to 5.30 p.m., how would you like to stand up in the streetcar and hang on a strap for thirty to forty-five minutes almost every morning on the way to work and again on the way home at night...? What would you think of a streetcar system that caused such conditions as this?

In reply, Couzens echoed the reassurances of Chicago transit officials that the introduction of new streetcars would reduce overcrowding.[23]

Like other mayors across America, Couzens was struggling to respond to the problems generated by rapid urban growth. Detroit had entered the twentieth century with a population of 285,000. By 1920, its population exceeded one million and its area had tripled in two decades to nearly eighty square miles. Detroit was the fastest growing city of the decade prior to 1926 when Los Angeles displaced it as the boom town of the Twenties. As a result, the warning given to Couzens when he first became mayor in 1918 that the city had 'outgrown practically every public utility and most every private facility' remained true for the rest of the decade. Despite these difficulties, the civic leaders of Detroit, like those studied by Blaine Brownell in the cities of the 'New South', regarded growth and increasing size as basic indicators of the health and character of a city, even while they strove for order, civic unity, and stability.[24]

With a large population scattered over a wide area, Detroit needed extensive transport facilities to link up the specialised functional areas within it. This need was recognised most vociferously by the city's middle classes, who, true to their appellation, regarded a detached suburban home as their proper habitat yet still required speedy access to the workplace. While Detroit's population growth averaged out at 60 per cent over the decade of the Twenties, that of its most fashionable suburb, Grosse Pointe, stood at 725 per cent. For the United States generally, as *National Geographic* pointed out in 1923, the more rapid relative growth of suburban to central city areas was linked to the spread of automobile ownership. Whereas in 1920 there had been one car for every thirteen Americans, by 1929 there was one for every five. In Detroit, the ratio was even higher: a motor car for every four residents; in Los Angeles, it was higher still: a car for every three inhabitants. No European nation even approached this level of mass car ownership until the mid-1960s.[25]

Given the contrasting social characteristics of Detroit and Los Angeles, their rejection of plans to improve mass transit facilities and high levels of car ownership during the 1920s provides an opportunity to study the sources of mass motoring in America. By the early 1920s Detroit ranked third behind New York and Chicago in terms of national industrial centres as measured by the dollar value of its manufactured goods. A blue-collar city, Detroit was also a city of immigrants. Native-born whites of native parentage comprised less than a third of the city's population in 1920. Detroit's population grew because its factories attracted migrants from rural America as well as further afield. Of the 528,000 people added to the city's population between 1910 and 1920, 412,000 were migrants. This influx provided the largely unskilled labour force needed by Detroit's automotive industrialists, yet the high rate of labour turnover and linguistic difficulties associated with such a polyglot and newly urbanised workforce also prompted Detroit's leaders to supplement their methods of subordination in the workplace by sponsoring programmes of cultural assimilation. Most strikingly in the case of the celebrated 'Five Dollar Day', the Ford Motor Company used the prospect of relatively high wages for unskilled labour as an incentive for the immigrant to shed his ethnic identity, and an important part of this assimilationist strategy was residential relocation: away from the walk-to-work ethnic neighbourhood to a new suburban lot. Such a pattern of home relocation had potentially significant repercussions for Detroit's transit facilities. Concurrently, the changing means of production pushed the city's leading manufacturers to relocate their operations as existing factory sites became unsuitable for their purposes. While this peripheral relocation of industry stimulated peripheral residential construction around these new plants in the conventional walk-to-work pattern, it also obliged workers to accept either immediately or for the future the necessity of commuting a long distance from peripheral residential location to another outlying industrial workplace. Moreover, for the rapidly growing black population of Detroit, the possibilities of residential resettlement were curtailed by increasingly rigid racial discrimination.[26]

Detroit's black population of fewer than 7000 in 1915 had risen to 40,000 by 1920 and had doubled again by 1925. The bulk of this population was confined to an inner-city ghetto north-east of downtown around St Antoine Street. There were secondary black enclaves in Highland Park and in Inkster near the River Rouge complex, a reflection of the employment offered to blacks by the Ford Motor Company. By 1926, the Ford Motor Company employed 10,000 blacks and the residents of the main ghetto among them faced long journeys to work. Their presence on Detroit's streetcars, it shall be argued, became a significant factor encouraging the switch to auto commuting by racially prejudiced whites.[27]

Less constrained in their movements than Afro-Americans, ethnic workers had traditionally solved their commuting problem by living close to the factory. This practice was still evident in Detroit in the case of Hungarians and Poles who had both arrived in large numbers when the auto industry developed its industrial districts after 1900. Hungarian settlement had been attracted to Delray Village on the west side by job opportunities at the Solvay Process Company's chemical plant. Within the city limits, following Delray's annexation in 1905, the working-class residents were increasingly employed at the giant Ford River Rouge complex after 1920. The Poles dominated the east side of Detroit, extending northwards into the industrial satellite city of Hamtramck. Dissected by railway lines, the east side attracted industrial plants like Dodge Main which provided jobs for the surrounding residents. Communal efforts and individual self-denial procured the homes of the Polish east side yet left the area lacking in public utilities as residents sought to avoid special assessments for paving and sewers.[28]

However, given the instability of working-class employment, the prevalence of multi-income households, and the relocation of industries by the early 1920s, not all blue-collar workers lived close to their place of work. Indeed, some were obliged to commute from the far east side to the west every day using an essentially radial north – south street railway pattern. For these workers, Detroit's mass transit system provided only clumsy service, involving circuitous routes and frequent transfers. Moreover, their voluminous presence impaired the efficiency of the street railway system for the suburb-to-central-business-district commuter. As a consequence the grievances of Chicago's trolley-riders were echoed by the commuters of Detroit.

Across the continent in Southern California, users of the Pacific Electric (PE) and Los Angeles Railway (LARY) systems were equally discontented. Unlike the major metropolises to the east, Los Angeles had grown at a time when mechanised transit afforded the means to spread the city out horizontally in a pattern of residential neighbourhoods composed of single-family dwellings. By 1910, Los Angeles had more than three times as many inhabitants as it had possessed in 1900. These residents used mass transit intensively, taking twice as many rides as did the inhabitants of cities of comparable size (320,000). They did so because the streetcars represented the vital link between home and workplace. While industries and business grew up near the downtown railheads, workers' homes were spread out along the trolley tracks. Indeed, access to transit was so important a consideration that it was noted in 1911 that between the lines were 'long reaches given up to vacant lots – the home of the billboard, tin can and sheep-sorrel weed'.[29]

Robert Fogelson notes that the timing of Los Angeles' spectacular growth, the absence of topographical barriers to settlement, the development of urban technology, particularly for the distribution of essential services, and the associated evolution of corporate managerial structures for such large-scale enterprises all contributed to the distinctively horizontal dispersal of the city. Yet, above these factors, Fogelson places that of 'the exceptional character of its population'. As he explains, Los Angeles was populated principally by the American-born rather than by immigrants. These newcomers to the region frequently had capital resources and marketable skills. Relatively affluent and culturally secure, they had the means to build the homes and communities of their choice. Moreover, these American-born migrants brought with them a carefully nurtured vision of home and community, features of which we have already described. Fogelson sees this conception of the ideal community 'epitomized by the residential suburb – spacious, affluent, clean, decent, permanent, predictable, and homogeneous' as the antithesis of the crowded, improvised, dirty, immoral, transient, volatile and heterogeneous central city.[30]

Fogelson regards these sentiments as the common belief of native Americans everywhere, and Kenneth Jackson, in his recent award-winning study of suburbia, concurs. Jackson cites Dolores Hayden's observation that American civilisation is the first in history to base its utopian ideal on the house rather than the city or the nation. However, he qualifies this statement on the grounds that a similar propensity for detached housing is exhibited by many nationalities. Of greater significance in his view is the fact 'that in the United States the average family was more able to realize its dream of a private home'. In the largely white-collar settlement of southern California at the turn of the century, the landscape was littered with such realised dreams.[31]

Angelenos not only had the means to pursue the suburban dream, they also had an inclination to impel others to follow their lead.

Dana W. Bartlett, a leading Los Angeles reformer extolled the advantages of the 'laying out of subdivisions far beyond the city limits' where working men could 'build their bungalows or California houses'. Economically priced rapid transit was needed to induce the working man 'to locate his family far from the noisy city' where the 'family unit, the desire of the sociologist, can be recovered'. Like their counterparts in Detroit and elsewhere, the professional and managerial classes of Los Angeles believed that republican virtue was nurtured by the correct domestic environment. Most Angelenos deemed single-family homes 'the foundation of this country's security' and so incorporated into the original deeds of the subdivisions clauses prohibiting the construction of multi-family dwellings, or, in some instances, the rental of the property to more than one family. As a result, even after the influx of single persons encouraged the construction of outlying apartment houses during the 1920s, Los Angeles in 1930 remained a city of almost entirely (94%) single-family dwellings in contrast to New York, Chicago, or Boston where multiple-family units nearly equalled single-family homes. Motoring embodied this social preference more readily than did mass transit.[32]

Prior to World War I, the southern Californian economy depended heavily on agriculture and tourism, neither of which encouraged high-density urban development. Yet even when Los Angeles began to emerge as a leading West Coast industrial centre after 1920, it retained its reputation as a white-collar town. Despite a manufacturing output worth $1.3 billion in 1929, the city's manufacturing workforce actually declined as a proportion of the total labour force during the 1920s. Two major local industries, the motion-picture and oil-refining industries, grew rapidly during the wartime period. By 1930, movies employed 15,000 persons while oil refining gave work to 5000 more. After World War I, rapid population growth and rising cross-country shipping costs encouraged the establishment of regional assembly plants on the West Coast. This relatively belated growth of major industry in Los Angeles helped to ensure its absence from the downtown area. The city's small manufacturers were mainly located around the Plaza, the old heart of Los Angeles and their Hispanic, Black and Oriental workforce congregated in the dilapidated houses of this area and the adjoining neighbourhoods of Boyle Heights and East Los Angeles. However, the large industrialists regarded such congested central locations in Los Angeles, as elsewhere, as disadvantageous for them and so preferred to locate their plants on large undeveloped tracts between the Southern Pacific, Santa Fe and Pacific Electric tracks in south-eastern Los Angeles or at Long Beach close to the waterfront and Los Angeles harbour. By 1930, the growth of automotive enterprises like the Ford assembly plant at Long Beach and the Goodyear, Goodrich and Firestone tyre factories in south-eastern Los Angeles pushed the metropolitan area ahead of rival Western manufacturing centres such as San Francisco and Seattle in terms of value of output. These factories expressed both the existing high level of demand for automobiles and the commuting patterns behind that demand.[33]

The manufacturing output of Los Angeles was less than half that of Detroit in 1929, although their respective workforces – 581,000 and 689,000 – were closer together in size. This discrepancy reflected the relative white-collar and blue-collar preponderance within the two labour forces. Los Angeles had 12.2 per cent of its workforce classed as professional service workers compared to 6.2 per cent of Detroit's workers. In equally sharp contrast, Los Angeles had 26.2 per cent of its workers engaged in manufacturing whereas Detroit had 48 per cent. However, notwithstanding these differences, both cities experienced a level of mass motoring which was to prove fatal for their rail transit systems. We have already noted that the ratio of people to automobiles in Detroit (4 : 1) and in Los Angeles (3 : 1) exceeded the distinctively high US level (5 : 1) in 1929. We have also noted that the geographical distribution of workplaces and residences was predicated on some mechanical means of daily commuting, particularly in the case of the middle and upper classes, but that this pattern of two separate spheres was also promulgated as a model for all classes. Thus, the automobile was produced and marketed in a society already committed to a life-style which necessitated commuting. Indeed, the relocation of industry in the context of a working-class culture founded on multiple wage-earners made the practice of commuting more common for workers than it had been in the earlier 'walking' city.[34]

Given the social pressures impelling daily commuting, the growth of motoring becomes a function in part of the public dissatisfaction with mass transit. We have noted that the pursuit of home ownership by low-income groups required sacrifice, persistence, and above all, the opportunity to stay in the same neighbourhood. In Detroit, remaining in the same place while industry moved further out might require workers to ride the trolley cars rather than walk. In Los Angeles, the commuting imperative meant that housing was only sought within a few blocks of the streetcar stop. In both cities, this reliance upon mass transit bred resentment as the quality of service declined and public expectations rose. The long history of speculation and political deception in the transit industry ensured that the general public viewed the local traction companies with profound suspicion. The industry had grown on the basis of short-term particularistic decisions principally relating to the profits from realty sales in suburban districts linked for the first time to the city centre. As a result, it provided only a circuitous route for the increasing number of riders who wished to travel across the city rather than from the periphery to the centre.

The industry had also expanded on the basis of lavish promises about its ability to alleviate the working-class housing problem. By bringing more land into the market, the street railway was supposedly ensuring that the supply of housing expanded to meet the pressing demand. In practice, it proved easier to remove the affluent from the discomfort of the central city than to bring adequate housing within reach of the lowly paid. Moreover, in cities like Detroit, where the level of home ownership was high at the turn of the century, ownership alone was not sufficient to produce the climate of domesticity desired by middle-class social reformers. The optimistic environmental determinism of early Progressive advocates of moral uplift was tempered therefore by a more resigned acceptance of social segregation.

By the time the automobile had demonstrated its practicality and affordability – a period dominated by the rising production of the Ford Model T – the mass-transit industry was financially bankrupt and nationally unpopular. Unable to attract enough new investment, it was therefore incapable of placating its critics. Unwittingly, William Knudsen, a senior figure at the Ford Motor Company and later at General Motors, summed up mass transit's failure when he declared that Americans had adopted the automobile because they wanted to get from A to B quickly sitting down. The archetypal streetcar line had once enabled the residents of point A to travel swiftly to a given point B in comfort, but as a fixed rail system, it could not readily accommodate any relocation. As the system expanded, it did provide access, albeit indirectly, to numerous other places by the development of one or more focal points of transfer. Yet this entailed delay and for economic and systemic reasons, congestion. By 1920 fewer Americans were confident that mass transit could get them from A to B quickly sitting down; just as often the journey was a slow one spent standing up.

The transit experts and urban planners who advised American cities on traffic matters as congestion worsened after World War I were well aware of mass transit's limitations, yet they also believed it to be a valuable source of order, civic unity and stability. Even in cities with a high level of car ownership, the traffic authorities regarded the trolley as the backbone of the urban transport system. Mayor Couzens of Detroit appointed former Packard executive, Sidney Waldon as chairman of the Rapid Transit Commission (RTC) in December 1922. A traffic survey undertaken by the RTC informed Waldon that motor vehicles accounted for 93 per cent of traffic in Detroit's one square mile central business district. During the evening rush-hour, 25 per cent of commuters occupied 91 per cent of the available street space in their efforts to drive home by automobile, while the remaining, and indeed the overwhelming majority of, travellers crowded aboard the streetcars. On this basis, Waldon argued that the trolley was the backbone of any urban transport system and that its successor should be underground rapid transit rather than mass motoring. Indeed, he noted that already in 1924 the advantages of the motor car as a means of individual rapid transit were being negated 'by the very number of persons trying to take advantage of this new medium of transportation'.[35]

Donald F. Davis has suggested that the established social elite in Detroit at the turn of the century always envisaged motoring as a practice of the leisure class. Consequently, its members invested only in those car companies, such as Packard, that produced automobiles for their social peers. Up to 1906 this high-priced market of models priced $2275 or more represented 43 per cent of US car sales. Ten years later, however, automobile companies of this class had a market share of less than 2 per cent while one low-cost producer, the Ford Motor Company, commanded 45 per cent. Thus, Waldon, although he was appointed by former Ford executive James Couzens, represented the old civic elite who patronised Packard rather than the new gasoline aristocracy epitomised by Henry Ford. He therefore sympathised with the goal of securing the economic interests of the downtown area and was anxious to find a means of separating the motorist from mass transit.[36]

Around the same time as Detroit deliberated on its traffic problems, three of America's most renowned urban planners – Frederick Law Olmsted, Jr., Harland Bartholomew and Charles H. Cheney – concluded a survey of Los Angeles traffic. This revealed that nearly as many people (48%) reached the downtown area by automobile as came by streetcar. Despite a much larger number of commuting motorists than Detroit, Los Angeles' consultants echoed the Detroit RTC's advice. 'The streetcar', the professional planners argued, 'owing to its economy of space and low cost of operation per passenger, must take precedence over other forms of vehicles in the congested district whenever the traffic capacity of the arteries approaches its limits.' Giving priority to the streetcar meant in practice providing it with its own separate right of way. A year later, transit consultants, R. F. Kelker and C. De Leuw, insisted that such a rapid transit system was essential for the orderly development of Los Angeles and pointed to the current congestion downtown as proof that the automobile could not provide mass access to the central city. Meanwhile, the Detroit RTC, under the guidance of New York transit planner Daniel Turner, also proposed a small elevated railway system around the downtown area linked to a far more extensive network of surface lines running along the centre of express highways: the so-called 'Superhighway' scheme.[37]

Both Detroit and Los Angeles were faced in the mid-1920s by recommendations for massive public investment in rail transit made by authoritative figures. Yet neither metropolis took its experts' advice. In Los Angeles, this was partly due to public hostility to the transit companies. Neither the memory of their past conduct nor their current standard of service aroused the sympathy of Angelenos. Rapid transit in the form of elevated lines also had a notorious reputation for damaging the values of abutting property and so it faced vociferous opposition. Moreover, the notion of population dispersion which mechanised transit had already advanced in southern California was so deeply rooted that it facilitated the area's emergence as the nation's premier motor-car market. As traffic congestion worsened in the central Los Angeles area, motorists patronised other regional retail and service centres. Population diffusion was followed by economic deconcentration. This was in turn facilitated by public investment in roads and highways.[38]

In Detroit, too, rapid transit was spurned. Yet Turner had stressed that his proposals took account of the needs of the city's overwhelmingly industrial workforce. It included cross-town lines running near working-class districts and linking the River Rouge complex on the west side and the east-side Hudson, Continental and Chalmer automobile companies as well as passing the Cadillac Motor and Michigan Central railcar plants. Indeed, the system was geared to the delivery of labour to Detroit's industrialists. None the less, it failed. As transit was municipally owned, public suspicions of the transit companies was less intense than in California. However, the proposed elevated lines and superhighways faced fierce local property-owner criticism. As in Los Angeles, elevated lines were seen as environmentally harmful by Detroiters. They were also expensive and the cost of the project ($126 million for the initial elevated sectors) alienated taxpayers. Moreover, to be financially self-supporting the system would require higher fares and high passenger loads. The superhighway proposal's biggest obstacle was the feasibility of obtaining the street width of 500 feet required to accommodate the lanes of cars and transit. The necessary condemnations of property in built-up areas would only be possible to secure in areas of low-income housing. Thus, it was easy to persuade residents to vote against the RTC's ambitious plans.[39]

However, the opposition of low-income groups might have been offset by the spirited advocacy of the scheme by the industrial and civic leadership of Detroit. Eventually, areas of low-income housing, such as that in the black ghetto, were bulldozed to make way for expressways. On this occasion, neither the downtown elite nor the automobile magnates backed rapid transit. Members of the downtown Business Properties Association (BPA) complained that property assessments in Detroit were already higher in 1923 than in other cities because of recent public works from which BPA members had received little tangible benefit. To such men, the RTC's superhighway plan was extravagant. Members of the automotive elite were less short-sighted than these downtown businessmen. They realised that infra-structural investment on a massive scale was needed, but this need not involve rail transit. Their plant managers had noticed for several years an increase in the number of workers commuting to work by automobile. Thus, when Sidney Waldon visited E. G. Liebold in November 1924, he was informed by the Ford Secretary that 30 per cent of the company's workforce drove to work in their own cars and that the company intended to encourage this trend.[40]

Rapid transit was not only rejected by powerful interests because it appeared to run counter to their own concerns at the time, it was also, it must be said, rejected by ordinary individuals. As William Knudsen declared, average Americans wanted to get from A to B quickly sitting down. They might live at point A because it was the best accommodation they could afford. They might work at point B because there was the only job they could find. They might get there slowly on a streetcar and they might have to stand but as the price of motoring declined, more and more Americans chose not to do so. A quantitative study of the cost of commuting in Baltimore in 1925 when the ratio of automobiles per citizen stood at one car per eight persons argues that the motor car 'provided the most economical way for many to meet their transportation needs'. However, the urban adoption of the automobile did not simply rely on an elaborate systematic calculation of relative costs. It was also a product of social prejudices.[41]

The overcrowding on urban streetcars has already been noted as a major public grievance in the period when mass transit faced increasing competition from the private motor vehicle. This crowding was in part a product of the economics of mass transit which encouraged congestion at the hub in order to maintain high average passenger loads. However, as industry and workers relocated away from the inner city after 1918, the centripetal direction of the transit system became a source of resentment since it took travellers not simply out of their way but into areas of the city which they would otherwise avoid. The associated social tensions can be highlighted by a brief examination of racial tensions in American cities as they were manifested on the mass transit systems.

The Great Migration of black Americans to the nation's urban centres between 1910 and 1930 made racial conflict a truly national rather than Southern concern. Detroit's black population of a mere 5741 in 1910 soared to 40,838 in 1920 and 120,066 in 1930. Chicago's black population was already over 44,000 in 1910 but it also rose dramatically to 104,000 in 1920 and 233,903 in 1930. Los Angeles' black population of 7500 in 1910 exceeded Detroit's black population. By 1930, it was significantly less than in the Motor City, namely, 38,894. However, this neglects the presence of other minorities facing white racism in the Los Angeles population. When Orientals and Hispanics are added, Los Angeles' non-white population was the second highest in the nation in 1930 as a proportion of the city's total population (14.2%); significantly higher than Detroit's (8.2%) or Chicago's (7.6%). Baltimore's long-established black community gave it the highest proportion of non-white citizens (17.8%).[42]

Racism in all of these cities prevented blacks from settling wherever they chose either by restrictive covenants forbidding the sale of houses or by force. Consequently, unlike other newcomers to urban America, blacks could not relocate easily as their circumstances changed. In Detroit, they were confined principally to a ghetto to the north-east of downtown around St. Antoine Street. However, there were secondary enclaves near the Cadillac plant on West Grand Boulevard, near the Dodge complex on the East Side, in Inkster near the Ford River Rouge and around Ford's Highland Park plant. Local philanthropist Henry Stevens had also sponsored a black suburban subdivision on Eight Mile Road, a precarious development which faced increasing pressure from surrounding white settlement.[43]

In Chicago, the black ghetto was on the South Side and wherever blacks lived, it seemed that train tracks hemmed them in. However, while the tracks served as communal boundary lines, the streetcars that ran along them brought the hostile parties face to face. Black spokesmen were conscious that the journey to work for ghetto dwellers was often a passage through hostile territory inhabited by whites ready to take offence. They feared especially that the uncouth mannerisms of newly arrived Southern blacks would inflame the racial situation. With the encouragement of the white civic elite in Detroit, the Urban League undertook to train such greenhorns how to behave under public scrutiny via such initiatives as the Dress Well Club, an organisation whose sartorial principles were difficult to practise because blacks were customarily assigned the dirtiest, most unsavoury jobs.[44]

Anxious about inter-racial relations, Forrester B. Washington, head of the Detroit Urban League, warned club members in 1917 that he was receiving complaints from transit officials 'regarding the unclean clothing, etc of Negro workers on the car lines. This sort of carelessness in regards to dress', he cautioned, 'will lead to discrimination and segregation unless steps are taken to improve conditions'. He advised those blacks returning from work in dirty, greasy overalls either to stay on the platform away from other passengers or to wear a clean coat over their work clothes. Chicago's black newspaper, *The Defender*, which had encouraged the northward migration by its reports of job opportunities in the manufacturing centres, was equally insistent that rural migrants should abandon their 'obnoxious' habits and adopt 'the customs of their new homes'. A headline of 17 March ordered: 'Keep your mouth shut, please! There is entirely too much loud talking on the street cars among our newcomers'.[45]

However, it remains doubtful whether proper etiquette would have been enough to mollify white hostility to the increasingly conspicuous black presence. Regardless of costume or conduct, all blacks were 'low-grade' in the eyes of the majority of whites. As one Chicagoan put it, white men did not like to think of their wives and daughters riding on streetcars 'breast to breast with Negroes'. Even middle-class Americans like mechanical engineer Charles L. Samson would refuse to buy the house of his wife's choice because the State Street trolley-line serving this all-white Chicago neighbourhood was 'jammed with niggers'.[46]

Ultimately, such blind hatred manifested itself in a series of race riots in 1919. Much of the violence in the Chicago riot took place on main thoroughfares and at streetcar transfer points as whites attacked blacks seeking refuge in their home districts. Indeed, the eventual decline in physical clashes in the city was due in part to an unrelated strike by streetcar workers that confined blacks to their residential ghetto. In the wake of the riot, the inflammatory mixing of the races on public transit was still seen as a contributory factor to the conflict along with the acute housing shortage. Writing in the national magazine *Outlook* in August 1919, Charles W. Holman argued that race relations in Chicago had noticeably deteriorated once blacks became an important part of street and elevated railway traffic. He contended that the distribution of blacks throughout the trains or cars was such that 'Whites thought that they did it on purpose to force whites to sit down besides them [sic]'. The resentment provoked by this action laid the basis for later confrontations.[47]

Such paranoia found expression in the early 1920s in the growing membership of the revived Ku-Klux-Klan. Membership in the Detroit area Klan grew from 3000 in the autumn of 1921 to 22,000 eighteen months later. On Christmas Eve, 1923, a six-foot cross was set alight on the steps of the Wayne County Building and in the mayoral primary of September 1924, Charles Bowles, a local attorney, running as a write-in candidate with the active support of the Klan, was narrowly and controversially defeated. The Klan's popularity reflected not only concern over the growing black population but a more diffuse antipathy to the polyglot character of most American cities. To minds animated by such fears, mass transit was too inclusive for safety and the outcome of expensive rapid transit systems would be simply the spread of this blight.[48]

Once perceived and presented by the middle classes as the cure for urban pathologies, the streetcar had become a model in miniature of the vices of city life. By aggregating different classes and racial and ethnic groups together, it confronted Americans with precisely the claustrophobic social nightmare that they were striving to avoid. In Midwestern metropolises, like Chicago, avoiding blacks was a significant aspect of the process of selecting one's mode of travel. The largely Midwestern 'Anglo-Saxon' population of Los Angeles shared the alarm at the large wartime migration of blacks. A Santa Monica newspaper spelt out the white reaction. 'We don't want you here', it declared in 1922, 'now and forever, this is to be a white man's town.' The coloured minorities were either confined to deteriorating neighbourhoods, such as those around the Plaza, or West Adams or Boyle Heights, where the whites no longer wished to reside or they were housed in undesirable areas such as Watts which were subdivided exclusively for them.[49]

The largest minority group in Los Angeles was Hispanic. At first centred on the original heart of Los Angeles, the Plaza, the Latino community spilled into the former white ethnic neighbourhoods of East Los Angeles as industrial activity in this area increased. Transit lines enabled the Hispanic population to commute readily to the industrial districts of downtown Los Angeles and as traffic congestion in the narrow streets of the central business district slowed the progress of trolley cars, the same problems of unwanted inter-racial proximity arose. The negative association of mass transit with the lower castes in Los Angeles was reinforced by the practice of the Pacific Electric of housing its Mexican track workers in labour camps along the tracks in suburban districts. However, the concentration of the coloured minorities – black, Oriental and Hispanic – in the dilapidated houses of the old city centre had its most adverse effect on transit as a deterrent against the creation of a central focus for Los Angeles' divided transit systems. Construction of a union station was the essential preliminary to the establishment of a modernised rapid rail transit system and its logical location was the old Plaza. Yet agreement on this vital first step was blocked by racial fear. An editorial in the *Los Angeles Examiner* declared: 'If there is ever to be a union station, let it at least not be located between Chinatown and Little Mexico.'[50]

The Los Angeles newspapers with large circulations usually articulated the opinions of the middle and upper classes and as mass transit ceased to meet their needs, the press painted its weaknesses in ways which played upon deeply rooted social fears. The West Coast's great fear was, of course, the Yellow Peril, and so its castigation of transit took on an Oriental hue. The *Los Angeles Record* of 10 December 1912 reported:

> Inside the air was a pestilence; it was heavy with disease and the emanations from many bodies. Anyone leaving this working mass, anyone coming into it ... forced the people into still closer, still more indecent, still more immoral contact. A bishop embraced a stout grandmother, a tender girl touched limbs with a city sport, refined women's faces burned with shame and indignation - but there was no relief. Was this an oriental prison? Was it some hall devoted to the pleasures of the habitués of vice? Was it a place of punishment for the wicked? No gentle reader, it was only the result of public stupidity and apathy. It was a Los Angeles streetcar on the 9th day of December in the year of grace 1912.[51]

As this report suggests, it was the contact between the sexes as much as between the races which made the crowded streetcar offensive. Certainly the rush-hour crush of bodies provided an opportunity for sexual harassment. Paul Barrett recounts the experience of one Chicago shopper who was jammed tight in the crowd on an open platform for eight miles one December evening in 1913. In such conditions, what another woman termed 'unpleasant circumstances' were likely to arise. Even before boarding the streetcar, women were at risk because of the location of stations and transfer points. One Chicago elevated railway station, said to be in the 'vice' district, was a source of complaint because 'the stenographers and businesswomen who were obliged to go into that neighborhood do not like to get off at that station'.[52]

Just as racial tensions contributed to the political rejection of transit modernisation in Los Angeles by blocking the construction of a union station at the Plaza, so notions of female purity intruded into the 1918 Chicago referendum on transit development. During the week prior to the vote, the Association of Commerce's women's auxiliary encouraged its upper-class members to venture forth on rush-hour trolleys in order to discover whether transit services needed the improvements proposed. Their indignant reports were prominently featured by newspapers seeking approval of the new ordinances. One society matron, Mrs Joseph Coleman, was reported to be confined to her bed 'ill from the experience'. Complaining to a *Daily News* reporter about the 'awful men on the back platform', she exclaimed, 'Why are people allowed to sell such odoriferous whisky, I wonder?' Other members of the expedition denounced the incivility of trolley conductors, and reported unwanted brushes with greasy strangers caused by an inability to 'free our persons from indecent contact with the struggling mob'. 'If Chicago does not pass the traction ordinance', the *Tribune* declared sternly, 'it will be committing a crime against its womanhood.'[53]

Chicagoans voted down the proposals, none the less; instead they, like Americans elsewhere, turned increasingly to the automobile as a substitute for the discredited streetcar service. There had been a motor car for every sixty-one residents of Chicago in 1915 but by 1925 this had risen to one car per eleven Chicagoans. A traffic survey of 1926 indicated that auto ownership was diffused throughout the city with only the inner west side of the city showing a disproportionately low level of car registrations for its population. A Chicago Elevated spokesman complained in 1923 that 'anyone who can scrape together $100 and put up a scrap container in his yard' could own his own car and thus turn his back on transit. The declining number of rides per capita both in Chicago and as a national average after 1926 documented this fall from public favour.[54]

During the 1920s Americans rejected mass transit in favour of the private motor vehicle. However, their demand for automobiles was neither automatic nor simply motivated. It was not a 'natural' preference but rather the product of distinct historical circumstances. The preceding pages have attempted to examine the conditions which simultaneously undermined the appeal of mass transit as they spurred the adoption of the automobile. The production of the built environment under capitalism guided American urban development along contradictory paths which required yet feared the aggregation of labour; which sought the functional integration of the city even while it nurtured those social antipathies which divided worker from worker; which recognised long-term needs for infrastructural investment both in terms of the social reproduction of labour and of the enhanced circulation and accumulation of capital, yet opposed such plans according to a diverse range of short-term calculations of personal interest; and which legitimised policies of peculiar advantage to a minority capitalist class using a rhetoric of concern for the people as a whole.[55]

As a result, innovations in transport technology were pursued under capitalism with a view to improving its operation, and their social application became ensnared in a process which advocated their adoption for reasons of democratic social welfare at the same time as their use became linked to processes of social control. Thus, mass transit improved the operation of capitalism by expediting the circulation of suburban real estate as a commodity and by functionally integrating the urban market by its delivery of workers and consumers. Yet, it had promised to improve the social welfare of urban residents by allowing a reduction in population density and facilitating the economical construction of healthy homes for all. However, it proved disappointing and inflexible in these terms. Deeply ingrained in the Progressive campaigns for social justice was the assumption that the amelioration of the condition of the working classes ought to entail their simultaneous *embourgeoisement*. Consequently, until the other half lived in a manner similar to that approved by the professional and managerial stratum of society, the desire to unite the community was restrained by an urge to keep its apparently healthy elements uncontaminated. The ideology of domesticity evaluated mass transit in increasingly negative terms after 1910 at precisely the time when its inflexibility made it vulnerable because of the relocation of industry and of other social institutions. In the years prior to 1914 when the private motor vehicle was proving its practicality to the American upper and middle classes, mass transit was increasingly judged to be inefficient both as a system for the delivery of labour and as a social filter. As labour used the system more intensively, traffic congestion required more fixed investment. Detroit, Los Angeles and other cities needed special rights of way to carry transit commuters swiftly to their destinations without the impediment of other traffic. But the mobility of industry meant that there was no guarantee that such an investment would be of durable value, given its inflexibility. Moreover, mass transit threatened to undermine the hegemonic position of the capitalist class. The abuse of power in public utilities mobilised public discontent in an alarming way at the turn of the century, giving credence to socialistic ideas.

However, the persistence of atavistic forces of race hatred, ethnic rivalry, male chauvinism, and other more personal psychoses diverted this threat. The fault, it seemed, lay not in the constellation of capitalism as a process but in the people themselves who were not comfortable using a mass-transit system which duplicated the social clashes at work in the urban aggregation as a whole. The automobile had inherited by the mid-1920s the key attractions of transport under capitalism as a delivery system and as a social insulator. Its flexibility enabled capitalism to change gears by making labour more mobile and it still promised to reform human nature by facilitating the move from socially 'undesirable' districts to more wholesome surroundings. Yet the mesh into which motoring fitted was even more finely wrought, as the next chapter shows. To use personal motor vehicles for mass transport required mass production and it is to the development of this manufacturing system that we now turn.

Notes

1 C. H. Cooley, 'The social significance of street railways', *Publications of the American Economic Association*, VI, 1891, pp. 71–3.
2 K. T. Jackson, *Crabgrass Frontier*, 1985, p. 174.
3 Jackson, loc. cit.; C. W. Cheape, *Moving the Masses*, 1980, pp. 23–6; Ernest Ingersoll, 'Getting about in New York', *Outlook*, LVIII, 2 April 1898, p. 834.
4 Cheape, loc. cit.
5 Adna Weber, *The Growth of Cities in the Nineteenth Century*, 1899, p. 224; D. Harvey, *The Urbanization of Capital*, 1985.
6 Jackson, *Crabgrass Frontier*, p. 43.
7 Ibid., pp. 61–2.
8 M. Corbin Sies, 'The city transformed: nature, technology and the suburban ideal, 1877–1917', *Journal of Urban History*, XIV, 1, November 1987, pp. 81–111.
9 Thernstrom, *Poverty and Progress*, 1964, pp. 115–22; O. Zunz, *The Changing Face of Inequality*, 1982, pp. 142–71.
10 Jackson, *Crabgrass Frontier*, p. 129.
11 L. Morris, *Incredible New York*, 1951, p. 197.
12 For transit entrepreneurs' promise to relieve population congestion, see F. Sprague, 'The future of the electric railway', *Forum*, XIII, September 1891, pp. 122–3; T. Johnson, *My Story*, 1911, p. xxxi; F. Howe, *The City: the Hope of Democracy*, 1905, p. 131. For New York annexation, see Jackson, *Crabgrass Frontier*, p. 143.
13 Jackson, op. cit., p. 153; J. D. Buenker, *Urban Liberalism and Progressive Reform*, 1973, p. 25.
14 Weber, cited by C. McShane, 'American cities and the coming of the automobile', unpublished PhD, University of Wisconsin, Madison, 1975, p. 199.
15 Cheape, *Moving the Masses*, pp. 107–25; for higher costs, see US Bureau of the Census, 'The relative economy of cable, electricd and animal motive power for street railways', *Eleventh Census of the United States: 1890, Bulletin 55*, 1892.
16 Jackson, *Crabgrass Frontier*, pp. 120-2.
17 S. L. Bottles, *Los Angeles and the Automobile*, 1987, p. 29.
18 P. S. Barrett, 'Mass transit, the automobile and public policy in Chicago, 1900–1930', unpublished PhD, University of Illinois, Chicago, 1976, table 2.2, p. 119.
19 For the popular journalistic view of the traction barons, see Burton J. Hendrick, 'Great American fortunes and their making', *McClure's Magazine*, XXX,

November 1907 – January 1908, pp. 33–48; Alfred H. Lewis, 'Owners of America, II: Thomas F. Ryan', *Cosmopolitan*, XLV, May 1908, pp. 141–52; and Charles E. Russell 'Where did you get it, gentlemen?', *Everybody's*, XVIII, January 1908, p. 122.

20 Jackson, *Crabgrass Frontier*, p. 110; Barrett, 'Mass transit', pp. 87–8.

21 Barrett, op. cit., pp. 342–6.

22 Bottles, *Los Angeles*, pp. 33, 37, 40–1; P. S. Barrett, *The Automobile and Urban Transit*, 1983, p. 181.

23 For manouevres in the battle for municipal transit, see J. E. Schram and W. H. Henning, *Detroit's Street Railways: Volume I: 1863–1923*, 1978, p. 94; Anonymous to Couzens, 26 September 1922, Mayor's Papers, 1922, Box 5, 'Street Railways' folder, Detroit Archives, Burton Historical Collection, Detroit Public Library (hereafter BHC).

24 Zunz, *Inequality*, pp. 286–8; E. Kocher, 'Economic and physical growth of Detroit, 1701–1935', Division of Economics and Statistics, Federal Housing Administration, Michigan Historical Collections, Bentley Library, Ann Arbor. Quotation from Rupert E. Paris to Frank E. Randall, 30 July 1918, Papers of James Couzens, Special Correspondence, Box 6 Library of Congress, cited by John Chavis, 'James Couzens, Mayor of Detroit, 1919–1922', unpublished PhD, Michigan State University, 1970, p. 103; B. Brownell, *The Urban Ethos in the South, 1920–1930*, 1975, p. 127.

25 D. Levine, *Internal Combustion*, 1976, p. 12; Jackson, *Crabgrass Frontier*, p. 176; Mark S. Foster, *From Streetcar to Superhighway*, 1981, p. 59.

26 Zunz, loc. cit.; T. J. Ticknor, 'Motor City: the impact of the automobile industry upon Detroit, 1900–1975' unpublished PhD, University of Michigan, 1978, p. 162. For Five Dollar Day, see Chapter 6 below.

27 Levine, *Internal Combustion*, p. 130.

28 Zunz, *Inequality*, pp. 349–54.

29 Bottles, *Los Angeles*, pp. 32, 33, 40; M. Wachs, 'Autos, transit, and the sprawl of Los Angeles: the 1920s', *Journal of The American Planning Association*, L, Summer 1984, pp. 297–310, esp. p. 298.

30 R. M. Fogelson, *The Fragmented Metropolis: Los Angeles: 1850–1930*, 1967, pp. 143–4.

31 Fogelson, op. cit., p. 145; Jackson, *Crabgrass Frontier*, p. 288.

32 Jackson, op. cit., p. 117; Fogelson, *Fragmented Metropolis*, pp. 145–6.

33 Wachs, 'The Sprawl of Los Angeles', p. 302; Fogelson, op. cit., pp. 127, 132, 148, 150.

34 Fogelson, op. cit., p. 133.

35 Rapid Transit Commission, *Vehicular Traffic in the Business District of Detroit*, 1924, pp. 14, 9–10, 21–2, 16, RTC Papers, BHC.

36 Donald F. Davis, 'The price of conspicuous consumption: The Detroit elite and the automobile industry, 1900–1930', *Journal of Social History*, XVI, Fall 1982, pp. 21–46, esp. pp. 32–6.

37 Foster, *Streetcar*, pp. 143–4; Minutes, Rapid Transit Commission (RTC), 11 April 1923, Box 9, RTC Papers, BHC.

38 Bottles, *Los Angeles, passim.*

39 Turner Report, 26 June, Box 9, RTC Papers; 'Proposed Financial Plan for a Rapid Transit System for Detroit', 27 November 1923, Box 3, Mayors' Papers

(1923), Detroit Archives; 'Memorandum on Division of Rapid Transit Costs', 10 December 1923, Box 1, RTC Papers.

40 Meeting of RTC with BPA, 4 December 1923, Box 9, RTC Papers, Memorandum of meeting with E. G. Liebold of the Ford Motor Company, 14 November 1924, Box 17, RTC Papers.

41 D. O. Wise and M. Dupree, 'The choice of the automobile for urban passenger transportation: Baltimore in the 1920s', *South Atlantic Urban Studies*, II, 1978, pp. 153–79: quotation, p. 174.

42 Levine, *Internal Combustion*, p. 59; Fogelson, *Fragmented Metropolis*, pp. 76, 83.

43 Levine, op. cit., p. 129.

44 T. L. Philpott, *The Slum and the Ghetto: Neighborhood Deterioration and Middle Class Reform, Chicago: 1880–1930*, 1978, p. 147.

45 Levine, op. cit., p. 89; A. H. Spear, *Black Chicago: the Making of a Negro Ghetto*, 1967, p. 168.

46 Spear, op. cit., p. 165.

47 L. E. Williams and L. E. Williams II, *Anatomy of Four Race Riots: Racial Conflict in Knoxville, Elaine (Arkansas), Tulsa and Chicago, 1919–1921*, 1972, pp. 74, 86, 93.

48 Levine, *Internal Combustion*, p. 137.

49 Fogelson, *Fragmented Metropolis*, p. 200.

50 Bottles, *Los Angeles*, pp. 182, 151.

51 Ibid., p. 22.

52 Barrett, *Urban Transit*, pp. 113–14, 252.

53 Ibid., p. 198.

54 Ibid., pp. 131, 162, 141.

55 R. E. Fogelsong, *Planning the Capitalist City: the Colonial Era to the 1920s*, 1986, Chapter 1.

Chapter 5

The Columbian Exposition – manufacturing, planning and the consumer culture

Thus far, this study has been devoted to the historical circumstances which conditioned the American adoption of the automobile. The demand for automobiles has been interpreted as part of the evolving historical geography of industrial capitalism: expanding the market's influence over the culture of the rural hinterland, and permitting both the flexible delivery of labour and consumers and the segregation of the population in a way which public mass transit could not. However, the same imperatives of extending the market, of increasing the ready supply of labour, accelerating the rate of circulation, that is, the cycle from production to sale; and of structuring social conditions so that they maintain the hegemony of the capitalist classes and reproduced the social base of capitalism; all of these impulses were at work equally in other capitalist societies. However, only the United States used mass motoring as a response to these pressures prior to 1930. What factors encouraged this earlier onset of mass motoring by bringing automobiles within the means of the average American wage-earner?

The gasoline-powered motor vehicle was a European invention which Americans adopted and refined. It was first exhibited to Americans at the World's Columbian Exposition or Chicago's World's Fair of 1893. By careful examination of the Fair's exhibits, this chapter seeks to establish more clearly the cultural context within which the automobile was introduced. In particular, the technological bias of American culture at this stage will be explored in terms of the strengths of different sectors of the economy and the tension between the emerging organisational dominance of the corporation and the individualistic values of the American democratic republican tradition.

The great expositions of the nineteenth century celebrated the idea of progress. Their exhibits recorded past achievements and heralded further advances. The Chicago World's Fair of 1893, held to commemorate the four-hundredth anniversary of the discovery of the

New World – albeit a year late – was firmly in this tradition. Indeed, its display of past successes and future prospects was so encouraging that it heartened even those social critics who had been dismayed by the nation's recent course. Chicago anti-monopolist, Henry D. Lloyd, congratulated the Fair's Director of Works, Daniel Burnham, on having 'revealed to the people possibilities of social beauty, utility, and harmony of which they had not even been able to dream'. The chief portent of this grand potential was the Exposition's architectural plan, and subsequent discussion of the Fair's significance has focused on whether Burnham's neo-classical design was a sound model for American urban planners or a debilitating retrogressive step. More certain is the Exposition's appeal to the professional – managerial classes and their intellectual associates who were eager to endorse the ideal of planning and the value of expertise. Charles E. Norton of Harvard took the Fair's systematic design as 'a great promise, even a great pledge'. The same seeming commitment to order and rationality prompted Henry Adams to believe, at least for a time, that the future would be shaped by his friends and peers; in short, by men who could realize visions beyond the masses' dreams.[1]

This 'search for order', to use Robert Wiebe's familiar phrase, is an important part of this interpretation of Progressive America. In 1893, the possibility of widespread automobile ownership was so fanciful that it occurred only to a handful of Americans, yet within thirty years it would be achieved, thanks to an arrangement of industrial production as integrated and systematic as the model city hailed by Lloyd, Norton and Adams as they admired the Exposition's Court of Honour. By the 1920s, Fordist mass production represented 'modern times' just as the Exposition, the so-called White City, had done in the 1890s. The former, as we shall explain, imposed control through an enveloping architecture of production which was based on the recognition of the regulatory possibilities of design. However, mass production was derived not simply from the latent authoritarianism of the City Beautiful's pioneering showcase, nor from the technical exhibits on display, but also from the subtler forms of social manipulation at work in the Chicago Fair's sideshow, the Midway Plaisance. Seeking relief from the austere symmetry of the Exposition itself, visitors had flocked to the Midway to see Little Egypt dance the 'hootchy-cootchy' or to take a ride on the world's first Ferris wheel. Considered as a whole, the Fair offered a prophetic foretaste of the culture of the 1920s: in which corporate power wielded authority and expertise in the workplace while providing the compensations of mass consumption.[2]

As if forecasting the automobile's ambiguous role as corporate product and cherished medium of escape, there were automobiles in both the Exposition's halls and its Midway amusements. The organisers of the Columbian Exposition had studied carefully the example of the Universal Exposition of 1889 in Paris which had included a display of steam- and gasoline-powered vehicles featuring a Serpollet – Peugeot steam tricycle and a Daimler quadricycle. Despite arriving late, the Daimler vehicle with its new V-twin engine impressed French automobile experimenters. After the Paris Exposition, Peugeot abandoned steam power in favour of the Daimler engine, which was produced under licence by French automotive engineers, Panhard et Levassor. Impressed by this example, Willard Smith, head of the Fair's Transportation Department, announced that 'a special place will be provided in the rear of the transportation building for showing electric carriages in operation'. Alluding to the weight problem that had blocked the adoption of steam and electric vehicles, Smith promised a display of 'fine carriages' rather than 'heavy lumbering affairs'. In the event, the Fair's *Official Catalogue* defined the automotive vehicle exhibit as 'Steam and electric vehicles and all vehicles for carrying passengers on common roads, operated by other than steam power'. This encompassed gasoline-powered vehicles and even sedan chairs, but the emphasis on steam and electricity was both justified and significant. The only American automobile on display was an electric vehicle which was displayed in the Electrical rather than Transportation Building, where its exhibitor, Harold Sturgis, gave demonstration rides.[3]

As at the Paris Exposition in 1889, the gasoline automobiles at Chicago were German. American pioneering car-maker Ransom E. Olds claims to have seen a Benz at the Exposition, though this is challenged by a *New York Sun* report on the arrival of the first Benz automobile in America after the Exposition had closed. Olds perhaps mistook the Daimler quadricycle for the Benz Viktoria. Although it too arrived late, too late to be included in the *Official Directory*, the quadricycle was definitely at the Fair, offering American automotive pioneers the same chance to appreciate its potential as that seized by French car-makers in 1889. In marked contrast to the French, however, American experimenters present overlooked the Daimler car. The one exception to this was Charles Duryea, who visited the Exposition with his brother, Frank, shortly after the successful trial run of their own gasoline-powered car.[4]

This was not the first time that Charles Duryea had studied the Daimler engine, since he recalled seeing a display of Daimler motors at the National Machine Company in Hartford, Connecticut where they were being produced under licence by the New York-based Daimler Motor Company owned by the piano manufacturer, William Steinway. Short of capital and anxious to uphold his own status as an inventor, Duryea dismissed the Daimler engine as too heavy, too low-powered and too costly for automotive use. Two years later the Duryea automobile finished ahead of an imported Benz in the Chicago Thanksgiving Day Race but this success for American internal combustion engineering was overshadowed by the intervening acute economic depression which inclined capitalists to invest in the more proven technologies of electric power.

Any visitor to the Exposition's Transportation Building could judge for himself which modes of transport had attracted capital investment. Row upon row of railroad exhibits dominated the vast hall, testifying to the proven power of steam and the economic power wielded by those who controlled the nation's rails. By 1893, the exploitative nature of this corporate influence had excited widespread resentment, particularly among American farmers who depended on the railroads for the distribution of their produce. As Henry Adams concluded, the 'generation between 1865 and 1895 was already mortgaged to the railways and no one knew this better than the generation itself'. Steam dominated not only the nation's rails but also its stationary engines as well. The familiar sight of steam traction engines in rural areas at harvest times reminded Americans of the practicality of steam locomotion off the tracks. The automobile to be seen on the Midway Plaisance was a steamer belonging to the circus clown Philion, and this may have been the same Roper steamer from Massachusetts which Ransom Olds claims to have seen at the Exposition. Certainly, steam road vehicles continued to be produced in New England where the Locomobile and Stanley companies gained favourable publicity from the performance of steam cars in endurance trials at the turn of the century. Nevertheless, the appeal of steam automobiles proved temporary.[5]

If the generation leading up to the Exposition acknowledged the domination of the railroads over daily life, as Henry Adams claimed, then the next generation envisaged by the Fair seemed destined to rely on the electrical manufacturers; a prospect immortalised somewhat later by Adams's own deification of the Dynamo at the Cleveland Exposition of 1902. Electricity's status as the most modern of power sources had been evident from the Columbian Exposition's opening when President Cleveland had thrown an electrical switch to illuminate the Fair whilst intoning: 'As by a touch, the machinery that gives life to this vast exhibition is set in motion, so at the same instant, let our hopes and aspirations awaken forces which in all time to come shall influence the welfare, the dignity and the freedom of mankind.'[6]

The Fair depicted electricity as just such an awakened force. Electrical illumination enabled the Fair to remain open after dusk allowing more visitors to attend, reducing the hazards of fire from oil lamps, and releasing the nation's oil reserves for other uses. To provide its electricity, the Fair had a central generating station transmitting power on command to an array of machines in a less cumbersome manner than that used by the giant Corliss steam engine at the Philadelphia Centennial Exposition of 1876. Without appreciating the Chicago Fair's fascination with electricity, expressed in its electric lighting, elevated railway, and even electric launches on the central lagoons, one cannot accurately interpret the Exposition's transport exhibits. The Sturgis Electric, intended to carry twelve passengers, powered by 24 storage batteries, which produced 4 horse power with which to propel its 768 pounds, becomes a profound disappointment outside of this context, exemplifying the 'heavy lumbering affairs' dismissed by Willard Smith in 1892. However, in the context of the Fair's other exhibits, it becomes part of the larger contemporary search for an efficient mechanical means of urban transit.[7]

In sharp contrast to the paucity of exhibits in the automotive category at the Chicago World's Fair, the display reserved for 'streetcars and other shortline systems' attracted fifty exhibitors, who were willing to bring their necessarily large displays to Chicago. Of these, twenty had a clear interest in electric traction while the remainder included not only cable-car companies and equipment dealers for the still active horse-car lines but companies offering street railways powered by such diverse means as ammonia and compressed air. Reflecting the slowly emerging recognition that congested routes impeded urban transit as much as inadequate means of propulsion, a number of exhibitors offered equipment for elevated lines and subways.[8]

This provides an alternative perspective on the Daimler exhibit at the Columbian Exposition. In strictly automotive terms, it was a disappointment. Not only did it fail to impress American automotive interests, but even Daimler's established American backer, William Steinway, seemed to lose interest. Steinway's dwindling concern in the Daimler Motor Company of New York between 1893 and his death in November 1896 can be partly explained by his deteriorating health. However, alongside this may be placed the recognition that Steinway's interest in the Daimler internal combustion engine was not as the basis for a private motor car but as a power source for urban transit. Steinway's interest in mass transit was evident in his majority share-holding in the Long Island City Street Railway Company. Like other industrialists, Steinway had been alarmed by the industrial unrest of the late 1870s and had responded by moving his piano factory from Manhattan to Astoria, Long Island. He believed that the removal of his largely German-born workforce to a suburban location would stabilise industrial relations by reforming their temperament, preserving virtues and eliminating incipient vices. He also saw an opportunity for real-estate speculation and to speed the profitable sale of residential properties in Astoria he established his street railway. Steinway's German background meant that he learnt of Daimler's experiments as early as 1876 but it was not until 1888 that he visited Cannstadt to examine the potential of Daimler's invention. By this stage, the high cost and operational difficulties of cable-driven transit were becoming evident, while electric street traction remained unproven. Circumstantial evidence suggests, therefore, that Steinway regarded Daimler's gasoline engine as a potential power source for streetcars.[9]

Supporting this view is Steinway's intensifying interest in New York's transit system. Despite a public reputation of being reluctant to accept public office because of the heavy demands of his business interests, Steinway not only accepted his appointment to New York's Rapid Transit Commission in 1891 but showed a profound commitment to the RTC's work. Indeed, while confined to bed with what proved to be his final illness, he implored fellow commissioners to hold a forthcoming meeting at his bedside so that he might join in their deliberations. Moreover, Daimler himself was aware that his gasoline engine might be seen as applicable to mass transit. At both the Paris and Chicago Expositions, one of the Daimler engines was shown powering a model streetcar, and when the Daimler Motor

Company of New York published its first prospectus in 1891, it listed streetcars first among applications of the Daimler motor. In addition to this evidence linking the Daimler engine to the search for a new propulsive power source for mass transit in America, we have the negative evidence of William Steinway's apparent neglect of its automotive potential. Given Steinway's long-standing and distinguished record as an international exhibitor, it seems unlikely that he would have allowed the Daimler quadricycle to arrive so belatedly in Chicago if it had been the centrepiece of the display.[10]

Moreover, if one accepts that Steinway's investment in the Daimler patents was founded on their possible application for mass transit, his declining interest after 1893 can be readily explained by the emergence of electric traction as the preferred mode of mechanisation. The feasibility of electrification was widely accepted following the success of Henry Whitney's West End Company in Boston. By 1892, electric trolleys accounted for two-thirds of the West End's total car mileage; by 1894, more than nine-tenths. Once electric traction proved its worth, the prospect of a rapid return on investment in transit powered by the internal combustion engine seemed to have passed, and so Steinway withdrew. This incident is of more than antiquarian importance since it challenges the assumption that the triumph of the internal combustion engine was predicated on a quest for individualised transport. On the contrary, it would appear that its foundation was the desire for swifter, more extensive transit.[11]

The gloss of individualism came later. When one also considers that even the founding father of American mass motoring, Henry Ford, was initially intent upon designing a truck or delivery wagon to convey farm produce, then the traditional linking of the motor car with personal freedom, self-reliance, independence and other key words of American ideological rhetoric becomes a product of later propaganda efforts. The sources of the demand which prompted research and development of the automobile were rooted in the social relations of the congested city and of the attenuated, depopulating rural community.[12]

Consistent with this interpretation is the history of US automotive experimentation in the 1890s which confirms the preference for electrical power among leading financial interests located near the first major electric traction markets in the East. The General Electric (GE) Corporation was the result of a merger between Edison General Electric and Thomas-Houston, both of whom held valuable patents in the electric traction field. Newly formed at the time of the Columbian Exposition, GE regarded the Chicago Fair as a vital opening to its sales campaign against rival electrical manufacturer, Westinghouse. The contract for the Exposition's intra-mural electric elevated railroad went to GE, which also secured more elaborate entries in the Fair's *Official Catalogue* than did Westinghouse. This publicity gained results. The Metropolitan Elevated Railway of Chicago, the first American elevated to be electrified, gave GE its order which included 110 GE-2000 motors at $2700 each shortly after the Exposition. Orders for the GE-800 motor also rose from 3000 in 1893 to 5500 in 1894. However, the economic depression which caused banks to close their doors almost at the same time as the World's Fair opened its gates, prevented GE from collecting payment on many of these orders. The ensuing cash-flow crisis forced GE to accept the purchase of local company securities by a syndicate of bankers, headed by J. P. Morgan. However, this intervention was itself a sign of confidence in the electrical industry. It would be at least fifteen years before gasoline-powered automotive technology could command similar interest in high financial circles in America.[13]

None the less, entrepreneurial capitalists were alert to the possible return from automotive technology. They were eager, as William Steinway had been, to secure patent rights in the field in order to establish control over the application of a new technology. As legal assets, such patents encouraged the growth of oligopoly either through mergers or cartels. In the automobile industry this strategy was followed by the founders of the Association of Licensed Automobile Manufacturers on the basis of the generic gasoline automobile patent claim of George B. Selden. However, the larger investment interests were inclined to back enterprises with a perceived synergy with their established interests. Consequently, since the largest investment was in mass transit and electrical manufacturing, the first venture into the automotive field by major capitalists was the Electric Vehicle Company which aimed to establish electrically powered taxi-cab fleets in major American cities as a complementary investment to their electric traction interests.[14]

The potential of electric power, so evident in the Chicago Fair's exhibits, temporarily overshadowed the possible applications of the internal combustion engine. However, this did not impair the urge to find new faster means of transport. Urban transit was profitable because it was essential to the imperatives of industrial capitalism.

Just as the developing factory complex sought an increasingly smooth flow of material from operation to operation, so the new industrial society produced a need to link specialised functional areas by a transport system which carried not only the raw materials and goods but also workers and clients to their respective stations. As late as 1900, recalled journalist – historian Frederick Lewis Allen, 'to put one's money into street railroad development was to bet on the great American future'. Even the outcry against the traction barons' profiteering was a reminder that urban transit had proved highly remunerative. However, as we have seen, the rhetoric of transit, promising population dispersal, contradicted its operational economics in terms of high passenger loads per car, and the resulting failure to meet genteel standards of social segregation encouraged the more affluent to adopt private forms of personal transport. This resulted in a proliferation of carriages and bicycles, produced in volume under conditions which foreshadowed the later development of the automobile industry. By 1893, the introduction of the safety bicycle and the pneumatic tyre had reduced the dangers and increased the comfort of cycling. The demand for cycles prompted the industry to expand, notably in the Midwest where new processes such as steel presswork were tried, and in New England where manufacturers adapted an already highly developed manufacturing tradition to the needs of the new product.[15]

The cycle displays at the Columbian Exposition testified to the strength of the American bicycle industry in 1893. When the popularity of the bicycle declined in the late 1890s, a number of bicycle makers such as Alexander Winton, Thomas B. Jeffrey, George N. Pierce and John and Horace Dodge turned their efforts to automobile production. Other automotive pioneers came from either the carriage and wagon industry like the Studebaker and Fisher families and General Motors' founder, William Durant, or from the machine-tool trade like Henry Leland, founder of Cadillac, and Walter Flanders who was influential in the development of Ford and Studebaker. In different ways, these three branches of manufacturing represented the so-called 'American system of manufactures' and were the avenues by which it was transmitted to the automobile industry. One feature of the American system, extensive mechanisation, was evident in all three sectors as well as in other American industries. However, a more esoteric tradition of interchangeability of parts in the federal armouries, particularly in New England, was more applicable to the metal-working industries of bicycle making and machine-tool building than to the predominantly wood-working trade of carriage and wagon manufacturing. The distinctive interchangeability of parts was achieved in the armouries by the continual and careful application of hundreds of specially designed jigs, fixtures and gauges. The exacting nature of such practices made the armoury tradition time-consuming and expensive to apply. Tooling-up was extremely expensive under such a system and had to be constantly maintained in order to achieve a long enough production run of interchangeable parts at a low unit cost in order to justify the heavy initial costs.[16]

The Pope Manufacturing Company and its wholly owned subsidiary, the Hartford Cycle Company, were among the representatives of the armoury tradition at the Columbian Exposition. Colonel Albert A. Pope, known as the father of American cycling, attended the Exposition not only to oversee his companies' large exhibits, but also to inspect a comprehensive road construction display which he had pressed the Fair's management to include. Pope was keenly aware, as we have seen, not only that highway improvement was a profitable cause for any manufacturer of vehicles, but that it also constituted a vital area of infrastructural investment serving to accelerate and synchronise the circulation of goods within the economy, and thus improve the pace of capital accumulation. Due largely to the lobbying of the League of American Wheelmen, a cycling organisation founded by Pope, it was announced at the Fair that the federal government had established an Office of Road Inquiry.[17]

The Good Roads movement was a reflection of the role of transport in the changing gears of a more integrated corporate economy. Pope's business success was founded on his perception of the profits to be made from expediting the flow of commodities. Good roads would bring produce from and manufactured items to rural America more efficiently as well as extending the range of the cyclist. Besides bicycle manufacturing, Pope was involved in electric street railways as one of the original investors in Henry Whitney's West End Company in Boston. Like Whitney, Pope owned real estate in Brookline and regarded the street railway as a means of rapidly increasing demand for this commodity. The same middle-class clientele that bought suburban lots in Brookline in order to acquire the space necessary for wholesome domesticity, had earlier been persuaded to buy Pope bicycles as a means of removing themselves from the corrupting throng of the metropolis and enjoying the 'recuperative relaxation' of metropolitan Boston's system of parks and landscaped avenues or 'parkways'. Indeed, following his decision to produce bicycles in 1877, Pope had campaigned tirelessly to ensure that the bicycle was admitted to the parks by the nation's park commissions. He also founded a park near his factory in Hartford, thus sharing Boston landscape designer Stephen Child's belief that giving workers ready access to parks would help to 'relieve the strain of the numerous labor troubles now confronting us'.[18]

Within his factories Pope was more concerned about increasing the pace of production and securing interchangeability than about workers' recreation. He began bicycle manufacturing in Hartford at the Weed Sewing Machine plant some of whose workforce and machinery had formerly been associated with the Sharp Rifle Manufacturing Company on the same site. George H. Day, manager at Weed, and Hayden Eames, a former US Navy contract inspector, discovered that the switch to bicycle manufacturing made the established practice of drop-forging parts much more complicated than it had been for rifles or sewing machines. The drop forges had to be bigger and the dies more intricate for the Columbia bicycle's larger, more complex parts. During the 1880s Pope's ownership of key patents for the 'ordinary' high wheel bicycle or 'penny-farthing' had provided a cushion against these manufacturing difficulties which had slowed production and increased labour costs. However, the introduction of the 'safety' bicycle by competitors forced Pope to overhaul his operations. By the mid-1890s, the market for the more comfortable 'safety' exceeded one million and this volume of demand increased the Pope managers' desire to control the pace and quality of production.[19]

Pope strove to realise his objective of interchangeability of parts for rapid assembling by developing special tools and inspection procedures in the machining departments. One of these tools, a wheel 'truing' stand, was praised in the trade press as 'a thoroughly Yankee machine, adjustable all over, and having every essential for the avoidance of unnecessary labor'. Similarly, the inspection procedures which Pope used to boost consumer confidence in the reliability of his product were also a means of ensuring closer managerial supervision of the workforce. While large established firms like Pope were able to develop their own specialised machinery, most of the smaller bicycle firms listed in the Columbian Exposition's *Catalogue* would have relied upon the expertise of machine builders. By 1893, the sustained growth of bicycle production had encouraged the US machine-tool industry to respond to the technical challenges facing bicycle manufacturers in their pursuit of profitable high-volume production. In most cases, this meant simply adapting a general machine, such as a screw-machine, by making it heavier or giving it a new cutting edge, but in other instances entirely new machines were designed to perform such tasks as threading spokes or drilling holes in cycle wheel rims. By 1895, the would-be bicycle manufacturer could buy a complete set of machine tools from Pratt & Whitney. The same pattern of response was repeated after 1907 when the automobile industry's surprising resilience during the financial panic of that year encouraged the machine-tool industry to cater for its distinctive needs.[20]

The refinement of machine tools, like the refinement of mechanised vehicles, was inadequate by itself to overcome the problems of congestion and control evident in high-volume manufacturing plants as in the major population centres. Assembling and finishing operations remained so intricate and laborious a part of manufacturing as to become bottle-necks where the flood of parts from the highly mechanised machining departments accumulated. A potential solution to this 'traffic' problem had been developed by Henry Leland in the 1880s during his time as head of the sewing-machine department of the Rhode Island tool-makers, Brown & Sharpe. Leland instituted a strict procedural approach to sewing-machine production by the use of pre-calculated operations sheets. These detailed in advance the operations required for each part, along with the necessary tools, jigs, fixtures and gauges. Given the relatively low output of Brown & Sharpe and of Leland's later automotive ventures, the prestigious Cadillac and Lincoln Motor Car Companies, these plans were not a reaction to the pressure of attempted mass production but rather an expression of a desire for order and discipline within the workplace. Leland's interest in the cause of Temperance and in the open-shop drive of the Detroit Employers' Association substantiates the view that operations sheets arose as much out of a desire for social control as from any inherent technical imperatives. The logical application of these production planning documents was the laying out of machinery according to the sequence of production. When American auto makers began to switch from being assemblers into integrated manufacturing itself, they developed sequential production arrangements well beyond the early efforts of the New England bicycle and sewing-machine makers until they became, as we shall see, part of a new architecture of production in which managerial imperatives were transmitted to the workforce through the built environment of the workplace.[21]

This would be the basic achievement of the Ford Motor Company at Highland Park rather than of the Cadillac Motor Company. However, the successes of both firms were indicative of the Midwest's triumph in the automotive field. The manufacturing tradition of New England, so evident in the gun-making, sewing-machine and bicycle industries, faltered when it came to the gasoline automobile. A portion of the blame for this may be attributed to the Pope Manufacturing Company. When the bicycle craze waned in the late 1890s, Albert Pope was quick to perceive the automobile as not only its successor but potentially the dominant element in the road traffic of the future. However, Pope's interest in electric traction led him to invest the considerable resources of his manufacturing business in the unsuccessful electric taxi-cab scheme launched by a syndicate of New York traction magnates headed by Henry Whitney's brother, William. Pope's chief technical officer, Hayden Eames, encouraged Pope to hire Hiram P. Maxim from the American Projectile Company of Lynn, Massachusetts, to oversee automotive research at Pope. Maxim was unable to translate his own personal preference for gasoline power into a motor vehicle which was as reliable and easy to operate as an electric vehicle partly because he wasted time duplicating the research of earlier European automotive pioneers. Maxim was also unable to prevent the purchase of the Selden patent, thus providing the Electric Vehicle Company with its chief legacy. The patent formed the basis for the Association of Licensed Automobile Manufacturers, an organisation in which Pope veterans George Day and Hayden Evans were prominent officers. The ALAM's attempt to control the automobile industry was ultimately thwarted by the Ford Motor Company after many years of litigation, but not before the association's schemes to unite the industry by encouraging standardisation of parts had played a part in the evolution of mass production.[22]

Another businessman, prominent in efforts to integrate the auto industry, William C. Durant, was one of several carriage and wagon manufacturers who moved into the automobile field. The large number of carriage exhibits at the Columbian Exposition reflected the predominance of horse-drawn vehicles in road traffic at the turn of the century. The exhibits also testified to the significant technological and organisational changes that had taken place in the industry since the Civil War enabling it to offer an immense variety of vehicles in terms of style and comfort while at the same time producing carriages in unprecedented numbers. Contemporaries estimated that the number of horse-drawn trucks in New York City increased at a rate of a thousand a year between 1890 and 1895 to reach 65,000. Historian Clay McShane has estimated that the number of teamsters in ten selected US cities rose 328.4 per cent in these years while the population increased by 105.5 per cent. As the transport needs of industrial capitalism fuelled the expansion of the carriage and wagon industry as well as a search for alternative modes of transport, so the carriage industry took up production practices which would later be transferred to the automobile industry.[23]

Visiting America in 1893, Julius Lessing of the Berlin Museum of Industrial Arts praised the practicality of the American wooden articles displayed at the Chicago World's Fair. He declared that they were 'created in the same spirit as the railroads, ships and wagons'. Such functional design was compatible with extensive mechanisation and subdivision of labour geared to the ideal of rapid high-volume production. Like the furniture maker, the American carriage builder was becoming more of an assembler and finisher since it was cheaper to buy parts from specialised component makers. As the Columbian Exposition's *Catalogue* reveals, some of the latter were jobbers producing a variety of parts to order while others specialised narrowly on key components such as axles. The year after the Fair, the US Commissioner of Labor, Carroll D. Wright, singled out the carriage industry as an industry which had experienced dramatic changes. Whereas in 1865 every step in buggy making was done by hand, less than thirty years later each operation was mechanised. Foreshadowing the evolution of the car industry, this process reduced unit costs by lowering labour costs in terms of the labour time expended. The two hundred hours taken to make a buggy in 1865 had cost $45.67 in hand labour whereas the forty hours taken to build the same vehicle thirty years later cost only $8.10; such figures also indicated a drop in the hourly cost suggestive of de-skilling.[24]

The impact of such changes on the workforce is more apparent when one learns that buggy building in 1865 was the work of 6 men while the same task was shared out amongst 116 workers in 1894. Such large-scale operations evident in 1894 required a level of capital investment which few companies could afford. Between 1900 and 1905 the capitalisation of the carriage industry increased 15 per cent while the number of establishments fell 20 per cent. The giant producers such as Studebaker and Durant-Dort integrated their operations vertically, buying timber lands and establishing national dealer networks. Using advertising on an increasing scale, such producers aimed to stimulate the flow of customers to the dealers so that it matched the burgeoning flow of goods from the factories. William C. Durant, who was always more of a salesman than a manufacturer, built up the Blue Ribbon product line of the Durant-Dort Company of Flint, Michigan in the 1880s until it became 'from the standpoint of volume, the largest carriage company in the United States'. On the basis of this experience, Durant took over the faltering Buick Motor Car Company and in 1908 founded the General Motors Corporation.[25]

Although carriage parts were mechanically produced, they were not uniform and therefore required skilled fitting. In fact the unavoidable imprecision of wood-working in carriage bodywork made the body shops of the automobile industry bastions of skilled labour into the 1920s when pressed-steel bodies were introduced. They remained focal points of workers' resistance into the 1930s. Skilled labour was also required because of the carriage industry's strategy of trying to stimulate consumer demand by offering a wide range of models and options. This so complicated the production process that Durant's partner, Dallas Dort, remarked that Buick production was straightforward by comparison. Nevertheless, Durant retained a belief in the wisdom of offering a range of products to entice the unpredictable consumer and purchased an array of companies to form General Motors rather than concentrating on a single standardised car as Henry Ford did from 1909 onwards. Rationalised by Alfred P. Sloan into a model range of graduated price bands offering stylistic differences and optional accessories but still enjoying the economies of high-volume mass production, Durant's broader approach supplanted the rigid Fordist single-model strategy by the mid-1920s.[26]

Sloanism, the vital second stage in the development of the automobile industry in the United States, built therefore on the lessons of the carriage and wagon industry. Obliged by the nature of their raw material and the perceived capriciousness of their clientele in a saturated vehicle market sharply affected by short-term financial factors, carriage makers sought to offset the cost of the heavy inventories they carried by organising the work in ways which speeded production. This might take the form of sequential layout as reported at the Hiram W. Davis factory in Cincinnati in 1886 or of mechanical conveyors for the delivery of parts held in storage as recalled by Max

Wollering at Studebaker around 1910. Hence, although the emphasis on styling in carriage building foretold the marketing orientation of Sloanism, the concern with the flow of the work within the factory foreshadowed Fordist practices at Highland Park.[27]

One of the aims of this chapter has been to challenge the mythology of a virtually automatic American 'love affair' with the automobile. This myth explains the undeniable distinctiveness of the high level of automobile ownership in the United States by the 1920s in terms of the motor car's congruity with key American cultural values. Certainly, the automobile was marketed in terms of freedom, independence, self-reliance; indeed, all the virtues of frontier individualism, but allusions to these facets of the motor car's appeal were not the first reaction. More immediately, as our examination of the Columbian Exposition has tried to show, the gasoline-powered vehicle was just one option in a research programme intended to provide the means of speeding the flow of goods and services within the capitalist economy. Ironically, the internal combustion engine and the private vehicle were initially overshadowed by the promise of electricity and the profitability of bulk carrying, both of which promised a more systematic orderly arrangement of social and economic activities.

This mechanistic approach was not confined to American manufacturing and commerce. It lurked behind the many and varied attempts at social engineering in the Progressive Era. A rhetoric of social justice cloaked what were ultimately conservative objectives of social control. The brutal lives of many working-class Americans appalled middle-class Americans whether they saw the deprivation first hand as settlement-house workers or learned of it through the journalistic exposés of the period. The social reform efforts thus engendered were expressive of a sense of both crisis and confidence: crisis because the presence of such degraded conditions was a moral condemnation of the Republic and a potential source of revolutionary disorder; and confidence because these reformers were certain that their own values and customs were valid models for universal development and because they possessed a seemingly limitless faith in the efficacy of applied expertise: a problem thoroughly studied could be solved.[28]

On the eve of the introduction of the automobile, the grounds for apprehension were evident to a wide variety of Americans. The revolt of Populism in the South and West was simultaneously an outcry against the degradation of agricultural labour and a firebell in the night for the American establishment. The latter's remedy included a massive reduction in the Southern electorate to ensure that its participants conformed to established political plans to produce the solid South. Meanwhile the Western insurgency was contained by a mixture of coercion and co-operation to promote a politics of accommodation rather than resistance. Simultaneous to the agrarian revolt, America experienced widespread industrial unrest and an influx of immigrants from southern and eastern Europe into its industrial cities. As well as any other city, Chicago epitomised these disturbing trends. Already inhabited by over a million people, Chicago added a further 600,000 citizens during the 1890s. Typical of American industrial cities, this ebullient growth was largely made up of immigrant workers. One-third of the nation's total population increase between 1860 and 1900 was the result of immigration and their preponderance in the industrial workforce prompted one Chicago clergyman to remark that while not every foreigner was a working man, 'it may be said that every working man is a foreigner'.[29]

The immigrant presence encouraged Americans to accept the often hostile portrayal of the activities of the working classes as 'alien' and 'un-American'. Increasingly, personal experience did not correct such stereotyping, for the middle classes were withdrawing from the shop-floor into white-collar jobs, and from inner-city neighbourhoods to more homogeneous middle-class suburbs. The same magazines which saw labour as an alien force simultaneously depicted innovative entrepreneurs like Edison and Ford as models of American virtue. Moreover, since American industrial relations were redefined by turn-of-the century managers in terms of the immigration question, control of the workforce was tied to larger programmes of Americanisation, thus promoting the efforts to adjust the heterogeneous character of a polyglot labouring population to cultural norms supportive of managerial objectives. As we shall see, the automobile industry was a prominent advocate of these assimilationist strategies, and the motor car itself and Henry Ford, its leading producer, were presented as embodiments of American values derived from the Turnerian process of character-formation on the moving frontier. The automobile could convey urban Americans back to the regenerative realms of Nature, while businessmen like Ford could safely be trusted with the leadership of the nation for which a 'frontier' upbringing had trained them.[30]

However, as Frederick Jackson Turner pointed out in his

celebrated paper, 'The Significance of the Frontier in American History' which he presented to the American Historical Association at the Columbian Exposition's World's Congress Auxiliary, the frontier which had permitted America's progress hitherto, was now closed, and so some substitute had to be speedily devised. The conflict in American cities suggested that the infection of 'class' had been brought to America from Europe. Within a year of Turner's address, Chicago witnessed the Pullman strike with its burning railroad cars and bloody confrontations between the American Railway Union and federal forces. This was especially alarming because it discredited George Pullman's paternalistic efforts to plan a factory town so that the living environment instilled 'habits of respectability among his employees'. The commission established by President Cleveland to study the cause of the strike placed much of the blame on the company's policy of reducing wages during the acute recession of 1894 while holding rents for workers' houses constant. Thus, capitalists were shown the dangers of combining the roles of employer and landlord, or indeed, of supervising other community facilities such as transport.[31]

Even before the explosive clash of 1894, the reform community had adjudged Pullman's efforts to be heavy-handed, symptomatic of the need for the intelligentsia to educate what Francis Parkman called 'an ignorant proletariat and a half-taught plutocracy'. The editor of *Cosmopolitan*, John Brisbane Walker, an advocate of public ownership of the railroads, referred to the Columbian Exposition as a college for democracy, and its designers had an avowedly didactic intent. Explaining the Fair's design, one of its architects, Henry Van Brunt, remarked that: 'It is the high function of architecture, not only to adorn this triumph of materialism, but to condone, explain and supplement it, so that some element of "sweetness and light" may be brought forward to counterbalance the boastful Philistinism of our times.' The remark may be taken as an illustration of the Arnoldian tension between the 'genteel' intellectuals and their plutocratic patrons. Nevertheless, whatever their misgivings, such figures still sought to condone, explain and supplement the system of production as it stood.[32]

Van Brunt's designated superior at the Exposition, Daniel Burnham, was an outstanding example of such a sympathiser. According to Louis Sullivan, Burnham's ambitions paralleled the 'tendencies towards bigness, organization, delegation and intense commercialism' evident in the corporate age. Burnham had told Sullivan that designing the homes of the business class was not enough. 'My idea', he had declared, 'is to work up a big business, to handle big things, deal with big business men, and to build up a big organization.' At its peak in 1912, the Burnham firm had 190 employees and Burnham became the foremost planner of the City Beautiful movement. Sullivan was a hostile critic of this movement and the downward course of his own architectural career may be taken as proof of the astuteness of Burnham's recognition of the new profession of urban planning's dependence upon the support of the business class. A more friendly commentator on Burnham's career, Thomas Hines, views him as a Progressive Republican who believed that centralised planning was needed to limit the excesses of both democracy and capitalism. While basically a supporter of capitalist individualism, Hines declares, 'he also saw the need – perhaps in the interest of conserving that system – for greater social collectivization and co-operative sacrifice among individual citizens'.[33]

Van Brunt shared Burnham's belief in the need for regulation. 'Every block in our large cities', he complained, 'is made up of a series of independent uncompromising individualities' whose success 'is generally by virtue of superior audacity in height or vulgar pretense'. In contrast to this urban jungle of disorderly growth, the Exposition's design displays a unity and harmony which Van Brunt compared to that found in the classical music of his time. 'In this vast symphony', he enthused, 'no individuality forces itself into undue prominence to disturb the majestic symphony.' In the discourse of City Beautiful planners, such imagery captured the primacy of aesthetic judgement and also the need for a sovereign conductor to 'realize the unity of our city life', as the city planners of St. Louis put it in 1907, 'by bringing together the different sections of the city'. Accordingly, the stress on beautification may be seen as a tactic intended to ensure that the 'maestro' was an architect since only the latter could 'show the way to the City Beautiful'.[34]

Although the equation was too 'Philistine' for a man of Van Brunt's sensibilities to acknowledge, these principles of harmony and expert direction were also the key elements in the notion of efficiency popularised by the campaign for scientific management, whose discourse was more mechanistic in its choice of imagery. Factory managers shared Van Brunt's dislike of 'uncompromising individualities' who sought to distinguish themselves by 'superior audacity' or 'vulgar pretense' and who thus forced themselves 'into undue prominence' and disturbed the design. Just as Van Brunt vilified the competition between property owners to flaunt their autonomy so Ford managers viewed with hostility those workers who strove to stand out as individuals. The outward appearance of an employee, according to the *Ford Times* was symptomatic of his general conduct. Thus, the company journal declared:

> The dude employee stands in his own light. He wears a higher priced hat than his boss; he is immaculately neat; he looks like a fashion plate but at the same time his tailor's bill is unpaid; he is owing money left and right. He spends his evenings in cafés, and at off moments during the day dodges out to look over the racing form and smoke a cigarette. This dude employee sits up late at night. He spends his salary, and more too, in the gay life. He is tired next morning when he comes down.[35]

At the Ford Motor Company after 1914, a special Sociological Department was set up to investigate the life-style of the workforce and to encourage those workers whose habits were held to detract from their efficiency to reform, the company would withhold their profit-share, which when added to the basic wage brought workers' pay up to the celebrated $5 a day. As we shall see in the next chapter, this attempt at human engineering was begun when Ford managers realised that their plans for systematic mass production were as dependent upon a constancy of labour effort as upon the continuous flow of material or the precise synchronisation of machines. By stabilising the rate of labour turnover, instilling values which were deemed conducive to industrial efficiency, and providing a financial incentive for unskilled workers to accept the Ford managers' interpretation of the 'effort bargain', the labour relations programme condoned, explained and supplemented the architecture of production at Highland Park. The payments to Ford workers were generous by the standards of 1914 though the inflation of the First World War period soon eliminated this advantage. More importantly, the company's scrutiny of its workforce on and off the job was criticised as inconsistent with American notions of individual privacy and liberty. Thus, the ideology which was used to protect individual property-holders from the more totalitarian designs of urban planners made it impolitic to extend overt managerial social controls over the workforce beyond the factory gates. The Ford Motor Company disbanded the Sociological Department in 1922 but thereafter intensified its surveillance of the workers within the factory via its notorious Service Department.[36]

The technocratic ideal of order common to both city planners and factory managers during the Progressive Era was only part of the process of social stabilisation which emerged during the 1893 – 1923 period. Indeed, had the degree of regimentation of all classes been feasible in America in this period, one may presume that public transit with its schedules, routes and fares would have flourished as planners commonly hoped it would, whilst the automobile would have been less widely owned and used. However, the growth of motoring at the expense of mass transit should not be interpreted, as Scott L. Bottles has it, largely as a product of Progressivism's failure to democratise transit. In addition to its more rigid authoritarian elements, Progressivism contained advocates of subtler forms of social discipline which preserved the hegemony of the ruling order by reinvigorating a popular belief in its legitimacy. Utopian novelists such as Edward Bellamy and social commentators such as Simon Patten had suggested that the ability of industrial production to bring an increasing variety of commodities within the economic reach of the proletariat might form the basis for renewed social stability, but it was the mass production of the automobile which substantiated this claim.[37]

Motoring in America, as elsewhere, was initially a rich man's sport, and as such, it threatened to epitomise the contradiction between the egalitarian premisses of democracy and the inherent tendency to inequality of capitalism which Progressives feared would rend the nation asunder. Woodrow Wilson, while President of Princeton, warned that motoring was an incitement to class-hatred. It exemplified what Thorstein Veblen had dubbed 'conspicuous consumption' which was indulged in by the leisure class as a 'means of reputability'. Known to be expensive, an automobile on the common road testified to its owner's wealth. A more mobile symbol of wealth than other expensive items such as palatial homes, it could be used to bring guests to expensive feasts and entertainments, thus increasing their reputability. Moreover, as a novelty, the motor car gave its owner a reputation for trend-setting, enabling him to pioneer new branches of etiquette and fashion. Finally, like the owner's horse, the automobile could satisfy 'its master's impulse to convert the "animate" forces of the environment to his own use and discretion and so express his own dominating individuality through them'.[38]

Initially, therefore, the early and usually wealthy, American motorists incensed Progressive reformers as the kind of vulgar and audacious individuals whose impact on the architecture of American cities Van Brunt had deplored. Fortunately, like other transport innovations, the automobile could be presented to the public as a means of diminishing the pathological influences threatening the health of the Republic. The isolation, economic disadvantage and social dislocation experienced by rural Americans could all be alleviated by automobile ownership. While bringing rural Americans closer to each other and the corporate market-place, the automobile could also disperse the hazardous congestion of population in the nation's cities. The street railway whose task it had been to reconcile the conflicting requirements for aggregated labour and suburban residential spaciousness had become a deliverer of crowds rather than their dispersant. Accordingly, middle-class commentators anxious to legitimise their growing preference for motor commuting began to extol the automobile's potential blessings. As early as 1904, William Dix urged his readers to:

> Imagine a healthier race of workingmen toiling in cheerful and sanitary factories with mechanical skill and trade-craft developed to the highest, as the machinery grows more delicate and perfect, who, in the late afternoon, glide away in their comfortable vehicles to their little farms or homes in the country or by the sea twenty or thirty miles distant! They will be healthier, happier, more intelligent and self-respecting citizens because of the chance to live among the meadows and flowers of the country instead of in crowded streets.[39]

As industrial capitalism's thirst for abundant labour pushed American immigration figures to their zenith in the early years of the twentieth century, concern over the need to supervise the character-building of this proletarian mass remained both intense and committed to *embourgeoisement* in the guise of assimilation. The densely populated wards of the major industrial cities were focal points of this concern. The New York Committee on Congestion of Population (CCP) sponsored the Exhibition on Population Congestion in March 1908. The social workers and 'Social Gospellers' behind the CCP shared the 'conviction that back of all the evils of city life lay the dominant evil of congestion of population'. Accordingly, they argued for the relocation of factories and workers' residences. Factories should be moved close to rail or water freight lines at the edge of the city while working-class housing should be spread out by improving mass transit and lowering fares. More controversially, CCP spokesmen urged land-use zoning and fiscal reforms to deter land speculation. Indeed, when the CCP's efforts persuaded both the city and the state of New York to establish commissions to study the problem in 1910, it was the assault on property rights in its tax proposals that excited greatest opposition to reform.[40]

For reformers, congestion was a problem because of the social and potentially political ills it engendered. As late as 1922, housing reformer Lawrence Veiller endorsed Lord Bryce's warning that great cities were 'likely to become great dangers in a political sense, because the more men are crowded in great masses the more easily they become excited, the more they are swept away by words, and the more they form what might be called a revolutionary temper'. The remedy to such fears was already articulated in the contrasting image of labour contentment offered by William Dix. However, while capitalists were anxious to quell the stirrings of revolutionary temper in their workers, changing people by changing their habitat was not their only interest in the congestion question. The Progressive Era was a period of increasing competition for space on the part of retailing, banking, and various other service industries in the central areas that had formerly contained manufacturing plants. This competition between capitalists, together with the traffic congestion in these central districts, encouraged industry to relocate to the outer rail junctions and stimulated efforts by the civic elites to rationalise the transport system and stabilise the pattern of land use.[41]

The recommendations of the Reform Club of New York City at the Congestion Show illustrated the elites' concerns. It urged the locating of factories along the waterfront with intervening parks as 'breathing spaces' and along selected transport routes on Long Island. Workers' housing should be sufficiently near to allow them to walk to work, thus prompting the removal of some workforces to suburban residential locations like that of Garden City, Long Island, home of publishers, Doubleday, Page & Company. This dispersion of industrial and working-class neighbourhoods, it was argued, would allow central Manhattan to be reserved for office buildings, retail outlets and entertainment centres. By giving priority to the economy and efficiency of the land-use and transport systems in urban planning over the ideals of beautification in urban planning, this perspective gave rise to the so-called City Practical movement among planners. While hoping to restrain the indiscriminate and short-sighted development of private resources through such processes as functional zoning, this philosophy of urban design was also marked by a call for public investment in those public facilities, particularly streets, which as gears linking the different phases of capitalist production serve to enhance the expropriation of surplus value.[42]

This philosophical shift from City Beautiful to City Practical was evident at the first national conference on urban planning held in Washington DC in 1909. Almost all the speakers at the conference decried the aesthetic orientation of planning. Organised by New York's CCP the gathering retained a concern for the problem of urban congestion but was inclined to interpret the issue from a businessman's perspective rather than a radical housing reformer's standpoint. The radical implications of the latter in terms of the expansion of government and its antagonistic relationship to private property holders were evident in the controversial proposals of men like Benjamin Marsh. Planners recognised that they were more likely to secure powerful support by addressing the problem of congestion in terms of the zoning of land use, relocation of manufacturing districts, and provision of transport facilities, all of which enjoyed wide support within the business community. Such support would back the formation of city planning commissions, staffed by the profession, across the country. Planners thus resembled their fellow professionals, highway engineers, at this stage.[43]

Daniel Burnham, although absent from the Washington conference, retained his prominence within the profession in 1909 by the publication of his Chicago Plan which mixed the City Beautiful's insistence upon parks, boulevards and a monumental civic centre with the City Practical's emphasis upon infrastructural investment in streets. Burnham's plan called for a regional system of highways centring on Chicago; a system of freight handling which by its location at the outskirts of the city would facilitate the 'ultimate removal of the wholesale and heavy business interests from the downtown district'; a complementary consolidation of railroad facilities and the creation of elevated, surface and subway loops around an enlarged business district. As Paul Barrett demonstrates, the politics of transit in Chicago ensured that Burnham's proposed street improvements were more swiftly realised than his mass-transit recommendations. As significant for our purpose was Burnham's conception of the city as principally a place of business, a view of the collective purpose of urban life which legitimised the rationalisation of land use and transport under the auspices of business and thus foreshadowed the triumph of business Progressivism of the Hooverite type in the 1920s.[44]

Without ignoring the input of urban politicians from immigrant wards, it may be said that Progressivism had always venerated the virtues of middle-class government, for the honorable members of this class were the vital stabilisers and intermediaries in society. Standing between labour and capital, the unenlightened masses and the irresponsible few, the middle classes were the guarantors of decency, justice, wisdom and statesmanship – at least, that was their conviction. On the basis of such moral self-assurance, Progressives embraced planning as one vital process in their campaign to make American democracy safe for business and business safe for American democracy. As wealthy merchant and permanent secretary of the Chicago Plan Commission, Charles H. Wacker declared proudly: 'First know you're right, then go ahead.' Helped by former Columbian Exposition publicist, Walter D. Moody, Wacker advanced the Chicago Plan by orchestrating a $200,000 propaganda campaign 'to show conclusively that the plan advocated is a plan not for a class but for all the people, and a plan not for a section, but for the entire city'.[45]

The crowning accomplishment of Moody's brilliant campaign for the Chicago Plan was the adoption of *Wacker's Manual*, summarising the plan, as an eighth-grade text to be learned by rote by Chicago's schoolchildren. They memorised that the 'first three things of which our cities are demanding the conservation [are] the health of the people, the streets by which they may conveniently go from place to place [and] the parks within which they may conveniently find recreation'. Wacker himself explained to the Secretary of War that in its educational propaganda, the plan's advocates emphasised 'the health and happiness of the people, hygienic and social', and street improvement was presented as a major source of social amelioration. The Commissioner of Health, George Young, saw the major street projects proposed by Burnham as the foundation for good housing in the city since 'housing congestion is largely a result of our non-solution of Chicago's transportation problem as it affects our streets'. In *Wacker's Manual* only two transit improvements were specifically mentioned as compared to numerous major street projects, thus indicating the perceived greater importance of the latter for social betterment. The promotional efforts were rewarded by public support and the implementation of the plan began with those elements of street upgrading of greatest interest to its sponsors. Providing the southern baseline for the proposed central quadrangle of streets, the widening of Twelfth Street from the Ghetto to the lakefront was approved in a 1912 referendum. This was followed by the approval of schemes to improve Michigan Avenue at the east end of the central business district. Neighbouring property owners paid around $8 million towards the cost of this project in special assessments, a tax burden later planners justified by referring to increased property values totalling over twelve times the amount of the assessment. However, the planners had extended the benefited area to include a broad section of slum, whose residents had neither connection with, nor use for, the new boulevard. Thus, as implemented, the Chicago Plan favoured some citizens more than others, despite the protestations of Wacker and Moody to the contrary.[46]

As the Chicago Plan signalled, the city was viewed as 'a depot and a distributing apparatus' as Frank Koester defined it in 1912. Reflecting the same preconception, the plan prepared for metropolitan Boston in 1909 devoted the bulk of its pages to a study of the city's street system. Half the papers at the 1910 National Planning Conference were devoted to 'The Circulation of Passengers and Freight in Relation to the City Plan'. The American Academy of Political and Social Science devoted one of its meetings to streets in 1914 with the majority of contributors sharing B.A. Haldeman's opinion that streets should be rationalised according to industrial models. Given the increasing success of American industrialists in their efforts to reorganise the workplace in order to facilitate the flow of the work during the second decade of the twentieth century, urban planner Henry A. Barker could not understand their failure to transfer this strategy for efficiency in industry to the management of American cities, 'which are', he declared, 'but large workshops'. The force of this analogy was confirmed by the growing number of cities adopting the city-manager form of municipal government.[47]

If the problems facing urban planners and scientific managers were as similar in character as Barker believed, they included the problem of social control. However, imposing the same level of regimentation on urban life as that evident increasingly in major US manufacturing plants would be contrary to the public ideology of America in terms of individualism and hostility to the paternalistic state. Moreover, the crude subordination of working-class Americans in both workplace and neighbourhood threatened to engender increased militancy by linking the grievances of the shop-floor to the grievances of the home, as the Pullman strike had shown. A subtler strategy was required. The designers of the Columbian Exposition had noted with dismay that visitors to the Fair turned eagerly from the authoritative, edifying, yet oppressive spectacle of systematic monumentality in the Court of Honor and had sought relief in the amusements of the Midway. To genteel commentators like William Howells, the side-shows of the Midway may have symbolised the sordid shallow appetites of commerce, but the instant gratification and crude stimulation they offered formed the basis of a new entertainment industry in the form of the thriving amusement parks of the turn of the century.[48]

Just as municipal parks had packaged a civilised version of natural landscape as a sedative for urban anxieties, so places like Coney Island provided sharper treatment for more severe cases of urban debilitation. At least, that was how Jane Addams explained the popularity of the fun-fairs she deplored. 'Looping the Loop amid shrieks of stimulated terror [sic] or dancing in disorderly saloon-halls, are perhaps the natural reactions to a day spent in noisy factories and in trolley cars whirling through the distracted streets', Addams conceded, but she warned, 'but the city which permits them to be the acme of pleasure and recreation for its young people commits a grievous mistake'. On the other hand, Richard Le Gallienne with a more European sense of the ineluctability of vice, was more sanguine about the value of the new tools of conviviality as safety-valves for the release of social tensions. Le Gallienne explained that every 'nation has, and needs – and loves – its Tom-Tom. It has a need for orgiastic escape from respectability – that is, from the world of What-we-have-to-do into the world of What-we-would-like-to-do, from the world of duty that endureth forever into the world of joy that is graciously permitted for a moment.'[49]

As the link between the increasingly separate yet interdependent functional areas of urban society, the automobile acquired the same connotations of escapism as the amusement parks. The automobile industry depicted the motor car as a means of escape from the world of work and duty to a realm of free travellers where motorists became explorers, wandering knights, gypsies and vagabonds. By a simple country drive, or better yet a touring vacation, a motorist could allegedly touch his primal roots and satisfy an inherent nomadic urge. Similarly, speeding in a car, as on an amusement ride, was said to strike a primordial cord. M.C. Krarup remarked in *World's Work* that the 'most enthusiasm for the automobile comes solely from the introduction of the superlative degree of speed and from the absence of effort or fatigue. The automobile is a vehicle that touches a sympathetic chord in most of us.' Non-motorists, enthusiasts thus contended, need only to take the wheel and the chord of sympathy for motoring would sound for them too.[50]

Publicists were equally adept at contrasting the automobile's convenience to the inflexibility of other forms of transport. The motorist did not have to stick to a schedule, as was the case for the railway traveller. Trains, declared novelist and motor tourist, Theodore Dreiser, in 1916 were 'huge clumsy affairs, little suited to the temperamental needs and moods of the average human being'. Mass transit and trains represented the alienating forces of modern times by virtue of being impersonal, monopolistic and inflexible. How sad it was, the *American Motorist* opined, that 'the individual has had to sacrifice much of his liberty of action to take advantage of ... mass transit'. In contrast, the motor-car offered a new freedom which compensated its owners for the often harsh hyper-rationality of modern life by the mobility and associated access to other recreational facilities which it gave. Thus, the automobile in America was wrapped in positive cultural symbolism in the same manner as it was in France until its role as a central artifact of American civilization by the 1920s was interpreted largely through this imagery. However, another interpretation of the therapeutic effects of mass motoring was given by a prominent labour figure in Muncie, Indiana who growled: 'As long as men have enough money to buy a second-hand Ford and tires and gasoline, they'll be out on the road and paying no attention to union meetings.'[51]

However, the principal impulse behind the urge for transport innovation lay in the inherent dynamic of expanding the market-place under capitalism, which Marx captured in his phrase, 'to annihilate space by time'. The Columbian Exposition of 1893 testified to the varied fruits of that effort in the form of its rail-transport exhibits. Despite the mistaken belief in the easy development of electric automobiles among corporate figures of the 1890s the eventual triumph of the gasoline-powered vehicle was foretold by the Fair's bicycle, carriage and wagon, and machine-tool displays which provided the manufacturing tradition upon which mass production was founded. The ambiguity of that triumph was also implicit at the Fair both in the stern autocratic ideal of systematic planning to which American capitalists intermittently turned in their hope of bringing stability to a volatile economic system, and in the tempting commodities of diversion presented on the Midway. In a society which divided life increasingly into specialised tasks performed at separate locations, the automobile was a practical tool. But as the mass of Americans took up the automobile in the early 1920s motoring became a highly regulated habit contradicting the individualistic rhetoric increasingly associated with it. Nevertheless, the pockets of individual freedom, even of personal prejudice, which motoring permitted, became increasingly cherished as the alienation of modern life intensified, and so Americans of different classes accommodated themselves to the unsatisfying qualities of modern life by buying the avenues of escape from it: movies, radios, pulp novels and automobiles. In the next chapter we look more closely at the working environment that underpinned this 'social contract'.[52]

Notes

1 Lloyd, as cited by T. Hines, *Burnham*, 1974, p. 120; Norton, as cited by D. Burg, *White City*, 1976, p. 342; H. Adams, *Education*, 1931, p. 344.

2 R. Wiebe, *Search for Order*, 1967; for significance of the Midway, J. F. Kasson, *Amusing the Millions*, 1978; cf. Alan Trachtenberg's interpretation of the Exposition as a product of an alliance between businessmen and the 'genteel' intelligentsia: *Incorporation*, 1982, pp. 208–34. This overlooks the business–leisure-psychology complex signalled by the success of the Midway.

3 For the influence of the Paris Exhibition, see Hines, *Burnham*, p. 75; for the auto exhibits there, see J. Laux, *First Gear*, 1976, pp. 11–18; 'Electric boats and carriages at the Columbian Exposition', *Scientific American*, 6 August 1892, n.p.; Moses P. Handy, ed., *The Official Directory*, 1893, p. 788; 'An electric carriage', *Scientific American*, 9 January 1892.

4 May, *R. E. Olds*, 1977, p. 55; *New York Sun* article cited by Frederick Schildberger, 'Seventy-five Years of Mercedes-Benz ties with the USA', *Horseless Carriage Gazette*, September–October 1964, p. 10. For neglect of Daimler by US auto pioneers, see C. B. King to C. Sintz, letters, 20 April 1940 and 12 September 1940, Acc. 80, Box 1, Ford Archives; and testimony of Elwood Haynes in Selden Patent Case, Box 4, C. B. King Papers, National Automotive History Collection.

5 G. W. May, *Charles E. Duryea*, 1973, pp. 44–58; and G. S. May, 'The Thanksgiving Day Race of 1895', *Chicago History*, XI, Fall 1982, pp. 175–83.

6 Handy, *Official Directory*, pp. 781ff; Adams, *Education*, p. 240; cf. J. Bryce, *American Commonwealth*, 1888, II, p. 444; for Philion's car, see M. Denison, *Power to Go*, 1956, p. 85.

7 Adams, *Education*, pp. 380ff. Joint Committee on Ceremonies, *The Dedicatory and Opening Ceremonies*, 1893, p. 265.

8 On the fair's illumination, see F. McDonald, *Let There Be Light*, 1957, pp. 30–2.

9 Handy, *Official Directory*, pp. 796–7; for rapid transit development, see Cheape, *Moving the Masses*, 1980.

10 Schildberger, 'Seventy five years', p. 10; E. Hubbard, *Steinways*, 1926, pp. 25–8; T. E. Steinway, *People and Pianos*, 1953, pp. 32–3, 37; William Steinway's obituary, *New York Times*, 1 December 1896, p. 9; C. Cheape, *Moving the Masses*, pp. 6, 76, 81.

11 Schildberger, loc. cit.

12 Cheape, *Moving the Masses*, pp. 112–19; A. Jardim, *The First Henry Ford*, 1970.

13 Passer, *The Electrical Manufacturers*, 1953, pp. 328–9; Duboff, *Electric Power*, 1976, p. 16; J. W. Hammond, *Men and Volts*, 1941, chap. 26.

14 J. B. Rae, 'The Electric Vehicle Company: a monopoly that missed', *Business History Review*, XXIX, December 1955, pp. 298–311.

15 F. L. Allen, *The Big Change*, 1952, p. 14; R. Smith, *Social History of the Bicycle*, 1972, pp. 13–14; Hounshell, 'American system', 1978, pp. 280–330.

16 Handy, *Official Directory*, p. 800; J. B. Rae, *American Automobile Manufacturers*, 1959; N. Rosenberg, ed., *The American System of Manufacturers*, 1969; Hounshell, loc. cit.

17 Handy, *Official Directory*, pp. 514–18; Rae, *The Road and the Car*, 1971, pp. 31–3.

18 Cheape, *Moving the Masses*, pp. 112–19; R. Fogelson, *Capitalist City*, 1986, p. 117.

19 Hounshell, 'American system', pp. 283–4, 289–93.

20 For more information on technological innovation in the bicycle industry, see Hugh Dolnar, 'Bicycle tools – XXVIII', *American Machinist*, XIX, 16 July 1896, p. 677; idem., 'Bicycle tools XXIX', ibid., 6 August 1986, two articles on Pope's machinery from a series by Horace Arnold (alias Dolnar) who later co-authored, *Ford Methods and the Ford Shops*; Handy, *Official Directory*, pp. 455–6; Hounshell, 'American System', pp. 295–300.

21 Hounshell, op. cit., p. 110.

22 Flink, *Car Culture*, p. 19; Rae, 'Electric Vehicle Company', *passim*; H. P. Maxim, *Horseless Carriage Days*, 1937, p. 165; Greenleaf, *Monopoly on Wheels*, 1962, *passim*.

23 Handy, *Official Directory*, Group 83; C. McShane, 'American cities', 1975, pp. 69, 72–4, 83; cf. 'Horseless carriages and sanitation', *Scientific American*, LXXIV, 18 January 1896, p. 36.

24 S. Giedion, *Space, Time and Architecture*, 1949, pp. 204, 209, 315; Handy, *Official Catalogue*, pt. VII, pp. 19–24; *Thirteenth Annual Report of the Commissioner of Labor*, vol. I, pp. 36–7, 160; ibid., vol. II, pp. 714–21; and J. D. Ritterhouse, *Horse Drawn Vehicles*, 1948, p. 5.

25 *Thirteenth Report*, I, pp. 36–7; US Bureau of the Census, 'Carriages and wagons and the steam and street car industry', Bulletin 84, *Census of Manufactures 1905*, 1907, p. 9; L. Gustin, *Billy Durant*, 1973, p. 43.

26 Interview with L. W. Haskell, Ass. Mgr. of Operations Plant, Chrysler Corporation, 6 November 1936, Box 10, Edward A. Wieck Collection, Archives of Labor and Urban Affairs, Detroit; Editors of the *Flint Journal*, unpublished 'History of Flint', Flint Public Library; cf. Durant-Dort Carriage Company Catalogue No. 20, 1907, 150 in National Automobile History Collection.

27 For Sloanism, see A. P. Sloan, *My Years With General Motors*, 1967, pp. 28–9; E. Rothschild, *Paradise Lost*, 1973, pp. 26–53.

28 S. Haber, *Efficiency and Uplift*, 1964; H.F. May, *End of Innocence*, 1979; D. Danhom, *'The World of Hope'*, 1987; R. Crunden, *Ministers of Reform*, 1982; P. Boyer, *Urban Masses*, 1978.

29 L. Goodwyn, *The Populist Moment*, 1978; J. Strong, *Our Country*, 1885, p. 40; Trachtenberg, *Incorporation*, p. 88.

30 For the impact of immigration, see D. Ward, *Cities and Immigrants*, 1971, pp. 105–43; cf. O. Zunz, *Changing Face of Inequality*, 1982, *passim*; and G. Korman, *Industrialization, Immigration, and Americanizers*, 1967, *passim*. For role models, see Warren Susman, '"Personality" and the making of twentieth century culture' in J. Higham and P. Conkin, *New Directions*, 1980, pp. 212–26. For industrial relations, see D. Nelson, *Managers and Workers*, 1975; R. Edward *et al.*, *Segmented Work, Divided Workers*, 1982; and S. Mayer, *Five Dollar Day*, 1981. For middle-class return to Nature see P. Schmitt, *Back to Nature*, 1969; and for Ford, see R. Wik, *Henry Ford*, 1972.

31 F.J. Turner, *Significance of the Frontier*, 1893, 1963 edition; A. Lindsey, *Pullman Strike*, 1943, *passim*; S. Buder, *Pullman*, 1967, pp. 70, 61; R. Fogelsong, *Capitalist City*, p. 193.

32 Parkman, cited by Trachtenberg, *Incorporation*, p. 215; John B. Walker, 'The World's College of Democracy', *Cosmopolitan*, XV, 5, September 1893, pp. 584–90; Van Brunt, see Trachtenberg, op. cit., p. 216.

33 L. Sullivan, *Autobiography*, 1926, pp. 321–5; Hines, *Burnham*, 1974, pp. 269, 172.

34 Van Brunt, 'The Columbian Exposition of 1893 and American civilization', *Atlantic Monthly*, LXXI, May 1893, pp. 577–88; Fogelsong, *Capitalist City*, pp. 150–61.

35 Fogelsong, op. cit., pp. 213–14; Haber, loc. cit.; *Ford Times*, I, 15 May 1908, p. 3.

36 John R. Lee, 'The so-called profit-sharing system at the Ford plant', *Annals of the American Academy of Political and Social Science*, XLV, May 1916, pp. 297–310; for concern and paternalism, see William Pioch's Reminiscences, Oral History Collection, Ford Archives; Meyer, *Five Dollar Day*, pp. 169–94.

37 Bottles, *Los Angeles and the Automobile*, *passim*; E. Bellamy, *Looking Backward*, 1888; S. Patten, *The New Basis of Civilization*, 1907, pp. 143, 213, 215; cf. A. Siegfried, *America Comes of Age*, 1927, *passim*.

38 For Wilson's remark of 1906, see F. Donovan, *Wheels for a Nation*, 1965, p. 8; T. Veblen, *Leisure Class*, 1899, pp. 64–5, 104.

39 Dix, 'The automobile as a vacation agent', *Independent*, LVI, 6 February 1904, pp. 1259–60.

40 Fogelsong, *Capitalist City*, pp. 168, 172–4.

41 Fogelsong, op. cit., p. 175; Veiller, 'Are great cities a menace? The garden city as a way out', *Architectural Record*, LI, 1922, pp. 175–84.

42 Fogelsong, op. cit., p. 176; Edmond Preteceille, 'Urban planning: the contradictions of capitalist urbanization', *Antipode*, VIII, March 1976, p. 70.

43 Fogelsong, op. cit., pp. 202–6.

44 D. Burnham and E. Bennett, *Plan of Chicago*, 1909, p. 4; Fogelsong, op. cit., p. 209; Barrett, *The Automobile and Mass Transit*, 1983; S. Kaplan, 'Social engineers as saviours: effects of World War I on some American liberals', *Journal of the History of Ideas*, XVII, June 1956.

45 On the urban immigrant input into reform, see J. Buenker, *Urban Liberalism*, 1973; Wacker, cited by Fogelsong, *Capitalist City*, pp. 210–11.

46 Barrett, op. cit., pp. 75–6; Fogelsong, op. cit., p. 212.

47 Koester, 'American city planning – Part 1', *American Architect*, CII, October 1912, p. 142; Fogelsong, *Capitalist City*, p. 216; Haldeman, 'The street lay-out', *Annals of the American Academy of Political and Social Science*, LI, January 1914, pp. 182–91; Barker, 'The need of a city plan commission', *The American City*, IV, February 1919, pp. 64–5.

48 I. Katznelson, *City Trenches*, 1981, *passim*; W. D. Howells, 'Letters of an Altrurian traveller', 1893, in *The Altrurian Romances*, 1968, p. 249; Kasson, *Amusing the Millions, passim.*

49 Addams, *The Spirit of Youth*, 1909, p. 69; Le Gallienne, 'Human need for Coney Island', *Cosmopolitan*, XXIX, July 1905, p. 243.

50 Compare W. Belasco, *Americans on the Road*, 1979, pp. 7–17; Krarup, 'Automobiles for every use', *World's Work*, XIII, November 1906, p. 8170; for the conversion of non-motorists, see comments of Frank Munsey in *Automobile Topics*, VI, 2 May 1903, pp. 162–3.

51 Belasco, op. cit., pp. 19–22; for French auto advertising, see Nicolas Spinga, 'L'introduction de l'automobile dans la société française entre 1900 et 1914; étude de presse', Master's thesis, University of Paris–Nanterre, 1973, cited by J. P. Bardou *et al., Automobile Revolution*, 1982, p. 310. J. and H. Lynd, *Middletown*, 1929, p. 254, footnote 7.

52 W. Lewchuk, *American Technology*, 1987, *passim*; T. J. Jackson Lears, *No Place of Grace*, 1981, *passim.*

Chapter 6

Fordism and the architecture of production

Widespread car ownership came to the United States between 1912 and 1923. Registrations in the earlier year equalled only 4.2 per cent of US households but by 1923 registrations had soared to 50.3 per cent of households. Although nearly half of American households did not possess automobiles in 1923 according to these figures, President Warren Harding declared that 'the motorcar has become an indispensable instrument in our political, social, and industrial life'. The Ford Motor Company was at the heart of this transformation. During its first year of full operation at its Highland Park complex (1911), Ford had 20 per cent of the US car market in terms of the number of vehicles sold. The dramatic production innovations of the next two years boosted Ford's share of the market to 48 per cent. Preparedness, mobilisation and demobilisation for World War I interrupted this expansion, but Ford entered the Twenties as America's premier auto maker with 55.45 per cent of the industry's output in 1921. This mass production, exceeding 5 million cars by 1921, underlay the unjustified assumption of universal automobile ownership since it was accompanied by price reductions which made the Ford Model T affordable to lower income groups. The price of the Model T was $690 in 1911 but by 1923 it could be bought for $265. Moreover, and ultimately fatally for the future of the Model T, the increasing number of used Model T's in circulation provided a growing supply of cheap vehicles for the second-hand car market to which the lowest income groups were forced to turn in their pursuit of automobility.[1]

Fordist mass production legitimised American capitalism in a period when respect for 'business' was particularly high. When Americans of the 1920s looked for models of success, Henry Ford's public image came to mind. Letters to the Dearborn auto magnate testified to the potency of this image as a means of stimulating a process of identification with Ford among working-class people. When

Ford sought control of the Muscle Shoals hydro-electric power site in Tennessee, he secured the endorsement of the American Federation of Labor's 1922 convention. When *Collier's* magazine conducted a poll for President in the summer of 1923, its readers placed Ford first, well ahead of incumbent President Harding. Thus, at the conclusion of our period of study, the nation's leading automobile personality was also its choice for President. A year earlier, Detroit had lost its own auto industrial executive when Mayor James Couzens had accepted the offer to take over as one of Michigan's US senators following the suspension of Truman Newberry (due to electoral misconduct in his contest with Henry Ford). Discussing the need for an expert successor to the hard-headed, former Ford executive, the Motor City's reform journal, *Civic Searchlight*, cast its argument in terms of automotive imagery. 'Popular government', it remarked, 'is like an automobile. Success depends on both car and driver. A lack of either factor may spell defeat.'[2]

Municipal reform for Detroit's Progressives had culminated in a revision of the city's charter intended to eliminate the inefficiency and corruption of ward-based machine politics by concentrating authority in the office of the mayor. According to *Civic Searchlight*, this had given Detroit the governmental equivalent of 'a high-powered modern car' but it also obliged the electorate to select 'only the most competent driver'. With such a chauffeur, the vehicle of government could 'confer vast blessings on the people', but in the wrong hands, it was equally 'capable of producing a most spectacular "smash-up", far more spectacular than happens when the "tin-lizzie" [Model T] goes astray'. Such imagery was not simply appropriate to Detroit but was also revealing about the notion of democracy for Progressives. Referendum, initiative, and recall legislation, the direct election of senators, and female suffrage were all measures sponsored by Progressives in order to restore government by the people rather than by special interests. However, they were also passed in the belief that the public could be educated to use these devices wisely. Thus, alongside these Populist measures, the Progressives had contradictory elitist aspirations. They wanted this electoral machinery of popular participation to legitimise government of the people and for the people by experts. Americans ought to feel that they were in the vehicle of state but not all of them should take a turn at the wheel. Moreover, Progressives were divided and individually inconsistent as to the rate of intellectual progress which might justify greater mass influence.

One faction retained a traditional republican faith in a field open to talents and the efficacy of education and uplift and saw all impediments as temporary hurdles destined to be overcome in the onward march of God's Chosen Republic. Others were more ready to see social stratification as immutably fixed and to see their role as a paternalistic supervisor of those less fortunate: the desperate plight of black Americans in the Progressive Era illustrates the limits of these conceptions of democracy.[3]

Within the Ford Motor Company, a similar division of opinion was evident. Ford himself was deeply autocratic. 'The average employee in the average industry is not ready for participation in the management', Ford declared in his autobiography of 1922, and he went on to admit that industry 'at this stage in our development, must be more or less of a friendly autocracy'. Other Ford engineers among the top managers were equally comfortable with the idea that their authority over the workforce was an inherent necessity based on naturally determined inequalities of ability. As engineer–journalists, Horace Arnold and Fay Faurote summarised it: 'the only reason why any one man works for another man is because the hired man does not know enough to be the director of his own labor'. To such men, traditional shop knowledge was an obstacle to progress. It was better to employ workers who were malleable, who, in Arnold's words 'have nothing to unlearn' but 'will do what they are told, over and over again, from bell-time to bell-time'. Ironically, many of the senior managers at Ford in the second decade of the twentieth century were machinists who had moved up. They shared, therefore, the social background and social prejudices of the craft workers who dominated the American Federation of Labor, particularly an attitude of condescension, verging on contempt for the largely 'new immigrant' unskilled labourers. This attitude encouraged Ford managers to dictate the character of work and made it difficult for the remaining skilled workers to mobilise mass support against de-skilling initiatives which opened up more jobs for the unskilled.[4]

The other faction at the Ford Motor Company emerged only after 1910 when the expansion of production so increased the workforce that the company began to consider a more systematic approach to personnel management. As the latter term suggests, this faction was rooted less in the company's manufacturing supervisors than in a new breed of administrator, typified by John R. Lee who came to Highland Park from Ford's steel-pressing plant in Cleveland in 1912. The growth of the workforce from just over 1000 in 1900 to 5000 in 1912 and 14,000 on the eve of mass production in 1914 forced Ford to reform its supervisory structure and procedures. The direct face-to-face discipline of the early years of the company was no longer appropriate. Indeed, its benevolent aspects had already withered under the pressure of demands to increase workers' output after 1908. Foremen had been given more authority in order to compel workers to meet output schedules. This had included control over hiring and firing, pay, and job allocations in their department. The consequent 'arbitrary, prejudiced and brutal' conduct of some foremen produced chronic problems of labour turnover and absenteeism. This provided the opportunity for Lee and his supporters to argue in favour of a welfare capitalist approach. The harshness of relations on the shop-floor, they argued, could be reduced by the establishment of a more centralised bureaucratic approach to discipline, which would limit the authority of foremen and other figures with whom the workforce came regularly into contact and so eliminate the immediate focal points for dissent. An appeals procedure would defuse discontent still further. Most important of all, other welfare initiatives aimed especially at the large number of immigrant workers would promote habits conducive to regular working practices. This programme of social control advocated by the 'welfarist' faction culminated in the work of the Sociological Department in connection with the Five Dollar Day.[5]

What both factions, the authoritarian and the welfarist, shared at Ford was a common recognition that the workforce was potentially harmful to the work process as management conceived it, in much the same way as Progressives perceived the people as potentially a threat to democracy because of what their vices might lead them to do or fail to do. The aim therefore was to design a set of structures which would prevent harmful interference by the workforce: first, by steadily reducing the individual worker's control or discretion within the work process; and secondly, by dissuading the worker from contending for control. However, this strategy of social control was itself subordinated to another overriding aim: profitable mass production of a standardised motor car. Thus, changing the gears of production necessitated an attempt to change people. However, as in the case of Progressivism, it proved easier for Fordism to change gears for higher production than to change people. We begin, therefore, with the change in manufacturing methods.

Prior to 1906, Ford was predominantly an assembler, fitting

together major components such as axles, engines, transmissions and bodies bought from outside parts suppliers such as the Dodge brothers. As the Census of Manufactures for 1905 observed, the automobile at this stage was a combination of components already being produced for other purposes. The gasoline engine had marine and manufacturing uses and the early auto bodies were carriage-like, as were the wheels. Like bicycle makers and carriage builders before them, early auto manufacturers were troubled by difficulties in the assembling and finishing process. Ford veteran, Fred Seaman, who had previously worked at the Globe Cycle Works in Cleveland, stresses in his reminiscences that assembly work was slow, skilled work at Ford's first plant on Mack Avenue in 1903 and both he and fellow veteran, John Wandersee, remark that some machining was necessary in order to repair 'some misfit pieces'. Leading General Motors engineers similarly recalled in 1932 that the 'early automobile was essentially a handmade mechanism'. They explained that because of 'errors in specification and because of further inaccuracies in fabrication the per centage of misfits was enormous; hence the extensive use of craftsmanship in order to obtain a working machine from a collection of dissimilar parts'.[6]

The highly skilled nature of the work left factory owners dependent upon artisanal labour. It was these skilled workers who determined how fast the job was done. Such workers' control was not particularly problematic as long as auto production was planned on a small scale. However, having sold 1708 cars in the 1903 – 4 season, the Ford managers wanted to expand. Fred Seaman recalled that working conditions were so crowded at the Mack Avenue shop that there 'was a lot of material left outside'. Moving to a larger plant on Piquette Avenue, the company managers became more attentive to the challenge of increasing output and holding or lowering costs after 1905. Net income as a per centage of sales declined between 1903 and 1906 and as a per centage of total assets it dropped back to 1903 levels. While retained earnings remained steady at 40 per cent of total assets, there was no dividend for stockholders for the first time in 1906. All of these things concentrated the minds of Ford stockholders and made them more combative in their approach to each other as well as to the workforce. One faction on the board led by Alexander Malcolmson wanted to introduce a new luxury car, the Model K, as a prelude to joining the Association of Licensed Automobile Manufacturers (ALAM). Another faction comprising Ford himself and James

Couzens wanted to concentrate on the relatively inexpensive Model N, a strategy which would mean not only continuing to contest ALAM patent claims but also dramatically changing current manufacturing practices. As part of this boardroom struggle, Ford and Couzens set up the Ford Manufacturing Company on Bellevue Avenue to supply parts exclusively for the Model N just as Malcolmson's allies, the Dodges, supplied parts for the Model K. The implications for workers at Ford were soon evident.[7]

One of the many areas of disagreement between Henry Ford and the Dodge brothers stemmed from the latter's use of piece-rates to secure an adequate output from their workforce. Ford believed that this practice encouraged inconsistent standards of work. However, Ford himself had so little experience in manufacturing prior to 1905, that while he could recognise the importance of interchangeability as a goal not to be forsaken in the pursuit of high output he had very little knowledge of how the two goals of accuracy and speed were to be reconciled. While purchasing equipment for the Ford Manufacturing Company in 1905, Ford became acquainted with machine-tool salesman Walter E. Flanders. Flanders had the experience that Ford lacked. He had seen high-volume manufacturing at Singer and had built tools for Landis, a pioneering firm in precision grinding. According to Charles Sorensen, Flanders took a keen interest in the tooling-up process at the Bellevue plant, ensuring that the machinery was properly set up and training the Ford men in its proper use. Flanders's charm and expertise attracted to him a series of protégés. Consequently he was able to provide Ford with an experienced superintendent, Max Wollering, to oversee operations at the new plant. Wollering had been superintendent of the drafting, engineering and tool-room section at the International Harvester plant in Milwaukee and he used his knowledge of the American system of manufactures to try to move Ford Manufacturing towards the interchangeability that Ford himself recognised as the foundation for mass production.[8]

Wollering ordered the mechanics under him to build jigs, fixtures and gauges for all the parts made by the Ford Manufacturing Company. He referred to these devices as 'farmers' tools' because, as explained to Fred Seaman, one could bring 'in a farmer, Fred, and put him on the machine and he can do as good a job as a first class mechanic'. The most immediate benefit of such an innovation was a reduction in labour costs due to the displacement of skilled labour by more abundant unskilled workers. Equally important, however, was the cumulative potential of such steps towards interchangeability, for once the latter was achieved, de-skilling in the subsequent assembling operations, which currently required skilled fitting, might commence. Despite the preponderance of skilled labour, there was already evidence that unskilled or at least lower-paid workers were becoming more numerous at Ford by late 1905. These efforts to reduce the role of skilled workers at Ford occurred in the context of a wider industrial relations struggle in Detroit centring on the successful 'open-shop' drive of the Employers' Association against local labour organisers. Men such as Henry Leland, whose Cadillac car company relied heavily on skilled machinists, were leading the open-shop campaign which was orchestrated by the National Association of Manufacturers presided over by D. M. Parry, head of the Overland Automobile Company. By 1907, with the defeat of the Machinery Molders Union, the craft unions had been crushed, leaving the workers in the emergent auto industry largely unorganised for thirty years.[9]

The most effective weapon of the Employers' Association of Detroit was its Labor Bureau. In 1906, this listed over 40,000 workers, virtually one-third, perhaps even a half, of the total Detroit workforce. Using such records, the bureau could blacklist union organisers, break strikes with non-union labour, and prevent a spiralling of wages caused by competitive bidding between employers. The latter danger could also be reduced by increasing the supply of workers. The Employers' Association actively recruited new labour and in 1907 encouraged immigration authorities to direct eastern and southern Europeans to Detroit. Advertisements in two hundred North American cities attracted what were known as 'Buckwheats', the surplus male labour from midwestern and Ontario farms: farmers for Wollering's 'farmers' tools'. The interruption of overseas immigration by World War I was offset by an influx of Southern black labour and more female employment. Whereas the earliest auto shops had been filled with experienced, second- or third-generation industrial workers, the larger shops, set up after the shake-out of auto companies during the financial panic of 1907, drew upon a larger supply of workers of more diverse ethnic, regional, racial and sexual characteristics. The census of 1910 revealed that over 27 per cent were of foreign parentage. A 1915 industrial survey in Cleveland, a centre of auto production where Ford managers such as Charles Sorensen, John R. Lee and William Knudsen had all worked, estimated that from 50 to 75 per cent of unskilled auto workers were immigrants. A 1914 survey of the national origins of

Ford workers revealed that nearly three-quarters were foreign-born and more than half came from southern and eastern Europe. Thus, in the words of one labour historian: 'From this mass of uprooted, unorganized immigrants and migrants divided by experience, custom, faith and language, the Ford Motor Company recruited the workers who manned the Highland Park Plant during its first historic decade.'[10]

Taking advantage of labour's weakness, capital in the Detroit auto industry pressed forward with its restructuring of working practices. In August 1906 the Ford Motor Company brought in Walter Flanders as 'a cost-cutting production manager'. Just as Wollering had begun to reorganise the work process at Ford Manufacturing so Flanders began to change assembly arrangements at Ford Motor. Flanders was accustomed to the New England practice of placing equipment according to the job to be done, like the crank job or hub job at the Pope bicycle works, for example. This logical sequence was not present at Ford where machine tools were grouped by type: milling machines in one area, drills in another, and so on. Even when victory for Ford and Couzens in the boardroom struggle with Malcolmson allowed the consolidation of Ford Manufacturing and Ford Motor in early 1907, the nature of the Piquette Avenue plant prevented a rationalised pattern of production. The heavy machinery remained on the ground floor, not because the production sequence dictated it but because the upper floors would not bear the weight. Accordingly, it may well have been at this stage that Flanders discussed with his managerial colleagues the need for a much larger custom-built plant. Certainly it was during Flanders's period at the company that Ford purchased the 60-acre tract on the northern edge of Detroit that became the Highland Park complex.[11]

In the absence of any contemporary records, the degree to which the arrangement of production was strictly sequential at the Piquette Avenue plant is debatable. However, the advantages to managers were quite clear. By arranging the hardware of manufacturing in a progressive sequence, managers not only eliminated the unnecessary shipment of parts to and fro within the plant but more importantly, they were also able to transmit the pace of production without interruption from one process to the next. The culmination of such principles came when conveyors and slides were installed to unite this drive system into an all-enveloping architecture of production. However, such an arrangement was a distant possibility in 1907. Before it could be attempted, the dangers of workers' control from the standpoint of management had to be reduced by other means. A first step in this campaign was to estimate what workers ought to achieve. Prior to Flanders's superintendency, there had been no such thing as a fixed monthly output at Ford. However, the success of the Model N ensured advance orders from dealers which enabled Flanders to 'set up a production program for twelve months ahead'. As a result, 'much of the confusion of the hand-to-mouth operation that the Ford Motor Company had been working under was now ended'. The results, wrote Charles Sorensen, 'were a revelation to us'. As a basis for his planning, Flanders introduced the practice of timing operations to establish output levels and as a corollary, consumption of inputs. Sympathetic workers, such as William Klann, were assigned to set work standards which were continually upgraded to take account of technical improvements. When Flanders departed in April 1908 to launch his own automobile company, he left the Ford Motor Company with the foundations for preparing for mass production in quantifiable terms.[12]

All the necessary details concerning tools, fixtures, gauges, material inputs, sequence of operations and estimated rates of production were available from operations sheets, providing Ford managers with a model of efficiency towards which to drive the recalcitrant workforce. Moreover, thanks to the popularity of the Model N and the manufacturing advances brought in by Flanders and his disciples, production had increased to 6755 units in 1907 and productivity in terms of output per employee had risen from 4.00 in 1906 to 11.78 in 1907. The company's net income had returned to an extremely healthy 83 per cent of total assets and the stockholders had received a modest 1 per cent dividend. Thus the company had the money and the demand to employ special single-purpose machinery more extensively as it tooled up for the Model T.[13]

Ford's confidence that the Model T was an automobile of sufficient quality to justify concentrating his entire operations on its production was a tremendous advantage to the company as it adopted new technology since it ensured long production runs. As Frederick J. Haynes of Dodge explained with the benefit of hindsight shortly before Model T production ended: 'To manufacture only one model offers the ideal conditions in manufacturing ... Because having one model, you are able to have designated special machines having to produce only one particular part of a kind.' Different changes of models could not be produced economically under such specialised arrangements at this stage because of the cost of the tools. According to Roy Chapin of the Hudson Motor Car Company, Ford had told other car makers in 1907: 'that he was going to produce a four cylinder automobile and that once it was produced, he was going to stick to the particular design without changing it every year, and that he was going to reach constantly towards a growing volume because it would actually cut his costs, standardization being his policy in 1907'.[14]

Ford was equally clear what his standardised car would have to offer. It would be: 'a light, low-priced car with an up-to-date engine of ample horse-power, and built of the very best materials ... powerful enough for American roads and capable of carrying its passengers anywhere that a horse-drawn vehicle will go without the driver being afraid of ruining his car'. The Model N had possessed some of these features but had needed refinement in terms of its power, lightness, and ease of operation. Throughout 1907, Ford engineers strove to improve these aspects in a new model and the result of their efforts, the Model T, was exhibited at the Chicago Automobile Show in December 1907. Its appeal was immediate. Even before production began, dealers' orders totalled 15,000.[15]

Having found his model for standardisation, Ford had to ensure that his output of vehicles expanded without boosting his costs. Initially, this entailed further mechanisation and subdivision of labour. As long as work assignments remained complex, machines and tools had to be universal so that they could be adjusted by a skilled operator to do different tasks. Once machine operations were broken down, it was possible to design and make machines to perform a single task with a speed and accuracy superior to that achieved by universal machinery. The use of jigs and fixtures had been a move towards specialisation by guiding machining operations on universal machine tools but the next steps of designing the work-table to hold only one type of part, or of rigidly fixing cutting-tools in one position, or setting spindles unalterably at one speed, required high volume to be economical, and so were not adopted until Ford standardised on the Model T. The accuracy obtained by specialised single-purpose machine-tools could be nullified by minor inaccuracies in the loading procedure since these were multiplied because of the extensive subdivision of labour. Consequently, auto manufacturers constructed multiple-operation machines to perform several metal-cutting operations with only one set-up and loading. Thus, around 1905 the multi-spindled drill press was adopted to drill the numerous holes in the cylinder block and cylinder heads. Around the same time what were termed 'complex machines' such as turret lathes were introduced so that several different machine tasks could be performed by a succession of cutting tools without reloading the rough part. Fixtures such as revolving fixtures and ganging fixtures were also introduced so that more than one part could be loaded, set up, and worked on at once. Table millers, for example, were commonly fitted with fixtures holding up to sixteen cylinder blocks at a time. The imperatives of management were thus incorporated in the machinery of production by design features that reduced workers' control.[16]

Automobile manufacturers strove to enforce their output and product specifications using the machinery described. They not only sought increased productivity by superior mechanisation but also demanded an intensification of worker effort. The discretionary time during which workers exercised skill and judgement was whittled away as tasks became more uniform and more easily timed. Equally, the formerly 'idle' time of the operator during which the mechanism was engaged and the worker waited to unload and reload was eliminated by the introduction of fixtures that forced the operator to set up and load one set of parts while another was being machined. As these innovations increased output in the manufacturing departments, managers turned their attention to the assembly operations and the parts delivery systems where delays continued to boost unit costs.[17]

Motor Age described assembling in 1907 as 'the first real point of differentiation between motor car manufacture and machine manufacture along any one of a dozen different lines'. In other words, whereas earlier phases of automobile production could be handled effectively employing methods familiar to the American system of manufactures, the assembly process could not. The *Motor Age* writer declared: 'Whatever advantage the automobile maker may have taken of past experience in other lines in the production of parts is thus lost sight of when the parts are put together, and though the process has the appearance of great simplicity, its difficulties are in reality very great'. *Motor Age* outlined two approaches to the assembling problem. The first approach, complete stationary assembly, followed the pattern of the building industry with materials being brought to the construction site and put in place as the work progressed. Under such arrangements, which were common practice in auto plants, including Ford prior to 1907, the assembling team of workmen had a brake on the pace of production. They determined the flow of parts. *Motor Age* deplored this 'old method of giving a single crew the entire work of assembling' because 'it prevented close time counting on each operation'. In short, because it failed to give managers full control.[18]

The recommended alternative was to subdivide the assembling process to make it easier to supervise each stage. The first step was to divide the task of assembling from that of parts delivery by hiring groups of unskilled workers to truck parts from the stockroom to the assembly floor. Initially haphazard, this transport of parts became gradually systematised by 1910. The next step, as *Motor Age* related, was that small work teams assembled major components such as motors, gears and axles in many auto firms and the magazine insisted that 'with proper system, the method is capable of further extension'. Underlining the advantages of this reorganisation to managers, the article pointed out that segmentation of the work developed 'specialisation among the assembling as well as in the elementary processes'. Thus, at the Ford Motor Company by 1907, 'in place of the jack-of-all-trades who formerly "did it all", there were now several assemblers who worked over a particular car side by side, each one responsible for a somewhat limited set of operations'. Further subdivision of tasks became possible once managers devised a linear layout allowing assembly gangs to work in rotation. One worker recalled the cars lined up in a row to be assembled at Ford's Piquette Avenue plant. Only one specialised assembly gang worked on a car at a time, completing its task before moving on to the next car and being replaced by the next specialised gang. Such specialisation, *Motor Age* claimed, would also simplify the task of synchronising the rates of output from elementary processes, thus eliminating stock shortfalls or stockpiling. Ultimately, such an integration of manufacturing operations would require an assured conformity to managerial targets not attainable while the workforce had the power to intervene. To eliminate such interference, the Ford engineers had to devise a new architecture of production in which the imperatives of management were transmitted and enforced not merely by foremen but by the very architecture of the workplace whose interlocking mechanical processes dictated the pattern and pace of the work.[19]

This new architecture of production was developed by the Ford Motor Company at Highland Park, its new, purpose-built plant which opened on New Year's Day, 1910. Engineer Fay Faurote recalled in 1927 that Highland Park was unique principally because 'it was laid out for the manufacture of one product, one car ... all the other plants in Detroit that I went through were attempting to make several models, five or six models, and they were also equipped so that they could change models yearly'. Ford's gamble of producing only the Model T simplified the task of organising production in terms of accelerating pace and volume but it relied upon his managers' ability to cut costs and get production out so that Ford could reduce his retail prices to attact new buyers while still maintaining or extending his profit margins. P.E. Martin, production chief at Highland Park, testified that 'Mr. Ford's chief desire in building Highland Park was to build a car ... as reasonably as we could, and get the cost down and make large quantities and we did everything in our power to carry that out'.[20]

Meeting this demand prompted a range of different measures. Initially, the demand for the Model T required the hiring of more workers. It was only after its introduction that the workforce at Ford first exceeded one thousand employees. During the first year at Highland Park, there were 2773 employees whereas smaller producers like the luxury car maker, Packard, employed 4640, and General Motors had 10,000 workers. The Michigan Department of Labor classified nearly three-quarters of the state's auto workers as skilled and a similarly high proportion of skilled workers is evident in figures from the 1910 census. Using a Ford Motor Company list of workers for 1910, Stephen Meyer has calculated that approximately 60 per cent of them were in skilled occupations (including foremen). Thus, the initial expansion of the workforce was not as great a dilution of its skills as the many rationalisation initiatives might have suggested. This meant that Ford managers still faced a workforce with established working habits which had to be broken. Long afterwards, Ford recalled their hostility. 'When', he noted in 1931, 'a few years ago, we made sweeping changes in our methods of manufacturing and greatly raised standards of accuracy, one of the largest obstacles that we met was the refusal of men to adjust themselves to the new standards. We had to change a very considerable portion of our personnel simply because so many of the men stubbornly refused to believe that the new standard of accuracy could be attained.'[21]

Ford was equally dismissive of workers' hostility to time-study which, like other aspects of scientific management, was extensively tried by American managers in the 'efficiency craze' of 1909 to 1912. 'Though they [the workers] suspected that it was simply a game to get more out of them', Ford declared, 'what most irked them was that it interfered with the well-worn grooves in which they had become accustomed to move.' It was the foremen in the different departments who had to deal with this resentment. Recalling the way the introduction of roller conveyors intensified the work in Ford's motor assembly department, its former foreman, William Klann observed: 'The men didn't like it because they had to work harder. The pieces were there and they didn't have time to walk back and take a rest in between.' As top management became more remote, the highest visible authority became the production superintendents, P. E. Martin and Charles Sorensen, representatives of the authoritarian faction at the company. Martin himself revealed something of the character of his supervision when he noted that the workers used to call the Ford plant the 'House of Correction'. Similarly, Charles Sorensen was a notoriously brutal figure in the Ford shops. Once, seeing a worker seated on a nail keg splicing some wires, Sorensen angrily kicked the keg out from under him on the grounds that the company prohibited workers from sitting at any time. When the worker leapt up and floored Sorensen in retaliation, the latter roared: 'You're fired'. 'The hell I am', responded the worker, 'I work for the telephone company'.[22]

Hiring and firing were crucial prerogatives of the foremen. Firing was their ultimate sanction but the foremen could also establish their sovereignty by favouritism in hiring practices. One investigator discovered that this built up 'cliques based upon nationality, religion, fraternal organization, etc., within the department, either because the foreman gives preference or because he hires such men unintentionally by asking men already employed to bring in friends'. Foremen were also commonly the technical trouble-shooters in their departments, performing the critical and as yet unrationalised tasks: machine setting, maintenance and repair; tool changing and sharpening; and work inspection. They were responsible for getting the production out and in return, senior management allowed them to wield absolute and arbitrary authority in their domain. To meet targets set, they turned increasingly to the impetus given by arranging the machinery in a progressive sequence.[23]

Production chief P. E. Martin recalled in 1927 that this idea of progressive sequence 'was uppermost in our minds as we went into Highland Park'. Edward Gray, the Ford engineer in charge of construction at the new complex, later claimed that this concern for the flow of production was even incorporated into the design of the buildings themselves. 'The thought', he recalled in 1927, 'was to hoist raw materials and start it [sic] as near the roof as possible and let it work down'. As a result there were 'thousands' of holes in the floors of the buildings: 'so that parts that are started in the rough on the top floor gravitated through chutes or possibly through conveyors or tubes and finally became the finished article ... on the conveyor on the ground floor'. Drawing on what Flanders had taught them, Sorensen and Martin laid out careful plans for the transfer of production to Highland Park from Piquette Avenue, including scale models of the layout of machinery which could have been used to incorporate delivery systems into the architectural designs of the building. Hand or gravity slides were the first step in the process of mechanising work-handling and consisted of bridging the space between work stations in a progressive sequence, yet when technical journalist Fred Colvin studied operations at Highland Park in the early spring of 1913, he noticed no gravity slides or conveyors and none appear in the photographs accompanying his articles.[24]

Whatever the extent of such work-handling devices prior to 1914, it is clear that progressive layout was a major objective of Ford managers at Highland Park because it offered a means of maintaining output by escaping workers' control. As long as line shafts and belts were used to power machines, it had remained difficult to mix machines with different power requirements. However, this was overcome by a switch to individual electric motors in the pre-war period. Edward Gray designed a large power plant at Highland Park consisting of a 3000 h.p. engine connected to a direct-current generator which powered the electric motors in the individual departments. When Colvin visited in 1913, an additional 5000 h.p. engine was being prepared. He visited the existing power plant which Henry Ford regarded as a show-piece. The generation and transmission of power fascinated Ford. After watching him on their camping trips together, naturalist John Burroughs observed: 'With him everything gets back to power'. In a lengthy interview with leading self-improvement author Ralph Waldo Trine in 1928, Ford himself declared that human beings were 'central stations with myriads of entities going and coming all the time with messages' from a central guiding consciousness. As a corollary to this, Ford was fascinated by energy-conversion processes, especially hydroelectric power and human digestion. Man, he once remarked, 'is just a human storage battery, that's all'.[25]

From this perspective, Ford looked down on the average workman as one out of tune with the universal brain and as a battery apt to lose power unnecessarily. Accordingly, he sought to minimise his company's reliance upon the thought and effort of individual workers by centralising control and skill in the hands of those he could trust, or rather embodying them in the design of production. Ford always denied that his company's efforts had de-skilled the process of automobile manufacturing. Rather, he insisted: 'We have put a higher skill into the planning, management, and tool building, and the results of that skill are enjoyed by the man who is not skilled.' Presumably, the latter's 'enjoyment' was not derived from the work process itself but from its end-product, which Fordist means made affordable to him. Indeed, elsewhere Ford declared that only under his strictly regimented system would the average worker 'get enough to live on his exertions'. Thus, the price of the Model T was the submission of the workforce to the demands of capital embodied technically in the managerially designed architecture of production. One is reminded of the corporate vision of a carefully integrated built environment offered by the designers of the Columbian Exposition. Behind the Fair and factory stood Platonic guardians, confident that they were among the few blessed with the intelligence needed to use power efficiently. Sorensen once implied that the 'laws' of mass production came from the machine, but Ford workers were well aware that they came from him and other members of Ford's elite entourage.[26]

As machine work became more specialised and work studies more prevalent, the direction and evaluation of work became more centralised. Some time shortly after the introduction of the Model T, Oscar Bornholdt was placed in charge of an engineering department which catalogued all existing machines and took control of plant expansion and machine purchases. From such staff, far removed from the shop-floor, foremen received the daily schedules of the work to be turned out by their departments as well as detailed written instructions regarding the set-up, methods and sequence of operations, the time of performance and the number of workers required. To monitor fulfilment of these commands auto companies established separate inspection and accounting departments. By 1914 some six hundred Ford inspectors kept surveillance over the process of production from start to finish.[27]

Walter Flanders had taught the Ford engineers the value of a more theoretical systematic approach. When interviewed in 1926, Oscar Bornholdt recalled how he would devise a work-scheduling system. He would begin by timing the production of each part and would then calculate the floor space, machinery, and sequence of production over the entire process, 'the production of all being so synchronised that there was no excess or shortage anywhere'. Another executive explained that such a calculation of output would include 'due allowance for mechanical defects and human indifference, as established by experience'. Rather than produce a surplus, certain rapidly producing machines would be shut down as the continuity of the entire system was monitored constantly by special time-keepers. By such methods, the Ford Motor Company secured a nearly tenfold increase in production between 1910 and 1913 from 19,233 to 183,572 vehicles. As the volume of production increased, so, strict interchangeability became more and more vital to the managers to ensure the speed, continuity and economy of the production system. Colvin noted that the main components of the Model T were machined in standard fixtures and checked by standard gauges to ensure accuracy by constraining and overriding the human element.[28]

As *Motor Age* had pointed out in 1907, special machine tools had the advantage of specialising the worker's task so that unskilled labour could be employed and supervised more readily. However, having broken the control of the operator by subdivision of labour, the Ford engineers then designed machine tools which did multiple operations in order to reduce the residual interference from the workforce in terms of loading and unloading the machine. Technical journalist O.J. Abell observed in 1912 a multiple-drilling machine designed to perform simultaneously what had once been forty-five separate operations. Production head, P.E. Martin, remarked that, with this machine, the managers 'obtained accuracy for the parts that dovetailed on to those surfaces ... if you had to switch those castings to four different machines, the workmen would not get them in the fixtures properly and they were lost'. By the time Fred Colvin visited Highland Park in 1913, not only had the idea 'of a single-purpose machine [been] carried to the limit', but he found that many machines were 'entirely automatic, except for placing the castings on the inverted spindle and starting the tools at work'. A year later, Horace Arnold observed a machine which did multiple operations and which had a magazine-like feed which fed the mechanism at a set pace. Ford workers thus served the machine in an increasingly restricted manner, while the ingenuity of Ford managers ensured that the machines performed intricate tasks at rapid speed without workers' control over pace or pattern.[29]

Both workers and machinery were media for power in Henry Ford's view and of the two, the 'average man' was less easily tuned for the efficient transmission of power. Without guidance, the common man's exertions would not even get him a living. Progress, measured in terms of mass production, depended therefore on the channelling of the ordinary worker's physical efforts by more gifted men and on the displacement of physical toil by mechanical ingenuity. Prophet of the consumer culture, Simon Patten, declared such technological substitution to be 'the next logical step in evolution'. The superiority of the machine was demonstrated in the eyes of Ford executives by its economy and speed. It used power efficiently. Building on their early lessons from Flanders and his associates, the Ford engineers measured efficiency in units of time. A. M. Wibel, who started work under Oscar Bornholdt in the Highland Park tool department in May 1912, recalled that the company's leading engineers 'wouldn't talk dollars and cents at all. They talked in terms of minutes that the thing cost. Not only with reference to a particular operation but with reference to how an assembly plant operated.' This obsessive concern with speed in reality reflected the capitalist drive to lower the labour time expended on a unit thereby increasing the rate of surplus value.[30]

While automobile production was artisanal, with a necessarily large measure of workers' control, hourly output per worker changed very little. However, the decade from 1909 to 1919 saw a phenomenal growth of nearly 300 per cent in output per worker-hour. For example, using data from the US Census of Manufactures and Bureau of Labor Statistics, David Gartman has calculated that, taking 1914 worker-hour output as 100, the figure for 1909 would be 35 but that for 1919 would be 141. By the end of our chosen period, 1923, worker-hour output was 265. Similarly, using data from Ford cost books, Wayne Lewchuk has attempted to calculate the labour hours expended on making the chassis and body of the Ford touring car. He estimated that 151 labour hours were used in 1906 compared to 39 in 1914 and 37 in the year ending March 1924. Another survey of unit labour time published in 1924 estimated that in 1923 it took only 813 worker-hours to build an automobile which would have required 4664 worker-hours in 1912: a decrease of nearly 83 per cent in unit labour time in only eleven years. A large part of this increase in the productivity of labour can be put down to the heightened efficiency produced by improved machines, greater division of labour, progressive layout and materials handling equipment, but increasing the intensity of effort from workers was also an important factor. Indeed, William Chalmers concluded his 1932 dissertation on employment policies in the auto industry by noting that 'working pace had increased along with improved techniques and was partly responsible for the increased man-hour productivity'.[31]

To set the pace of the work and to protect this rate from workers' interference, Ford managers needed working arrangements that impelled workers to comply with their demands and the key to such arrangements was a progressive layout which facilitated traffic flows. William Klann recalled that in the early days at the Highland Park motor assembly department, there were 'so many boxes around each bench that no one could work'. Journalist O.J. Abell found the principal machining shops orderly in 1912 but still grouped by machine type. However, the American Society of Mechanical Engineers reported in 1912 an upsurge of interest among its members in the traffic problems generated by the see-sawing of work between departments, and Fred Colvin praised Ford in 1913 for its logical sequence of production, which even mixed 'carbonizing furnaces and babbitting equipment in the midst of the machines' if the cycle of production dictated it. He applauded the close placement of the work and the absence of unfinished work in the aisles. Foremen were able to spot laggardly workers quickly by the accumulating parts at their station. Thus, this initiative to increase the continuity of the production process, not only boosted efficiency but enhanced the managers' control. Colvin was also impressed by the final assembly process, declaring that only a film could capture its smooth continuity. Truckers maintained a steady supply of parts to each station while highly specialised gangs moved down the row of static automobile frames performing narrowly defined tasks. Oscar Bornholdt, who left Ford in April 1913, recalled that when asked what their work was, Ford workmen would 'for example, say "My work was to put on bolt no. 46". This was all the man would do.' Hence when Ford reclassified its workforce according to skill in 1913, only 28 per cent of workers were considered skilled.[32]

Despite this rationalisation of tasks, it is easy to imagine how in 1913 the tardiness, resentment, or inexperience of a trucker or operative could seriously impede the Ford manufacturing process. As the productivity gains of the assembly-line experiments were shortly to demonstrate, the workers' efforts could be intensified by a more encompassing architecture of production. The first indication to management of the potential of the moving line as a pace-setter came in the Ford foundry in the course of 1913. Traditionally, foundries had relied on the skill and knowledge of moulders whose control over their work as craftsmen was expressed in their authority over the labourers who assisted them and in the uneven pace of their production. 'When we cast our first "Model T" cylinders in 1910', recalled Henry Ford, 'everything in the place [the foundry] was done by hand; shovels and wheelbarrows abounded. The work was skilled and unskilled; we had molders and we had laborers.' Neither group, in Ford's view, used power very efficiently. To eliminate these workers' restraints on production, Ford engineers took the skilled job of mixing sand for the moulds and replaced it with a centralised battery of machine-mixers positioned in a gallery above the foundry floor from where the standard sand-mix fell through chutes into moulds on a conveyor. The moulds then went under a bull-ladle designed for the continuous pouring of molten iron and then through an oven at the precise speed required to bake them for the proper time. When the castings were shaken out of the casting boxes over a grate, a second conveyor carried the sand back to the machine-mixers for recycling. Under these conditions, E.A. Rumley reported, the moulder 'is expected to place a finished mold upon each platform that bears his number, as it passes him in a continuous rhythm'. Incentive schemes were unnecessary as 'slacking' was immediately apparent to the foundry supervisor. In Rumley's words, the moulder 'must simply fill his place – be a link in the ever-moving chain'. Pointing out the advantage to management of such regimentation, Harold Slauson remarked that the 'output is regulated by the speed at which the traveling chains are operated'.[33]

This foundry incident illustrated the difference between Fordism and Taylorism. Frederick W. Taylor's approach to the foundry 'problem' would have been a scientific analysis of existing work assignments – the moulding, the shovelling, and the trucking of sand – in order to establish a standard rate of production achieved by the most efficient performance of each action. Workers would then have been encouraged to adopt this efficient mode of action by a piece-rate scheme. In contrast, Ford engineers were from the start anxious to displace human workers by mechanical alternatives which would be designed to circumscribe the conduct of the workers who remained. Thus, when the flywheel magneto assembly operation was reorganised in a linear sequence on 1 April 1914, the problem of sychronising the operators in an acutely segmented process was overcome not by a Taylorite piece-rate scheme but by a continuously moving belt arrangement which restrained the hasty and impelled the slow. Within a year this subassembly operation took 5 man-minutes instead of the previous twenty.[34]

Rationalisation of production methods allowed Ford to employ less skilled labour. By 1914, nearly three-quarters of its workforce was classed as unskilled and a similar proportion was foreign-born, mostly of southern and eastern European origin. The managerial approach to this immigrant workforce up to 1914 was summed up by William Klann when he recalled that the 'one word every foreman had to learn in English, German, Polish and Italian was "Hurry-up!"'. Authoritarian executives at Ford like Sorensen believed that the one sure way to get production and profits out of labour was 'to curse it, threaten it, drive it, insult it, humiliate it, and discharge it on the slightest provocation; in short – to use a phrase much on the lips of such men – "put the fear of God into labor"'. However, by 1914, top managers at Ford were beginning to see the disadvantages of such crude coercion because of the turnover of labour it produced. This labour crisis gave the welfarist faction at Ford an opportunity to present its case for a more sophisticated approach to personnel management.[35]

The tremendous expansion of industry in the Detroit area between 1908 and 1914 created an employment situation which encouraged workers to change jobs. As one observer noted: 'Demand for labor in Detroit in 1912 and 1913 was so keen that a man who quit a job in the morning might have employment in another factory at noon.' According to figures from the US Bureau of Labor for 1913 and 1914, labour turnover in fifteen automotive industrial plants averaged 156 per cent, much higher than the average of 93 per cent in the other eighty-four industries surveyed. The average rate of labour turnover in Detroit was 100 per cent, but at individual companies, it was higher. At Packard in its new plant on Grand Boulevard where the management had shown an interest in Taylorism, labour turnover was 200 per cent in 1913. However, this was small compared with the annual labour turnover rate at Ford, which was a staggering 370 per cent. Daily absences at Highland Park equalled 10 per cent of the total workforce, and John R. Lee, who was to head Ford's Sociological Department reported that monthly turnover rates as high as

69 per cent were common during 1913. Magnus Alexander of General Electric calculated that each new employee hired cost American industry on average $35 in clerical costs and waste from inexperience. At this rate, the labour turnover problem at Highland Park cost Ford $1,820,000 in 1913, which was almost one-third of the original investment in plant and machinery at the Highland Park site.[36]

Even at Ford, where rationalisation of tasks had produced a large number of jobs which were unskilled and easy to learn, there was an unavoidable training period during which workers became accustomed to their assignment, surroundings and general company policy. This required greater supervision and was commonly accompanied by a decreased rate of production as well as an increased level of wear and tear of equipment and of spoiled parts. Thus, the company managers had a powerful incentive to reduce the rate of labour turnover and of absenteeism which was similarly disruptive of the increasingly systematic arrangement of production. The new technology required a workforce that was, above all, stable and predictable. As trade journalists Horace Arnold and Fay Faurote wrote in their study of the Ford shops: 'It is of vital importance to successful factory management that workmen should be steady in their habits, and dependable in the point of continuous service'. The interdependence of the heavily mechanised, and therefore heavily capitalised, production process at Ford made a shortage of labour at any one point, or a slowdown for whatever reason, potentially very costly because of its disruptive impact. What Ford required was for workers to be links in the ever-moving chains of production, but by 1913 more and more workers refused to stay in place.[37]

It was apparent to several observers, such as John R. Commons, that the chronic volatility of employment among workers was deliberate. Commons declared: 'They [labour] are conducting a continuous, unorganized strike'. Commentators were equally clear as to the cause of discontent. A Detroit juvenile court judge declared himself unsurprised at the frequent shifting of jobs among the youths who came before him. Pointing to the acute specialisation in modern plants, he expressed the view that 'It is impossible to take a child and set him at one task and not have him chafe at that task'. Even Henry Ford was willing to concede that it was 'right for a man to resist being made into a machine', though more usually he gave the view that the average worker, above all, 'wants a job in which he does not have to think'. However, labour turnover peaked with the intensification of labour caused by the coming of the lines in 1913. James O'Connor, a foreman on one of the first Ford chassis assembly lines, recalled the exodus: 'We all would get new men every day. They kept coming and going.' O'Connor also remembered the alienating effect of the assembly line: 'There were a lot of people who wouldn't even try. They thought they couldn't do it', he recollected.[38]

Just as the foundry at Ford gained an odious reputation for its harsh discipline, so the Highland Park plant generally began to gain renown for its relentless pressure. As Jonathan Leonard wrote in 1932: 'in the Ford factory the worker found things very different indeed. The pace-maker was a machine, usually a belt or an overhead conveyor. The worker performed some simple operation. As soon as he had finished this, another part arrived. He had just time to grab it. There was no leeway, no variation. The belt was tireless.' In the booming labour market, workers need not endure this pressure for long. Other jobs were plentiful at plants less advanced in their efforts to mechanise and rationalise production. Given the Ford complex's peripheral location, these other factories might even be easier or cheaper to reach from home. Thus, as workers voted with their feet, John R. Lee and the welfare faction amongst Ford managers called for the reform of company policy. As a first step, the petty despotisms of the foremen in the company's several departments should be eliminated, thus reducing one contributory factor to the high labour turnover rate.[39]

The Ford Employment Department (FED) was established in October 1913 under the direction of George Bundy and given power over hiring, firing, absenteeism and wages. Instead of Ford foremen hiring at the plant gates, the FED took written applications and kept them on file. Selected applicants would be interviewed by the production superintendent to fill the vacancies reported by the foremen. The latter had also to fill out a standardised 'reasons for dismissal' form whenever they sacked someone, and the worker took this to the FED which was instructed that, whenever possible, the worker should be reassigned to another part of the factory rather than dismissed. The new department was also responsible for coping with absenteeism. Its response was illustrative of the welfarist faction's contention that successful personnel management required a concern for the worker's life beyond the factory gates. The factory departments reported all absentees to the FED each morning and a doctor, nurse, or investigator was sent to the homes of the absentees to establish the cause of their incapacity. If they were sick, medical attention was given. If they were not, they were required to explain their absence to the FED. As a result of this programme, Ford managers reported a large fall in absenteeism.[40]

The other major item placed under the FED's jurisdiction was wages. As early as 1908, when the production innovations surrounding the introduction of the single standardised model began, Ford had begun to increase wages. Given his abhorrence of piece-rates, Ford increased wages via annual bonuses based on seniority, thus attempting to encourage stability in his restless workforce. In 1911, the basis for calculating the bonus was changed from seniority to output, thus seeking to reward those workers who co-operated with the increased demands of new production methods rather than simply old-timers. Being paid annually to ostensibly daily-waged labourers, the bonus still retained an incentive for workers to stay. However, the bonus payments were also part of the arsenal of sanctions available to Ford foremen who were responsible for recommending workers for these extra discretionary payments. John R. Lee was convinced that this contributed to workers' resentment of shop-floor officials at Ford and so worsened the turnover of labour. The first act of the FED was to reorganise the wage structure completely on a rationalised skill basis. By reaching company output standards or otherwise demonstrating a recorded increase in individual efficiency, the worker could move to a new job classification and so secure a pay increase. Foremen were allowed to recommend a worker for a wage increase but it was the FED that made the decision, largely on the basis of its records.[41]

Other automobile companies adopted a similarly bureaucratic strategy for the problem of stabilising labour turnover. The Haynes Manufacturing Company claimed that the establishment of an employment department in 1915 had cut its turnover to only a quarter of its original rate in eighteen months. The Saxon Motor Car Company reported a reduction of 140 per cent in annual labour turnover during 1916, the first year of operation of its employment department. The Packard Motor Car Company, whose high labour turnover rate we noted earlier, also placed hiring, firing, absenteeism, employee complaints, and the monitoring of worker efficiency under the jurisdiction of an employment department. By placing the direction, evaluation and disciplining of workers on the characteristically centralised, depersonalised and rule-governed basis of a bureaucracy the auto manufacturers tried to use organisational mechanisms to regularise the performance of labour so that it could be co-ordinated with the mechanical instruments of production. Changing gears, it appeared, necessitated an attempt to change people.[42]

Emboldening this attempt by auto manufacturers to mould the character of their workforce along lines conducive to more profitable production was the preponderance of foreign-born immigrants. The first detailed ethnic survey of the Ford workforce revealed that American-born workers comprised only 29 per cent of the workforce. Southern and eastern Europeans predominated at the Highland Park plant as they did in the Detroit area as a whole by 1914. In contrast, the percentage of foreign-born in the total population of Michigan's second automotive centre, Flint, never exceeded the 17 per cent attained in 1910 and even among these, a significant proportion were English speakers from Canada and Great Britain. General Motors and its associates provided most of the jobs in Flint and its payroll was made up largely of native-born Americans. The financial troubles of Durant's ramshackle GM empire had resulted in a rationalisation programme sponsored by Eastern financial interests in the immediate pre-war years, which had reduced Buick's workforce by over 23 per cent and more than doubled production to 42,000 cars by 1914. The gap between Buick and Ford remained massive, none the less. With barely three times Buick's workforce, Ford's production of over 200,000 Model T's was five times that of Buick. However, even the limited degradation of labour's position at Buick produced a social climate in Flint which allowed a small Socialist faction to win three seats on the municipal council as well as the mayor's office before the business community could reassert its control by concessions to the 'labour aristocracy' so vital to the tooling-up process in companies that favoured frequent model changes.[43]

The organisational campaign of the International Workers of the World (IWW) at Highland Park in March 1913 was more swiftly diverted by arrests and by reducing the organisers' access to workers by ending outdoor lunch-breaks during which IWW speakers had previously attempted to address the workforce. Alarmed, none the less, by the spectre of labour militancy, senior executives were assured by John. R. Lee that 85 per cent of labour trouble could be attributed to 25 per cent of the workers who, like those in Flint, were native-born and English-speaking. Thus, the company had greater control over its immigrant workers which could be used to good effect by a carefully prepared programme of Americanisation which reinforced their deferential tendency towards management and guarded against less 'wholesome' influences. Peter Roberts, who developed the Ford English school programme noted approvingly that the new immigrants were 'hard workers, regular, uncomplaining and submissive'. What was needed was a company-sponsored scheme to eliminate the intemperance and poor diet that led to absenteeism, the poverty and thriftlessness that led to theft and deceit, and the inter-ethnic animosities that generated unproductive social friction on the shop-floor.[44]

John R. Lee included these negative traits in his 1913 report on the Ford workforce but placed them in the broader context of bad housing and a poor home environment. Although he also blamed poor factory-floor supervision, low wages and long hours for labour unrest, this emphasis on the welfare of the worker outside of working hours ensured that when the Five Dollar Day emerged as an experiment in the welfarist approach, it was accompanied by a detailed scrutiny of the workers' conduct outside of the factory. Such surveillance was already part of the company's strategy to reduce absenteeism. Similar investigations of the individual worker's domestic circumstances were also proposed in those instances where workers failed to progress in terms of the new rationalised pay structure. The company had also instituted an Employees' Savings and Loan Association in 1913 in order to alleviate the financial insecurities of working-class life primarily by 'the encouragement of the saving habit among employees'. Membership of the association required the personal depositing of at least a dollar each day, as an outward sign of the accumulating inner grace of thrift. However, any Ford worker, not just association members, could borrow up to $20 against their future pay at a rate of 2 per cent interest; principal and interest being automatically deducted from the worker's next pay-packet. Workers who availed themselves of this credit facility too regularly were subject to investigation by the company with a view to reforming their character. Seeing the facility as useful chiefly to the 'shifting class of labor', Ford managers hoped that the scheme would 'exercise some hold upon them', thus reducing labour turnover.[45]

The most celebrated example of Ford's new industrial relations strategy was the so-called Five Dollar Day. On 5 January 1914, with due fanfare, the company announced that it was reducing the working shift from nine to eight hours and giving its workers a share in company profits sufficient to boost the daily wage from an average $2.50 to a uniform $5. Senior Ford managers were said to have decided on the scheme at a meeting the previous day. While accounts of the meeting vary, the majority stockholding of Henry Ford and the pre-eminence of James Couzens in matters of company administration ensured that they were the key figures. When asked about the motivation behind the scheme by the Congressional Commission on Industrial Relations in 1916, Ford claimed that it sprang from a recognition that

> market rates of wages were not sufficient for men to properly care for self and dependents and that the environment in which its employees were thus made to live, gave rise to mental anxiety and a physical condition that made it utterly impossible for the human agency to deliver all of the effort that it was capable of in fulfilling the best and larger functions for which it was designed at work, at home, and in the community.

This corroborated Ford's insistence at the time of the plan's announcement that he expected 'to get better work, more efficient work, as a result'. A key aspect of this anticipated increase in productivity was a reduction in labour turnover, as we shall see. However, other longer-term advantages were perceived.[46]

James Couzens, for his part, seems to have hoped that higher incomes would promote thrift and so pre-empt calls for state-sponsored pensions schemes. Ford himself reportedly told Samuel Marquis, who at one time headed the Sociological Department, which administered the plan, that the wage increase sprang from fears that: 'By underpaying men we are bringing on a generation of children undernourished and underdeveloped morally as well as physically; we are breeding a generation of working men weak in body and in mind, and for that reason bound to prove inefficient when they come to take their places in industry'.

This suggests a recognition that the prevailing wage rates failed to reproduce labour power adequately. Inflation, and particularly the shortage of housing, was pushing up the absolute lower limit of income needed to meet minimal material needs in order to sustain the physical capacities of labour. Secondly, the demand for labour in the Detroit area and the growing culture of consumption were raising labour's perception of its standard of living. Indeed, Ford's vision of mass car ownership was predicated on the gradual inclusion of motoring among the essential activities to be supported by standard wages. Heightened expectations and a tight labour market were thus building up the pressure from labour to secure a better 'effort bargain' at the same time as the refinement of mass production required management to secure a stable level of effort in order to synchronise the interdependent phases of the production process. Ford was thus forced to raise wages in order to reduce labour turnover and raise labour effort up to levels commensurate with the potential of the managerially designed technology. By changing the wage system, Ford hoped to induce his workforce to change gears so that they might prove efficient links in the chain of production.[47]

The distinction between wages and profits was central to the operation of the Five Dollar Day scheme as a programme of social control. The provisional granting of a profit share gave the company a position of leverage over its workforce which a straight pay increase would not have secured. As Stephen Meyer has admirably demonstrated, the company stressed that the increase was conditional and might well be temporary. 'It is the Ford theory', John Fitch explained to the social-reform-minded audience of *Survey*, 'that a man is entitled to his wages if he is kept on the payroll at all, but that he is entitled to profits only in the case of his adhering very strictly to the rules laid down'. Thus a non-compliant worker could be kept on the Ford payroll at his low wage, which avoided the expense of replacing him, but at the same time he could be refused his profit share, thus disciplining him for his recalcitrance. There were four categories of workers eligible for the scheme; married men who lived with and took due care of their families; single men over 22 years of age and of proven 'thrifty habits'; men under 22 with dependents; and, after some controversy, women with dependents. Based ostensibly on 'need', this classification ensured that the profit-sharing scheme was targeted at those workers whose obligations made them less likely to leave than those for whom the extra cash would be 'discretionary income'. Another aspect of the plan clearly intended to stabilise the workforce was a minimum requirement of six months at the plant.[48]

The granting of profit sharing to those Ford workers eligible for the scheme was also subject to certification by Ford Sociological Department (FSD) investigators who secured details concerning the worker's nationality, religion, bank savings, property holdings, home environment, recreational habits, and much else. Only high-level managers were spared this invasion of privacy because it was assumed that such middle-class employees already possessed the character traits which the scheme was intended to nurture. In an early lecture to FSD investigators in 1914, John R. Lee explained that he shared Henry

Ford's belief 'that if we keep pounding away at the root and the heart of the family in the home, that we are going to make better men for future generations than if we simply pounded away at the fellows at their work here'. This linking of work performance to activities outside the factory was also evident in the words of Lee's successor as head of the FSD, Samuel Marquis, who declared that the family was 'the foundation of right industrial conditions' just as it was the foundation of church and state. 'Nothing', Marquis declared, 'tends to lower a man's efficiency more than wrong family relations.' While the Ford Motor Company established the most extensive welfare programme because of the need to adjust the general conduct of its workers in order to ensure the particular levels of desired effort at the factory, the insight that the culture of the working class needed to be reformed was not confined to one firm. As the trade journal *Automobile* explained in May 1914

> A man who works 10 hours a day for 10 years spends 4 years working, 3 years sleeping and 3 years eating and in recreation. The 4 years of work and the 3 years of recreation and eating are equally important to the company that employs this man. The remainder of his life is spent in sleep which automatically takes care of many of his bodily ills, but to make the 4 years of work as productive and effective as possible, the 3 years of recreation and eating should receive the attention of the employer and it is around this idea that the industrial betterment movement of recent years is centered.[49]

To the managers of the new mass-production industries, it was self-evident that middle-class habits were superior to working-class habits as a basis for industrial efficiency. Since new immigrants predominated among the working classes particularly in Detroit in 1914, and since Americanness was defined by middle-class cultural standards, assimilation, uplift and *embourgeoisement* became inextricably mixed. Labour discontent, evident in the high turnover of the workforce, absenteeism, and even organised strike action (at Studebaker in 1913), was interpreted by auto makers not as a signal that the new architecture of production was oppressive but rather as evidence of a need for a more systematic approach to personnel management which would adjust the unstandardised workers to fit them for their increasingly standardised role. In this respect, the Five Dollar Day programme and other corporate welfare programmes were similar to Progressivism as a whole in their paternalism and their preference for a politics of accommodation in which reform became a strategy for reformulation rather than innovation. Describing the FSD's objectives in 1915, Henry Ford stressed that it should 'counsel and help unsophisticated employees to obtain and maintain comfortable, congenial and sanitary living conditions, and exercise the necessary vigilance to prevent, as far as possible, human frailty from falling into habits and practices detrimental to substantial progress in life'.[50]

The welfarist faction at Ford gained an institutional base with the establishment of the Sociological Department. Beginning with 30 investigators, described as 'among the oldest and most trusted employees of the company', the FSD reached a peak of 120 employees around 1920, all of them committed to a solidly middle-class and assimilationist approach to social betterment. A couple of illustrative case histories confirm this. A German Catholic worker from a German area of Poland, for instance, was initially denied his profit share in January 1914 because he lived in a crowded, predominantly immigrant boarding house and because his personal habits (he drank and smoked) and family arrangements (his wife also worked and the children were dirty) were unsatisfactory. The investigator advised him to move to a single-family dwelling in a better (that is, less ethnic) neighbourhood. Accordingly, the Ford worker bought a suburban lot, built a three-room shack on it, enrolled in the Ford English School, and made sure his children washed regularly. Thanks to this metamorphosis, he was granted his profit share in August 1914. To prevent recidivism, the FSD continued to monitor his progress, and a year later, his investigator proudly reported that the house was now 'comfortably furnished', the family was 'neat and clean' and the worker could speak English and was seeking US citizenship. A second example corroborates the profit-sharing scheme's success as a means of Americanisation. M.G. Torossian, an Armenian member of the FSD was assigned, presumably on the basis of fluency in Turkish, to investigate a young Turkish worker, Mustafa. Given the inter-ethnic history involved, Torossian's report included an unflattering assessment of the Turks as a race, but he indicated that Mustafa might be an exception. 'Young Mustafa', Torossian wrote, 'unlike most of his race who mostly wander in the mountains and make money quickly robbing others, had a natural intuition for an honest living.' Torossian's view of the United States was that of a successful immigrant. Referring to America as 'this land of wealth and happiness', he explained that Mustafa had not yet felt the land's beneficent influence because currently he was living 'with his countrymen in the downtown slums in a squalid house'.[51]

Even despite Mustafa's attachement to his native culture, Torossian saw hope for improvement. Fortuitously, the ritual cleansing requirements of Mustafa's Islamic faith had instilled an admirable concern for cleanliness. Equally important, Mustafa showed a willingness to set aside aspects of his culture that conflicted with American customs. Thus, while retaining his concern for cleanliness, he none the less had reduced his prayer sessions from five to three times a day because in America time was too valuable. On his own initiative, Mustafa applied for preliminary naturalisation papers and Torossian recommended that he move to a better neighbourhood. The assimilation which followed Mustafa's receiving the Five Dollar Day allowed Torossian to conclude his report jubilantly; 'Today, he has put aside his national red fez and praying, no baggy trousers anymore. He dresses like an American gentleman, attend the Ford English School and has banked in the past year over $1,000.00. Now he is anxious to send for his young wife and child to bring her and live happily through the grace of Mr Henry Ford.' Just as discarding one's ethnic identity brought rewards from auto managers, correspondingly a stubborn attachment to it provoked harsh punishment. A few days after the Five Dollar Day was announced, the Ford Motor Company dismissed over eight hundred Greek and Russian workers who failed to come to work on 6 January, Christmas Day in the calendar of the Orthodox churches. A Ford official stated bluntly: 'if these men are to make their homes in America they should observe American holidays'.[52]

The mass production of a standardized automobile required the orderly attention of a stable, homogenised workforce; no unaccommodating minorities were permitted. To achieve this co-operation among the ethnically diverse Highland Park workers, the Ford company designed a variety of programmes to accelerate Americanisation. One of the chief of these, the Ford English School, coupled instruction in the English language with instruction in the norms of middle-class life in an attempt to produce a model American. Just 'as we adapt the machinery in the shop to turning out the kind of automobile we have in mind', Samuel Marquis of the FSD explained in 1916, 'so we have constructed our educational system with a view to producing the human product in mind'. In addition to the 'melting pot' school, as the Ford English School was also known, the company established the Henry Ford Trade School. Like the language school, this school for underprivileged boys aimed not only to train students in technical skill but also in terms of social mores conducive to industrial capitalism. Students were graded for their 'industry' which the school regarded as 'extremely important ... It includes "attitude" and is defined as "Industry – the effort put forth"; and "attitude – effort and conduct combined".'[53]

The wage and welfare programmes of the 'Five Dollar Day' scheme proved successful in their aim of securing the effort and conduct that the new architecture of production required. In its first two years of operation, the scheme reduced labour turnover by more than 90 per cent. Daily absentee rates fell similarly from 10.5 to 0.4 per cent in the first year. Monitored by the FSD, Ford workers were found to be adopting 'respectable' habits. By January 1915, home ownership had increased 85 per cent; the number of workers with bank accounts had risen 49 per cent and of those with life insurance by 124 per cent. Local judges, police officers and clergymen applauded the declining incidence of drunkenness, gambling and crime among Ford workers. Most important for the company managers was the tractability of the workforce in the plant. 'These pay conditions', Arnold and Faurote reported, 'make the workmen absolutely docile'. Thus, while mass-production methods were adjusted to speed up output, the workers, who, from the standpoint of management, were the weakest link, stayed in place. The company released details of worker-hour output in several departments in the first year of the scheme's operation to substantiate their claim 'that the large increases in production ... while made possible by constant improvement in methods and machinery, were due largely to the increases in wages'.[54]

Numerous articles on the Five Dollar Day appeared in the trade and business press explaining how the wage increase had reduced turnover and absenteeism while boosting morale, loyalty to the company, and deference to management. However, it should be noted that the pay rise's impact was heightened by the more extensive use of unskilled, lower-paid operators at Highland Park and that even here its force was undermined by inflation. In 1916, a skilled auto worker in Flint reportedly averaged up to $14 a day compared to the $2.30 to $3 a day earned by newly hired specialist operators. Such figures put the attractiveness of the Five Dollar Day in perspective. It represented a considerable increase in income for unskilled, inexperienced workers, but so compressed the distribution of wage levels that the gap between the lowest and highest factory wages at Highland

Park was reduced to 25 cents. Moreover, as World War I simultaneously reduced the flow of immigrant labour to the United States and increased US industrial orders, the demand for labour in the Detroit area remained sufficiently high to force auto manufacturers to offer high basic rates of pay. By 1916, the basic pay of $2.50 per nine-hour day which Ford had paid unskilled newcomers in 1914 had been raised to $3.40 for an eight-hour shift. While this attracted fresh labour, it effectively reduced the incentive offered by the Five Dollar Day since compliance with the scheme brought an increase of $1.44 in profit-share compared to the doubling of income in 1914. In 1918, the minimum wage at Ford rose to $4.00 per eight-hour shift, thus reducing the significance of the profit-share to only 20 per cent of the $5 a day. The following year, Ford announced the Six Dollar Day but in the context of wartime inflation, this gave no increase in real wages.[55]

Ford had also lowered the age qualification from 22 to 18 years and eliminated what it termed 'unnecessary' investigations in 1917. Nevertheless, other auto manufacturers took up the cultural offensive with regard to what Boyd Fisher called Ford's 'extension of factory influence into the whole life of the worker'. According to Fisher in 1917, Detroit industrialists recognised that the reduction of labour turnover 'is only the first step in a process of education and of economic pressure to elevate the standards of workmen. They aim not only to keep workmen, but to develop them. And they are prepared to go as far, even, as the workmen's home-life to solve their problem [of inefficient labour].' America's growing involvement in the global conflict provided an additional justification for the close scrutiny of the multi-ethnic industrial workforce and federal legislation in the form of the Espionage Act of 1917 and the Sedition Act of 1918 provided legal mechanisms for the enforcement of '100 per cent Americanism'. An editorial in *Automotive Industries* in 1918 explained the practical advantages of the intensified campaigns for Americanisation, declaring:

> it has been found to be a good, and in many cases a necessary, investment. Workers, to be good workers, to be the kind of workers that make for maximum production, must have the American point of view. They must have American ideals and ambitions. They must first of all speak and read our language. They must like our country well enough to become citizens of it. They must feel that their home is here and that this is the land in which they will experience the realization of their highest hopes.[56]

The identification of Americanism with capitalism evident in the above trade journal's references to 'our language' and 'our country' in contraposition to 'workers' made the IWW and the Socialist Party conspicuous targets for political suppression, especially in the wake of the Bolshevik revolution in Russia. In this climate of hysteria, major war-production centres, like Detroit, became focal points for the activities of vigilante patriotic organisations such as the American Protective League (APL). The surveillance, once confined to the Ford workforce under the Five Dollar Day scheme, became city-wide and less benevolent in intent. APL spies were stationed in every important factory in Detroit to check the loyalty of employees. Aided by the records of the Sociological Department, the APL operated at Highland Park from April 1917 until the Armistice in November 1918, and after a brief lull its operatives found work providing local industrialists with intelligence reports on the growing labour unrest in 1919. The supervision which had once expressed a paternalistic concern for workers' welfare became an overt tool of repression as the authoritarian faction at Ford became the dominant party once more. The war's end had brought a national recession at a time when Henry Ford's purchase of the minority stockholdings in the company had forced him to turn to Eastern financiers for loans. Like other industrialists, Ford began to regard his elaborate welfare programmes as an extravagance and to regain faith in coercion in the wake of the 1919 Red Scare expulsion of labour militants from Detroit.[57]

However, while Ford felt that he had adjusted his workforce to mass production by welfarist policies between 1914 and 1919, other auto makers were only just gearing up for mass production at the latter date and looked to wage and welfare programmes to mould their workers to fit their place on the line. Building on an annual Bonus Plan introduced in 1918 which awarded company stock to able, industrious and loyal employees, General Motors launched its Employees' Savings and Investment Plan in 1919. Having worked for GM for at least three months, workers could open an interest-bearing savings account and GM would match their savings with grants of GM stock which were redeemable according to the worker's length of service with GM. Another major auto-maker, Willys-Overland introduced a profit-sharing scheme in January 1919 which was calibrated to reward continuous service. The Studebaker Corporation also introduced a stock purchase plan in January 1919 and its president, Albert Erskine, emphasised that its aim was a stable workforce:

> Experienced, loyal employees do more and better work and are worth more than the prevailing wage rate which floaters also receive. Lower labor turnover, lower costs, and better products for the corporation and its customers result from the co-operative plans and the management naturally strives continually to minimize the turnover.

After numerous interviews with Detroit auto executives in the late 1920s, William Chalmers concluded that there was a general and deliberate policy of paying high wages to win the acquiescence of workers to the strain of mass production. This strain included that produced by the management's speed-up, as practised at Ford in 1921, and the associated practice of laying off workers when demand slackened. After laying off the entire workforce in January 1921, Ford rehired only 60 per cent of the labour force yet produced twice as many Model T's as in 1920.[58]

By comparison with comparable workers in other industries, auto workers maintained a decent income in the 1920s. In particular, their standard of living commonly exceeded that of Americans engaged in agriculture who flocked to Detroit in the war years and early Twenties to fill the gap left by the interruption of foreign immigration. In 1934, a Buick assembler was asked why he had left Michigan's Upper Peninsula for a job in the auto industry twenty years earlier. He replied that he had been working on a rented farm from which he couldn't scrape a living. It was in the face of these realities that working people chose to become human links in the ever-moving lines of production. The transfer of strength and skill from worker to managerially designed machinery encouraged the hiring of women, especially during the acute labour shortage of the war years. This meant that some families in Flint and Detroit had more than one wage-earner in the auto industry bringing home relatively high wages. Nearly two-fifths of Flint's working women in 1925 were married. These double-income households also tended to have smaller families and so could more easily afford home and car ownership. By 1929, federal investigators reported that Flint had become a city of detached houses and small apartments with four rapidly growing suburban townships. Similarly, the acute housing shortage of 1917 to 1919 in Detroit was relieved by a construction boom in the 1920s. The bulk of resources poured into residential construction was spent on the construction of single-family homes. After 1925 the number of unplatted acres in Detroit was too few to warrant a listing in the city's annual report. The semicircular periphery of the city was filling up and extending outward from Dearborn in the west via Ferndale and Royal Oak to Hazel Park and Grosse Pointe in the east, causing one commentator to remark that Detroiters evidently preferred to commute twenty miles a day to reach their work in the city rather than live within it and drive out on Sunday for relaxation.[59]

Mass production of automobiles, as we have noted elsewhere, allowed workers, who had formerly crowded the streetcars to the discomfort of the middle classes, to take to the streets in their own automobiles by the mid-Twenties. The suburban sprawl and metropolitan traffic jams bore witness to this diffusion of ownership. When the Ford Motor Company had built its factory at Highland Park in 1910, it had taken advantage of the terminus of one of the street railways there. However, when the company built the giant River Rouge complex it allowed space in the design for workers' car-parks. Together with a suburban home and a new variety of consumer goods and entertainments, such car ownership came to epitomise the American standard of living; a standard so much higher than that previously experienced by rural migrants, foreign immigrants, even de-skilled craftsmen, that it compensated for the stresses of a profoundly rationalised and alienating workplace. Thus, there emerged the profound paradox of a culture in which the system of production was deliberately designed to inhibit and direct the movement of individual workers in order to produce automobiles profitably in large numbers for the masses to move flexibly from home to workplace or retail outlet. Applying the principles of mass production, Henry Ford declared, had the net result of reducing 'the necessity for thought on the part of the worker and the reduction of his movements to a minimum'. Similarly, Ford explained the need for docile obedience. 'We expect the men to do what they are told', he explained in his 1922 autobiography, 'The organization is so highly specialized and one part is so dependent upon another that we could not for a moment consider allowing men to have their own way'.[60]

Given this restrictiveness and oppressive subordination at work, it was entirely proportionate that the freedom and independence carefully associated with motoring by auto publicists should become a vital feature of a therapeutic culture of consumption. This is where the insight of Italian communist, Antonio Gramsci, that Ford's high wage was 'the instrument used to select and maintain in stability a skilled labour force suited to the system of production and work' was only partially accurate. The successful development of the new methods of work did require a new type of worker, as Gramsci perceived. However, ultimately the attempt to dictate workers' morality was only partially and temporarily successful in terms of prescribed recreational activities. The connection between industrial rationalisation and Prohibition in America was undoubtedly present, a product of a nativistic impulse to compel a largely alien working class to conform to middle-class morality. However, just as the rigid solemn planning of the Columbian Exposition needed the entertaining safety-valve of the Midway amusements to attract the masses, so the Fordist architecture of mass production needed its antidote in the consumer culture of the 1920s of which the automobile was a key part. In this chapter, we have examined how the drive to change the gears of production in pursuit of more rapid output culminated in a campaign to change men. However, while the successful acceleration of the rate of capital accumulation by the 1920s indicated that a higher gear had been attained, the effort to change men was less successful. Co-operation was conditional, as auto worker Laura Nieminen revealed when he recalled: 'It was pretty hard work in Buick in 1916, 1917, and 1918 already, but we had such a big price'. The hegemony of capitalism rested less on the prescribing of pleasures, as Gramsci implied, than upon their redirection into consumer spending, less upon the inculcation of thrift than the extension of credit, principles more keenly appreciated by Alfred P. Sloan than Henry Ford and more effectively applied in the post-World War II period than before.[61]

Notes

1 H. Katz, *The Decline of Competition*, 1977, table 2-1, p. 41; for Harding, see J. Flink, *Car Culture*, 1975, p. 140; for Ford, see Case of John F. Dodge, Estate of Horace F. Dodge, James Couzens *et al.* vs. Commissioner of Internal Revenue before the US Board of Tax Appeals, Detroit and Washington DC (hereafter, Ford Tax Case), Exhibit 153, National Automotive History Collection; Accession 96, Ford Archives, Dearborn; Automobile Manufacturers Association, *Automobiles of America*, 1970, pp. 72, 78.

2 D. Nye, *Ignorant Idealist*, 1979, pp. 23–6; 'A high-powered car – who shall drive it?', *Civic Searchlight*, IX, December 1922, p. 1.

3 'A high-powered car', loc. cit.; for attitudes to blacks, see F. Henri, *Black Migration*, 1976, chap. 7.

4 Flink, *Car Culture*, p. 80; H. L. Arnold and F. L. Faurote, *Ford Methods*, 1916, pp. 43, 41–2. W. Lewchuk, *American Technology*, 1987, p. 37.

5 Lewchuk, op. cit., table 3.5, p. 46; G. Heliker, 'Detroit labor 1890–1910', Ford Archive, Acc. 958, 25; A. Nevins and F. Hill, *Ford: the Times*, 1954, p. 526.

6 US Bureau of the Census, *Census of Manufactures: 1905*, Bulletin 66, 'Automobiles and bicycles and tricycles', 1907; 'Reminiscences of Fred Seaman', Ford Oral History Collection (hereafter OHC); C. Kettering and A. Orth, *The New Necessity*, 1932, p. 39.

7 Seaman, loc. cit.; Lewchuk, *American Technology*, tables 3.1, 3.2, pp. 41–2; W. Greenleaf, *Monopoly on Wheels*, 1961, p. 101; K. Sward, *The Legend of Henry Ford*, 1948, pp. 21–2; Nevins and Hill, *Ford; the Times*, pp. 247, 278.

8 Nevins and Hill, ibid., p. 276; C. Sorensen, *My Forty Years*, 1956, pp. 46, 84, 92–116; 'Reminiscences of Max Wollering', Ford OHC.

9 Wollering, op. cit.; Lewchuk, *American Technology*, table 3.3, p. 44; D. Montgomery, *Workers' Control in America*, 1979, pp. 48–90; J. Russell, 'The coming of the line: the Ford Highland Park Plant, 1910–1914', *Radical America*, pp. 30–1.

10 Russell, loc. cit.; Nevins and Hill, *Ford: the Times*, pp. 513–17, D. Gartman, *Auto Slavery*, 1986, pp. 138–9.

11 Sorensen, *Forty Years*, p. 46; 'Reminiscences of Charles Sorensen', Ford OHC; Wollering, op. cit.; Walter E. Flanders, 'Large capital now needed to embark in automobile business', *Detroit Saturday Night*, 22 January 1910.

12 C. Sorensen, *Forty Years*, pp. 117–18, and 'Reminiscences of Frank Bennett, of Albert Smith, and of William Klann', Ford OHC. For Flanders, see Sorensen, op. cit., pp. 93, 96. For work standards, see Klann, loc. cit.

13 Acc. 166, Ford Archives; Lewchuk, *American Technology*, table 2.5, p. 46.

14 Haynes, Ford Tax Case, *Transcript*, II, p. 961; Chapin, Acc. 96, Box 3, Ford Archives.

15 Ford to the Editor, *Automobile*, XIV, 11 January 1906, pp. 107, 109; for Model T's debut, see testimony of N. Hawkins, Ford Tax Case, *Transcript*, IV, p. 1563.

16 D. Hounshell, *From the American System to Mass Production*, 1984, *passim*; D. Gartman, *Auto Slavery*, pp. 68–70.

17 Gartman, op. cit., pp. 76–8.

18 'Assembling: its relations to success and to failure', *Motor Age*, XVII, 24 October 1907, pp. 185–7.

19 'Assembling', loc. cit.; Sward, *Legend*, p. 32; 'Reminiscences of James O'Connor', Ford OHC; 'Reminiscences of Max Wollering and of Fred Seaman', op. cit.

20 I use the term 'architecture of production' to convey the enveloping character of the managerial design and to parallel this system of control to other Progressive schemes such as city plans which in their enthusiasm for expertise and efficiency sought to impose middle-class standards of behaviour on lower-class Americans to ensure a more stable social order. For Highland Park, see Nevins and Hill, *Ford*, p. 452; Faurote, Ford Tax Case, *Transcript*, III, pp. 1109–10; Martin, ibid., II, p. 853.

21 Nevins and Hill, op. cit., pp. 523, 380; US Bureau of the Census, *Thirteenth Census 1910*, vol. 4, 'Population, occupational statistics', 1911, pp. 336–9; Meyer, *The Five Dollar Day*, 1981, pp. 47–8; H. Ford, *Moving Forward*, 1931, p. 133.

22 S. Haber, *Efficiency and Uplift*, 1964, *passim*; H. Ford, *My Life and Work*, 1922, p. 43; Russell, 'Coming of the line', op. cit., pp. 39–40; Gartman, *Auto Slavery*, p. 184.

23 S. Slichter, *Turnover of Factory Labor*, 1919, p. 281; Gartman, op. cit., p. 185.

24 Martin, Ford Tax Case, *Transcript*, II, p. 885; Gray, ibid., III, pp. 1240–3; F. Colvin, 'Building an automobile every forty seconds', *American Machinist*, XXXVIII, 8 May 1913, pp. 761–2.

25 Lewchuk, *American Technology*, p. 53; Colvin, op. cit., p. 761; Nye, *Ignorant Idealist*, pp. 82, 61, 67.

26 Ford, *My Life and Work*, p. 78; Flink, *Car Culture*, p. 80; Sorensen, 'Reminiscences', loc. cit.

27 'Reminiscences of A. M. Wibel', Ford OHC; Arnold and Faurote, *Ford Methods*, pp. 97–101.

28 Interview with Oscar Bornholdt, factory manager, Wills-St. Claire Inc., Marysville, Mich., 26 July 1926, by Franklin Jones, Acc. 96, Box 2, Ford Archives; John R. Lee, 'The so-called profit-sharing system in the Ford plant', *Annals of the American Academy of Political and Social Science*, LXV, May 1916, p. 298; Lewchuk, *American Technology*, table 3.5, p. 46; Colvin, 'Building An Automobile', loc. cit.

29 'Assembling', *Motor Age*, loc. cit.; O.J. Abell, 'Making the Ford motor car', *Iron Age*, LXXXIX, 6 June 1912, pp. 1383–90; Martin, Ford Tax Case, *Transcript*, II, 359–60; Colvin, 'Machining the Ford cylinders – I', *American Machinist*, XXXVIII, 28 May 1913, pp. 841–6; Colvin, 'Special machines for making pistons', ibid., XXXIX, 28 August 1913, pp. 349–53; Arnold and Faurote, *Ford Methods*, pp. 208–9.

30 Nye, *Ignorant Idealist*, pp. 85–6; Flink, *Car Culture*, pp. 82–3; S. Patten, *The New Basis of Civilization*, 1907; Wibel, 'Reminiscences', loc. cit.

31 Gartman, *Auto Slavery*, pp. 143–4; Lewchuk, *American Technology*, table 3.4, p. 45; Mortimer L. LaFever, 'Workers, machinery, and production in the automobile industry', *Monthly Labour Review*, XIX, October 1924, pp. 3–5; Chalmers, cited Gartman, op. cit., p. 146.

32 Abell, 'Making the Ford', op. cit., pp. 1388–9; Klann, 'Reminiscences', loc. cit.; American Society of Mechanical Engineers [ASME], 'Developments in machine shop practice in the last decade', *Transactions, ASME*, XXXIV, 1912, pp. 847–65; Colvin, 'Building an automobile', pp. 759, 761–2; interview with Bornholdt, loc. cit.; O.J. Abell, 'Labor classified on a skill-wages basis', *Iron Age*, XCIII, 1 January 1914, p. 48.

33 Meyer, *Five Dollar Day*, pp. 62–4; Colvin, 'Continuous pouring in the Ford foundry', *American Machinist*, XXXIX, 27 November 1913, pp. 910–12.

34 Arnold and Faurote, *Ford Methods*, pp. 112–15.

35 Nevins and Hill, *Ford*, p. 648; Klann, 'Reminiscences', loc. cit.; S.S. Marquis, *Henry Ford: an Interpretation*, 1923, p. 141. Marquis was a key member of the welfarist faction who obviously reported the authoritarian approach in a hostile way.

36 S.M. Levin, 'Ford profit sharing, 1914–1920: I. The growth of the plan', *Personnel Journal*, VI, August 1927, pp. 75–6; B. Emmett, 'Profit sharing in the United States', *US Bureau of Labor Statistics Bulletin no. 208*, 1917, p. 115; Meyer, *Five Dollar Day*, pp. 83–4; J.R. Lee, 'Profit-sharing system', op. cit., p. 308; M. Alexander, 'Waste in hiring and discharging men', *Iron Age*, XCIV, 29 October 1914, pp. 1032–3.

37 Arnold and Faurote, *Ford Methods*, p. 42.

38 Commons, quoted by Lewchuk, *American Technology*, p. 59; Nevins and Hill, *Ford*, p. 520; Ford, *Moving Forward*, p. 39; *idem.*, *My Life and Work*, p. 103; O'Connor, 'Reminiscences', loc. cit.

39 J. Leonard, *The Tragedy of Henry Ford*, 1932, p. 25; Sward, *Legend*, p. 48; Lee, 'Memorandum on labor dissatisfaction', Acc. 940, Box 17, Ford Archives.

40 Gartman, *Auto Slavery*, p. 190; Arnold and Faurote, *Ford Methods*, pp. 43–58; Lee, 'Profit sharing system', pp. 300–1; Abell, 'Labor classified', op. cit., pp. 48–51; G. Bundy, 'Work of the Employment Department of the Ford Motor Company', *US Bureau of Labor Statistics Bulletin*, CXCVI, 1914, pp. 63–71.

41 Lee, 'Labor dissatisfaction', loc. cit.; Bundy, op. cit.

42 Gartman, *Auto Slavery*, p. 191; B. Fisher, 'How to reduce labor turnover', *Bulletin of the Bureau of Labor Statistics*, CCXXVII, 1917, pp. 29–31.

43 Meyer, *Five Dollar Day*, p. 77; R. W. Edsforth, 'A second industrial revolution: the transformation of class, culture and society in twentieth century Flint', unpublished PhD, Michigan State University, 1982, pp. 77, 114, 120, 80–100.

44 Gartman, *Auto Slavery*, p. 162; Heliker, 'Detroit labor 1900–1916', p. 18, quoted by Gartman, loc. cit.; Lewchuk, *American Technology*, p. 38; Roberts, quoted by Meyer, *Five Dollar Day*, p. 79.

45 Lee, 'Labor dissatisfaction', loc. cit.; Arnold and Faurote, *Ford Methods*, p. 44; Abell, 'Labor classified', op. cit., p. 51.

46 Nevins and Hill, *Ford*, pp. 532–4; Meyer, op. cit., pp. 109–21; Henry Ford's testimony, US Congress, Commission on Industrial Relations, *Final Report and Testimony*, 64th Congress, 1st session, Senate Doc. no. 415, vol. 7, 1916, p. 7629; *New York Times*, 9 January 1914, quoted by Meyer, op. cit., p. 118.

47 Marquis, *Ford*, pp. 149–51; Lewchuk, *American Technology*, pp. 17–21.

48 John A. Fitch, 'Making the job worthwhile', *Survey*, XL, 27 April 1914, p. 88; O. J. Abell, 'The Ford plan for employees' betterment', *Iron Age*, XCIII, 29 January 1914, p. 306; M. May, 'The historical problem of the family wage: the Ford Motor Company and the Five Dollar Day', *Feminist Studies*, VIII, Summer 1982, pp. 401–19; Gartman, *Auto Slavery*, p. 206.

49 'Mr Lee's talk to second group of investigators, April 16, 1914', Acc. 940, Box 17, Ford Archives; S. S. Marquis, 'Ford profit sharing', Acc. 293, Box 1, ibid.; 'Practical welfare in motor factories', *The Automobile*, XXX, May 1914, p. 959.

50 Ford testimony before Commission on Industrial Relations, op. cit., p. 7628.

51 Abell, 'The Ford plan', op. cit., p. 307; Gartman, *Auto Slavery*, p. 207; Emmett, 'Profit sharing', op. cit., p. 99; 'Human interest story, number 38', Acc. 940, Box 17, Ford Archives. Armenians seem to have been particularly responsive to the Five Dollar Day: cf. H. F. Porter, 'Giving the men a share', *System*, XXXI, March 1917, p. 267.

52 'Human interest story', loc. cit.; *New York Times*, 10 January 1914, section 4, p. 6.

53 'Preliminary Report of Work Done Teaching the English Language to Employees of the Ford Motor Company at Stevens School, Highland Park, Mich., June 12, 1914', Acc. 940, Box 17, Ford Archives; Meyer, *Five Dollar Day*, pp. 157–8; Marquis, 'The Ford idea in education', *Addresses and Proceedings of National Education Association*, LXIV, 1916, pp. 910–17; Edwin P. Norwood, *Ford Men and Methods*, 1931, p. 185.

54 Emmett, 'Profit sharing', pp. 116–19; A. Nevins and F. Hill, *Ford: Expansion and Challenge*, 1957, p. 339; Arnold and Faurote, *Ford Methods*, p. 328.

55 For Flint pay, see John Gilder, 'Flint: when men build automobiles who builds their city?', *Survey*, 2 September 1916, p. 556; Meyer, *Five Dollar Day*, pp. 167–8.

56 Fisher, 'How to reduce labor turnover', ibid., p. 15; Meyer, op. cit., p. 170; 'Americanization from the practical point of view', *Automotive Industries*, XXXIX, September 1918, p. 469.

57 R. Murray, *Red Scare*, 1955, pp. 215–16; Nevins and Hill, *Ford: Expansion*, pp. 324–54; H. Tipper, 'Fundamentals of labor question ignored', *Automotive Industries*, XLVI, April 1922, p. 878.

58 A. Pound, *The Turning Wheel*, 1934, pp. 395–404; J. E. Schipper, 'Willys profit-sharing plan on 50-50 basis', *Automotive Industries*, XL, May 1919, p. 944; A. R. Erskine, *History of the Studebaker Corporation*, 1924, pp. 119–21; Gartman, *Auto Slavery*, pp. 213–14; Meyer, *Five Dollar Day*, p. 197; Ford Tax Case, Exhibit 79, loc. cit.

59 Edsforth, 'A second industrial revolution', pp. 128–9, 133–5; D. A. Levine, *Internal Combustion: The Races in Detroit*, 1976, pp. 38–9; A. Player, 'Detroit: essence of America', *New Republic*, LI, 3 Aug 1927, p. 274, cited ibid., p. 42.

60 Edsforth, 'A second industrial revolution', *passim*; Ford, *My Life*, pp. 80, 111.

61 A. Gramsci, *Selections from the Prison Notebooks*, 1971, p. 303, quoted by Gartman, *Auto Slavery*, p. 207; Edsforth, 'A second industrial revolution', pp. 128–9; *passim*.

Chapter 7

Conclusion

In a recent review article, two leading practitioners of the history of technology complained of the neglect of science and technology evident in contemporary American history textbooks. By looking at the context in which the automobile was developed and adopted in the United States, this study has endeavoured to show how technological innovations may be related to the more familiar social and political trends of the Progressive Era. Both the production and the consumption of passenger cars, we have argued, may be best understood in terms of a specific historical context in which a Progressive bloc, middle-class in character and aspiration, sought to readjust social relations in a manner that ensured greater social stability. We have advanced the view that the automobile was embraced by Progressive Americans as a facilitator of many of their social objectives: ending rural isolation, establishing experts in local and national government, reducing urban congestion, avoiding potentially explosive or at least unpleasant social encounters, and controlling the workforce in the interests of efficiency in a way that legitimised that subordination.[1]

In his pioneering study of the automobile industry, Ralph C. Epstein provided lists of the first twenty buyers of Steam mobiles sold by William E. Metzger in Detroit in 1898–99, of Winton gasoline-powered automobiles produced in Cleveland in 1898, and of the first twenty Waverley Electrics sold in Detroit in that year. The purchasers' occupations confirm that at this stage, automobile ownership was a privilege of the business class: a majority of the vehicles was sold in each case to capitalists, manufacturers, merchants and physicians. A similar list for the 1903 curved-dashed Oldsmobile, a less expensive gasoline-powered automobile, recorded the popularity of the new vehicle with merchants and physicians, both social figures eager to expand the market and maintain social well-being. Epstein also notes, on the basis of admittedly incomplete data, that the purchasers of

Cadillacs in 1903 were of a similar social background, as were the first purchasers of Walter Flanders's new vehicle in 1907, the EMF. These members of the professional – managerial stratum were quick to purchase the automobile while it was still new and expensive, and found it compatible with their specific vision of social relations.[2]

The next phase in the diffusion of auto ownership was its adoption by the credit-worthy farmer and the man on a middle income. Thomas B. Jeffrey, Wisconsin manufacturer of the Rambler motor car which supplied this class of buyers, observed in 1909 that the 'mortgage has gone from the Middle Western farm, and to take its place there is the telephone, the heating system, the water supply, improved farm machinery, and the automobile'. Paul Barrett provides a portrait of early Chicago motorists as largely professionals, businessmen, and managers but with a significant scattering of skilled workers in this post-1907 period, residing largely in substantial neighbourhoods. Certainly, Chicago's Commercial Club regarded 'auto-owners' as 'people of means' whose 'hearts return to the country as eagerly as the pigeon seeks its loft, and they bring their pocketbooks with them'. The agri-businessman or at least the market-conscious farmer and his urban allies in the professional – managerial stratum thus bought automobiles early, and then on the basis of the mobility they enjoyed renewed their calls for the consolidation of rural social institutions, for more parking space downtown, and for better roads built by scientific road-builders.[3]

As late as 1924, the automobile industry continued to view families with annual incomes below $1500 as unlikely auto owners. One 1922 study reported that the average motorist held a $5000 equity in real estate, had personal property equal to $2000, a bank account and life insurance; and the following year the National Automobile Chamber of Commerce (NACC) discovered that the average car owner lived not in a city but in a substantial town, the 'half-way house' between open country and metropolis to which rural physician and suburbanite manager had gravitated in their pursuit of the stable yet 'progressive' community. The NACC had also conducted a survey of randomly selected motorists in 'ten widely selected states' in 1920 to ascertain how auto ownership was affecting their lives. Ninety per cent of respondents reported that 60 per cent of their mileage and the bulk of their motoring time were 'for business purposes'. Thus, the recreational or therapeutic use of the motor car, which received increasing emphasis in auto advertising, was a secondary function of the automobile in practice. Historians who stress the psychological appeal of the automobile as an instrument of autarky providing freedom, independence, and an exhilarating sense of personal power are failing to give due weight to the less romantic, practical functions to which the private motor car was put on a regular daily basis. In terms of practical utility, the NACC estimated the rank order of percentage gains in efficiency for different occupations as shown in Table 1.

TABLE 1. Percentage gains in efficiency for occupations

Occupation	*% gain in efficiency*
Real estate and insurance agents	113
Medical doctors	104
Salesmen	103
Clergymen	98
School supervisors	72
Farmers	68
Contractors	51
Manufacturers and bankers	33

Thus, the professional–managerial stratum whose role we have stressed in both the Progressive movement and in the development of a car culture in the United States was also the level of society whose members were most convinced of the car's advantages to their work. We have already discussed the nature of these advantages for doctors, farmers, clergymen and school supervisors in our consideration of the automobile's introduction to the rural areas. The benefits perceived by real-estate and insurance agents, salesmen, contractors, manufacturers and bankers are also consistent with our emphasis that the improvement of transport technology should be linked to the dual imperative to expand the market while simultaneously accelerating the circulation and accumulation of capital.[4]

In our discussion of the introduction of the automobile into urban America, we pointed particularly to the role of transport in the social production of a built environment in which land became real estate, a commodity for exchange in the market. Bankers, contractors, and real-estate agents were the logical beneficiaries of the automobile's expansion of the supply of real estate. As an expensive single purchase, increasingly bought on credit, and one which manifestly involved some risk in its use, the automobile was a great stimulus to the insurance industry not simply in terms of insuring the vehicle and its occupants against the dangers of collisions but also in terms of home insurance. The gasoline-powered automobile not only facilitated the residential redistribution of urban families into single-family owner-occupied homes – a Progressive goal with widely acknowledged benefits in terms of social stability – it also constituted a fire hazard whose close proximity to the home prompted a revision of actuarial calculations. However, in our view, the increased business of the insurance agent as a result of the demands of large-scale motoring was in part a reflection of the more generally accelerated circulation of capital produced by improved road transport. For the manufacturer, the production of the automobile was itself a major source of profit. By the mid-1920s automobile manufacturing was the premier US industry in terms of value of product. Other major industries such as steel and petroleum were dependent upon the auto industry and motoring as a major market for their product. As the second largest item of governmental expenditure during the 1920s, the construction of streets and highways was a major area of economic activity, and alongside the new auto highways countless new retail and service businesses were established. As the trade journal *Motor* concluded in 1923, 'certainly the automobile touched either a soul or some controlling springs and gears in our national life'.[5]

It is our contention that the automobile was itself a spring or gear in Progressive America transmitting a heightened pace in order to speed up the expropriation of surplus value, or what is more sympathetically termed 'the return on investment'. Robert Wiebe was one of the first post-war historians to reveal the significant role played by business groups in reform campaigns during the Progressive Era. In his seminal study of turn-of-the-century America, *The Search for Order* (1967), Wiebe saw three collective predispositions – the utopian, the idealist, and the bureaucratic – at work within Progressive thought. By 1900, the utopian strand, which, like Richard Hofstadter, Wiebe associated with the apocalyptic imagery of the Populist 1880s and 1890s, was being superseded by the confidence of Progressive intellectuals in a pre-ordained progress and in their own ability to create rational systems: that is, by the idealist and bureaucratic predispositions, respectively. The automobile's role in American society reflected these predispositions. As a symbol of progress and of new possibilities, it was welcomed by the idealists as a tool which would assist in the inevitable creation of an improved order: a less isolated rural community and a less congested urban and industrial metropolis. A reading of Progessive magazines such as *Munsey's* and *The Independent* confirms this welcome for the motor car among Progressive intellectuals. The bureaucratic mentality equally found expression in the car culture. First and foremost, it was the mood behind the managerial initiatives that culminated in the moving assembly-line and the Five Dollar Day but it also animated the Good Roads movement with its faith in expert administration. The welcome given to the innovations at Ford in 1914 by journals such as *Survey* and *World's Work* confirms their sympathy for a rationalised system of production coupled to a welfare programme for labour as the basis for a stable, well-administered society.[6]

Implicit within Wiebe's analysis of Progressive thought is the same emphasis upon industrialisation as a factor in social change that Samuel P. Hays made explicitly in his *Response to Industrialism* (1959). Progressive Americans are portrayed by Wiebe ultimately not so much as seekers after an ideal order, either nostalgic or futuristic, but as searchers for a coherent place within a new order which is already being shaped about them. The search becomes, in Jackson Lears's use of the term, a negotiation, a coming to terms with modern realities, and consequently, a movement predisposed to settle rather than eternally to struggle. Despite the importance of industrial development to Wiebe's analysis of the transition from an America of 'island communities' to a land incorporated by bureaucratic structures, *The Search for Order* does not investigate the technological changes which were a key part of that reformation. As an established focus for political and economic debate, the railroads attract Wiebe's attention but the automobile escapes it. Wiebe recognises that by the close of the nineteenth century the power-lines of a corporate economy criss-cross the nation's cities and penetrate the vast hinterland, yet he does not perceive how the incomplete nature of that network and the distended state of rural America might engender material innovations not as products of an immanent logic of technological development but as the outcome of social demand. In this study, we have tried to suggest how the isolation of rural America and the perceived pathology of America's overcrowded, industrial centres provided the sources of demand for technological innovation in the field of road transport. The imperatives of capitalism in terms of the functional specialisation of space had produced a genuine need for transport. However, the adoption of the automobile *per se*, even in the United States where mass car ownership came more rapidly than in other nations, was, we have argued, shaped by middle-class preferences.[7]

The metropolitan spatial pattern which evolved on the assumption of universal car ownership gave a better way of life according to one's economic station. The wealthy agri-businessman could afford not only an automobile but automotive agricultural machinery. He was the survivor of a process of farm consolidation and crop specialisation in the decade after 1914 that reduced the number of farms smaller than 100 acres and increased the number of farms of 500 acres or more. Yet in the agricultural depression of the 1920s his survival was precarious, and made more so by the capital costs of automotive technology. Between 1925 and 1930 farm tenancy, which had stabilised at about 38 per cent between 1910 and 1925, rose dramatically to 42.4 per cent of all farms, and the proportion of these tenants who were share-croppers also rose from 23 to 29 per cent. Whereas the successful agri-businessman – the 'Progressive' element in rural society – had the money with which to take advantage of the improved services which automobility had brought within his reach, the tenant farmer and agricultural labourer had to struggle to bear the burden of car ownership in order to gain access to relocated social institutions. Similarly, the urban manager or professional man could enjoy the complementary benefits of suburban respectability and industrial productivity and use his automobile as a safe, convenient, private link between the two. As we have seen, the Progressives encouraged lower-class Americans to adopt this life-style by buying single-family dwellings well away from the crowded tenements of the central city and adjoining industrial districts. The automobile was seen as assisting this process. The growth in car registrations, in the second-hand car market, in credit sales and in traffic volume all suggest that worker as well as manager had adopted the automobile in large numbers by the end of the Twenties. However, as in the countryside, ownership did not signify a uniform pattern of use. As industry relocated, some workers chose to drive to work as the Ford Motor Company indicated to the Detroit Rapid Transit Commission in 1924. Other car-owning workers preferred instead to continue the working-class pattern of residing close to the industrial districts and used their automobiles for recreational purposes and for shopping at relocated retail outlets which had moved initially in pursuit of the affluent customer who could no longer park conveniently in the congested downtown area. Thus, in Allegheny County around Pittsburgh, in the three heavy industrial steel-mill towns of McKeesport, Clairton and Duquesne, 38 per cent of chief wage-earners owned automobiles in 1934 but only 12.4 per cent used their automobiles to get to work. The need for an automobile for shopping was revealed by case studies of Baltimore and Detroit, and more recently of Atlanta, which showed how businesses reliant upon frequent patronage relocated to suburban locations to secure uncongested access and parking for their clientele prior to 1930. Thus, for the less affluent, the assumption that motoring was the universal practice made car ownership a costly necessity for which its subjective psychological delights were, arguably, slight compensation.[8]

The automobile's significance for Progressive Americans stemmed from its congruence with the particular interests of this influential social bloc. It promised to overcome the obstacles to modernisation in the countryside and it embodied the transport preferences of middle-class Americans more adequately than did public transit. Moreover, its association with other aspects of this middle-to-upper-class life-style, especially in terms of its public image, enabled automobile manufacturers to profit from the progressive hope that a new environment would produce a new man. The rebalanced social relations perceived in suburban living and a less isolated rural life established the idea that the automobile would be an instrument for the assimilation of the alien, disquietening working classes. Thus, it could act as a stabilising influence at the same time as it increased the efficiency of the economy by speeding up the transactions in the cycle of production. Thus, all Americans would come to resemble the Progressives themselves even though the rationalised, degraded work available to working-class Americans would require none of the ratiocination or individuality that the Progressive prized.

By 1923, automobile ownership had become sufficiently widespread to make large-scale motoring evident in American towns and cities. However, it was equally apparent that the hopes of Progressives regarding the reformation of the character of the impoverished country-dwellers or of the polyglot immigrant urban masses were substantially unrealised. The prospect of maintaining an agrarian nation continued to fade. The census of 1920 recorded for the first time that a majority of Americans (53 per cent) lived in urban areas. Moreover, the US Department of Agriculture was increasingly convinced that profitable agriculture required bigger farms. A study of farms in southern

Georgia in 1914, for example, concluded that 'food supplied by the larger farms furnishes a more varied and better quality of diet than smaller ones. In other words, the larger farms support a much higher standard of living as well as furnish larger net returns in other forms.' Larger farms in this case were over 250 acres, but the average white farm had 166 acres while the average black farm had only 54 acres. The resulting low incomes meant that, despite a widely publicised rush to buy automobiles among Southern farmers during the war, only 12 per cent of farmers in the eleven states from Virginia to Texas had acquired a car by 1920 compared to more than 57 per cent in the farm belts of the North Central states. Even by 1930, the more than a quarter of Southern farmers who owned cars indicated that the adoption of the automobile was still not on the same scale as in other sections of the nation. Even the farm owners and better-off tenants who were most likely to acquire an automobile remained less affluent, less informed of recent innovations, and more vulnerable to market swings than their national counterparts. Instead of producing a nation of 'Progressive Farmers', the diffusion of car ownership paved the way for the Depression landscape of the Joads in Steinbeck's *The Grapes of Wrath*, whose land is taken by the impersonal combine, whose shack is bulldozed by the machine man, and whose life continues on the road, feeding the car before they feed themselves because it represents the lifeline carrying them west to the agri-business state of California.[9]

In the cities, too, the acquisition of automobiles, while it encouraged suburban residential development did not produce the human metamorphosis desired by Progessive Americans. The competing influences of allegedly alien cultural traditions were seemingly spread more quickly by speeding cars. The gangsters of the Prohibition Era were readier to spend money on fast motor cars than were the police authorities charged with apprehending these racketeers. Auto theft became a major type of crime, while older offences, such as prostitution, which had faced tighter controls in the First World War period, took to the streets. As one *Middletown* judge explained: 'the automobile has become a house of prostitution on wheels'. However, once again, there is a danger of generalising on slight evidence, and of endowing technology with a deterministic role. The moralistic perspective evident in Progressive social-control efforts tended to confound all forms of extramarital activity into the single category of harlotry, and so any location where such activity occurred was a house of prostitution.

The Kinsey report indicates that of women born between 1900 and 1910 who reported having sex prior to marriage, 48 per cent had coitus with a fiancé only. As this was especially true of those who married young, the sexual activity on this evidence was a preliminary to matrimony. If the automobile did serve as accommodation for pre-marital sex – thanks to such necessary refinements as the closed car and interior heating – its eventual outcome – marriage – hardly justifies vilifying the car as an agent destructive to the home and family life. Moreover, in the case of prostitution, the automobile's use may be seen as a product of the Progressives' attempts to suppress brothels. Studies of prostitution reported that it was often a secondary source of income for women whose publicly declared primary occupation was poorly paid. Such part-timers were unlikely to be able to provide suitable accommodation of their own and so, with the suppression of the red-light district, a client's car became an economical substitute.[10]

Despite these notorious aspects of automobile use in the United States in the early 1920s, a more immediate and profound consequence of more widespread car ownership was traffic congestion. However much Progressive Americans may have cherished the hope that auto ownership would promote the *embourgeoisement* and assimilation of the immigrant proletariat, the consequences of many motorists attempting to use the same streets to reach similar destinations were daunting, indeed. By the end of 1916, the magazine *Automobile* fretted that 'everyday in big cities the parking problem grows more acute. If it is bad today … what will be the situation in 3 years?' The president of Atlanta's street railway company pleaded with the members of that city's automobile club in 1925. 'You don't appreciate the problem the automobile has brought to the City', he declared. 'Think of the 50,000 vehicles moving through Atlanta's streets! On this village plan. The builders of the town never dreamed of such a thing! And every year it grows worse'.[11]

Traffic regulation was gradually acknowledged to be a necessity as the practice of motoring spread from the respectable few to a more socially diverse range of motorists. Parking bans and speeding regulations which excited protests in Los Angeles, Chicago, and other cities in the early 1920s became an accepted part of urban life by the end of the decade. Foreign-born teamsters and other commercial drivers were blamed for many traffic problems, and were therefore subject to special scrutiny. In Detroit, the police compelled truck drivers to take a special driving test from 1921 onwards. Further study of the development of traffic regulation is needed, but it would appear that the weight of numbers which made traffic policing imperative also ensured that the experience of motoring for the less affluent was from its inception more subject to control than had been the earlier motoring practice of the well-to-do. Moreover, the relocation of both industry and retail establishments was encouraged by the advent of practical, economical motor-trucks and this relocation also altered the nature of the choice made when buying an automobile. The redistribution of employment, shopping and recreational facilities made the automobile less and less of a discretionary purchase and more of a necessity by the late 1920s.[12]

Further study is needed of this process of relocation, as are case studies of cities and of regions to establish the historical character of the change that took place. As the Lynds realised in their classic study of Muncie, Indiana, the way of life of average Americans in the mid-1920s was significantly different from that of the previous generation in the mid-1890s. As a conspicuous symbol of modernity, the automobile was easily associated with this transformation by laymen and social scientists alike. This study has attempted to switch attention away from the motor vehicle to its sponsors, away from mobility as an absolute facet of life and towards a consideration of its economic function in a given pattern of social relations. Many may deny the connections I seek to draw between the advent of the automobile and the emergence of corporate capitalism, but none I trust will hereafter neglect them. At a time when a new array of technological innovation has begun to change the gears once more so that the cycle of accumulation can take place at electronic speed, our attention should be carefully fixed on how the new information technology may be used to advance the interests of the powerful, for surely there will be people in the early twenty-first century willing to assert that what has changed society in the previous thirty years can be summed up in just two letters: 'I-T'. But neither 'A-U-T-O' nor 'I-T' is a sufficient explanation. Mankind makes its own history, though not always as it wishes.[13]

Notes

1 J.L. Heilbron and D.J. Kevles, 'Science and technology in US history textbooks: what's there – and what ought to be there', *Reviews in American History*, XVI; June 1988, pp. 173–85.

2 R.C. Epstein, *The Automobile Industry*, 1928, p. 95.

3 J. Flink, *America Adopts the Automobile*, 1970, p. 82; P. Barrett, *The Automobile and Urban Transit*, 1983, pp. 58–9, 62.

4 Barrett, op. cit., p. 140; J. Flink, *The Car Culture*, 1975, p. 160.

5 Flink, *Car Culture*, pp. 140, 141, 161.

6 Cf. S.P. Hays, *The Response to Industrialism*, 1959, and J. Weinstein, *The Corporate Ideal in the Liberal State*, 1968; R. Wiebe, *The Search for Order*, 1967, p. 144. For welcome of Fordism, see J.R. Commons *et al.*, 'Henry Ford, miracle maker', *Independent*, CII, 1 May 1920, pp. 160–1, 189–91; J. Fitch, 'Ford of Detroit: and his ten million profit sharing plan', *Survey*, XXXI, 7 February 1914, pp. 545–50; E.A. Rumley, 'The manufacturer of tomorrow', *World's Work*, XXVIII, May 1914, pp. 106–12.

7 Wiebe, op. cit., p. 295.

8 J. Interrante, 'You can't go to town in a bath-tub: automobile movement and the re-organization of rural American space, 1900–1930', *Radical History Review*, XXI, Fall 1979, pp. 156–7; Joel Tarr, 'Transportation innovation and changing spatial patterns in Pittsburgh, 1850–1934', *Essays in Public Works History*, VI, 1978, p. 36; H.L. Preston, *Automobile Age Atlanta*, 1979, p. 131.

9 G. Fite, *Cotton Fields No More*, 1984, pp. 99–100, 102; John Steinbeck, *The Grapes of Wrath*, 1939, cf. Steinbeck's comment that 'the highway became their home and movement their form of expression', p. 173.

10 Flink, *Car Culture*, p. 158; P.S. Fass, *The Damned and the Beautiful*, 1977, pp. 38–41.

11 'The parking problem', *Automobile*, XXXV, 21 December 1916, p. 1044; for Atlanta see Preston, op. cit., pp. 54–5.

12 'Safety council starts drivers' school', *The Detroiter*, XII, September 1921; 'Drivers' course proves popular', *The Detroiter*, XIII, November 1921; L. Moses and H.F. Williamson, 'The location of economic activity in cities', *American Economic Review*, LVII, May 1967, pp. 211–22; J.C. Nichols, 'The planning and control of outlying shopping centers', *Journal of Land and Public Utility Economics*, II, January 1926, pp. 17–22; Preston, *Atlanta*, pp. 131–6.

13 R.S. Lynd and H.M. Lynd, *Middletown*, 1929, p. 251; B. Brownell, 'A symbol of modernity: attitudes towards the automobile in Southern cities in the 1920s', *American Quarterly*, XXIV, March 1972, pp. 20–44; L. Winner, *Autonomous Technology*, 1977, *passim*.

Bibliography

Manuscript collections

Archives of Labor History and Urban Affairs, Walter P. Reuther Library, Wayne State University, Detroit. Edward Levinson Papers and others relating to Five Dollar Day.

Board of Wayne Country Road Commissioners, Central Records File, Wayne County Road Commission, Detroit. Annual reports and minute-books and pay ledgers.

Burton Historical Collection, Detroit Public Library. Papers used in collection:
Detroit Archives – various municipal papers, including Mayors'.
William S. Gilbraith Papers.
Henry B. Joy Papers.
William R. Stocking Papers.
Sidney D. Waldon Papers.

Flint Automotive History Collection, Flint Public Library, Flint.

The Ford Archives, Edison Institute, Dearborn.
Oral History Section and Accessions 63, 293 and 683 on Five Dollar Day.

Michigan Historical Collection, The Bentley Library, Ann Arbor. Roy D. Chapin Papers, Horatio S. Earle Diaries, Henry B. Joy Papers, UAW Oral History Project, Arthur Tuttle Papers.

The Transportation Library, University of Michigan, Ann Arbor. Thomas H. MacDonald Papers, Frank F. Rogers Papers.

National Automotive History Collection, Detroit Public Library. David Beecroft Papers, Charles B. King Papers, Ford Tax Case Papers, trade journal collection.

Periodicals consulted

American City, American Machinist, Automobile, Automotive Industries, Detroit Free Press, Detroit News, Saturday Night, Detroiter, Engineering, Engineering News-Record, Ford Times, Horseless Age, Iron Age, Machinery, Motor, Motor Age, Motor World, Popular Science, Scientific American, Survey, World's Work.

Official publications

Michigan State Highway Department, *Biennial Report of the State Highway Commissioner, 1905–6 to 1917–18* (1–7th Biennial Reports), Michigan State Printer, Lansing, 1906–1918.

US Bureau of the Census, *Census of Manufactures 1905*, Bulletin 66, Automobiles and Bicycles and Tricycles, Government Printing Office (GPO), Washington, DC, 1907.

US Bureau of the Census, *Historical Statistics of the US: Colonial Times to 1957*, GPO, Washington, DC, 1961.

US Bureau of the Census, 'The relative economy of cable, electric and animal motive powers for street railways', Bulletin 55, *Eleventh Census of the United States, 1890*, GPO, 1892.

US Bureau of the Census, *Thirteenth Census of the United States, 1910*, GPO, Washington, DC, 1911.

US Congress, *Report of the Country Life Commission*, 60th Cong., 2nd Sess. 1909, Senate Doc. 705.

US Department of Agriculture, Office of the Secretary, *Economic Needs of Farm Women*, Report No. 106, GPO, Washington, DC, 1915.

US Department of Agriculture, Office of the Secretary, *Educational Needs of Farm Women*, Report 105, GPO, Washington, DC, 1915.

US Department of Agriculture, *The Farm Woman's Problems*, Circular No. 148, GPO, Washington DC, 1920.

US Department of Agriculture, Office of the Secretary, *Social and Labor Needs of Farm Women*, Report No. 103, GPO, Washington DC, 1915.

US Department of Agriculture, *A History of Agricultural Education in the US, 1785–1925*, Miscellaneous Publication No. 36, GPO., Washington, DC, 1929.

US Department of Agriculture, *What Tractors and Horses Do on Corn Belt Farms*, Farmers Bulletin No. 1295, GPO, Washington, DC, 1923.

US Department of the Interior, Bureau of Education, *Consolidation of Rural Schools and Transportation of Pupils at the Public Expense*, Bulletin No. 30, GPO, Washington, DC, 1914.

US Department of the Interior, Bureau of Education, *Rural Schools Supervision*, Bulletin No. 48, GPO, Washington, DC, 1917.

US Department of Transportation, Federal Highway Administration, *America's Highways, 1776–1976: a History of the Federal Aid Program*, GPO, Washington DC, 1976.

US Senate, Commission on Industrial Relations, *Final Report and Testimony*, 64 Cong. 1st Sess. (1915), Senate Doc. No. 415, VII, 7626–38.

Books

Adams, Henry, *The Education of Henry Adams*, Modern Library Edition, Random House, New York, 1931.

Addams, Jane, *The Spirit of Youth and the City Streets*, Macmillan, New York, 1909.

Allen, Frederick Lewis, *The Big Change: America Transforms Itself: 1900–1950*, Harper & Brothers, New York, 1952.

American Association of State Highway Officials, *AASHO: the First Fifty Years, 1914–1964*, AASHO, Washington DC, 1964.

Arnold, Horace L. and Faurote, Fay L., *Ford Methods and the Ford Shops*, Engineering Magazine Co., New York, 1916.

BIBLIOGRAPHY

Atherton, Lewis, *Main Street on the Middle Border*, Quadrangle Books, Chicago, 1966.

Automobile Manufacturers Association, *Automobiles of America*, Wayne State University Press, Detroit, 1970.

Ayres, Leonard P., *The Automobile Industry and its Future*, Cleveland Trust Company, Cleveland, 1921.

Badger, R. Reid., *The Great American Fair: the World's Columbian Exposition and American Culture*, Nelson Hall, Chicago, 1979.

Bailey, Liberty H. (ed.), *A Cyclopaedia of American Agriculture*, Macmillan, New York, 1907.

Bancroft, Hubert H., *The Book of the Fair*, Bancroft, Chicago, 1893.

Bardou, Jean-Pierre, Chanaron, Jean-Jacques, Fridenson, Patrick and Laux, James M., *The Automobile Revolution: the Impact of an Industry*, University of North Carolina Press, Chapel Hill, 1982.

Barrett, Paul, *The Automobile and Urban Transit: the Formation of Public Policy in Chicago, 1900–1930*, Temple University Press, Philadelphia, 1983.

Belasco, Warren James, *Americans on the Road: from Autocamp to Motel, 1910–1945*, MIT Press, Cambridge, Mass., 1979.

Bellamy, Edward, *Looking Backward* (ed. John L. Thomas), Belknap Press, Cambridge, Mass., 1967 (first publ. 1988).

Berger, Michael, *The Devil's Wagon in God's Country – the Automobile and Social Change in Rural America*, Archon Press, Hamden, Conn., 1979.

Berkebile, Donald H., *American Carriages, Sleighs, Sulkies and Carts*, Dover, New York, 1977.

Betts, Herbert, *New Ideals in Rural Schools*, Houghton Mifflin, Boston, 1913.

Boorstin, Daniel, *The Americans: the Democratic Experience*, Vintage Books, New York, 1974.

Bottles, Scott L., *Los Angeles and the Automobile*, University of California Press, Berkeley, 1987.

Bowers, William L., *The Country Life Movement in America 1900–1920*, National University Publications Series in American Studies, Kennikat Press, Port Washington, New York, 1974.

Boyer, Paul, *Urban Masses and Moral Order in America, 1820–1920*, Harvard University Press, Cambridge, Mass., 1978.

Braverman, Harry, *Labor and Monopoly Capital: the Degradation of Work in the Twentieth Century*, Monthly Review Press, New York, 1974.

Brownell, Blaine, *The Urban Ethos in the South, 1920–1930*, Louisiana State University Press, Baton Rouge, 1975.

Brunner, Edmund de S., *Rural Communities*, George H. Doran, New York, 1927.

Bryce, James, *The American Commonwealth*, Capricorn Edition (ed. Louis M. Hacker), G.P. Putnam, New York, 1959 (first publ. 1888).

Buder, Stanley, *Pullman: an Experiment in Industrial Order and Community Planning, 1880–1930*, Oxford University Press, New York, 1967.

BIBLIOGRAPHY

Buenker, John D., *Urban Liberalism and Progressive Reform*, Charles Scribner's Sons, New York, 1973.

Burg, David F., *Chicago's White City of 1893*, University of Kentucky Press, Lexington, 1976.

Burnham, Daniel and Bennett, Edward, *Plan of Chicago* (ed. Charles Moore), Da Capo Press, New York, 1970 (first publ. 1909).

Burr, Walter, *Rural Organizations*, Macmillan, New York, 1921.

Burr, Walter, *Small Towns: an Estimate of their Trade and Culture*, Macmillan, New York, 1929.

Callow, Alexander B., *American Urban History – an Interpretive Reader with Commentaries*, Revised Edition, Oxford University Press, New York, 1973.

Calvert, Monte A., *The Mechanical Engineer in America, 1830–1910*, Johns Hopkins Press, Baltimore, 1967.

Chandler, Alfred D., *The Visible Hand: the Managerial Revolution in American Business*, Belknap Press of Harvard University, Cambridge, Mass., 1977.

Cheape, Charles W., *Moving the Masses: Urban Public Transit in New York, Boston and Philadelphia, 1880–1912*, Harvard University Press, Cambridge, Mass., 1980.

Clymer, Floyd, *Treasury of Early American Automobiles, 1877–1925*, Bonanza Books, New York, 1950.

Cohn, David L., *Combustion on Wheels: an Informal History of the Automobile*, Houghton Mifflin, Boston, 1944.

Colvin, Fred, *Sixty Years with Men and Machines*, McGraw-Hill, New York, 1947.

Crunden, Robert M., *Ministers of Reform: the Progressives' Achievement in American Civilization, 1889–1920*, Basic Books, New York, 1982.

Cubberly, Ellwood P., *Rural Life and Education: a Study of the Rural School Problem as a Phase of the Rural Life Problem*, Houghton Mifflin, Boston, 1914.

Curti, Merle, (ed.), *Probing Our Past*, Harper, New York, 1955.

Danhom, Daniel, *'The World of Hope': Progressives and the Struggle for an Ethical Public Life*, Temple University Press, Philadelphia, 1987.

Davenport, Eugene, *Education for Efficiency*, D.C. Heath, Boston, 1909.

DeForest, Robert W. and Veiller, Lawrence, *The Tenement House Problem*, 2 vols., Macmillan, New York, 1903.

Denison, Merrill, *The Power to Go*, Doubleday, New York, 1956.

Donovan, Frank, *Wheels for a Nation*, Thomas Y. Crowell, New York, 1965.

Duboff, Richard B., *Electric Power in American Manufacturing, 1889–1958*, Arno Press, New York, 1974.

Duryea, James Frank, *America's First Automobile: the First Complete Account of Mr J. Frank Duryea of How He Developed the First American Automobile 1892–1893*, D.M. Macauley, Springfield, Mass., 1942.

Earle, Horatio S., *The Autobiography of 'By-Gum' Earle*, State Review Publishing Co., Lansing, Mich., 1929.

Eastman, Edward R., *These Changing Times: a Story of Farm Progress during the First Quarter of the Twentieth Century*, Macmillan, New York, 1927.

Edson, Milan C., *Solaris Farm*, Arno Press, New York, 1971 (first publ. 1900).

Edward, Richard, Gordon, David M. and Reich, Michael, *Segmented Work, Divided Workers: the Historical Transformation of Labor in the United States*, Cambridge University Press, Cambridge, 1982.

Epstein, Ralph C., *The Automobile Industry: its Economic and Commercial Development*, A.W. Shaw, Chicago, 1928.

Erskine, Albert R., *The History of the Studebaker Corporation*, Studebaker, South Bend, Ind., 1924.

Ewen, Stuart B., *Captains of Consciousness: Advertising and the Social Roots of the Consumer Culture*, McGraw-Hill, New York, 1976.

Fass, Paula S. *The Damned and the Beautiful: American Youth in the 1920s*, Oxford University Press, New York, 1977.

Feinstein, Otto (ed.), *Ethnic Groups in the City: Culture, Institutions and Power*, D.C. Heath, Lexington, Mass., 1971.

Fite, Gilbert, *Cotton Fields No More: Southern Agriculture 1865–1980*, University Press of Kentucky, Lexington, 1984.

Fite, Gilbert, *The Farmer's Frontier, 1865–1900*, Holt, Rinehart & Winston, New York, 1966.

Flink, James J., *America Adopts the Automobile, 1890–1914*, MIT Press, Cambridge, Mass., 1970.

Flink, James J., *The Car Culture*, MIT Press, Cambridge, Mass., 1975.

Fogelson, Robert M. *The Fragmented Metropolis Los Angeles: 1850–1930*, Harvard University Press, Cambridge, Mass., 1967.

Fogelsong, Richard, *Planning the Capitalist City: the Colonial Era to the 1920s*, Princeton University Press, Princeton, NJ, 1986.

Ford, Henry (with Samuel Crowther), *My Life and Work*, Heinemann, London, 1922.

Ford, Henry (with Samuel Crowther), *Moving Forward*, Heinemann, London, 1931.

Ford Motor Co., *Helpful Hints and Advice to Employees to Help them Grasp the Opportunities which are Presented to them by the Ford Profit Share Plan*, Ford Motor Co., Detroit, 1915.

Foster, Mark S., *From Streetcar to Superhighway, American City Planners and Urban Transportation, 1900–1940*, Temple University Press, Philadelphia, 1981.

Fox, Richard U. and Jackson T.J. (eds), *The Culture of Consumption*, Pantheon, New York, 1983.

Fuller, Wayne E., *RFD.: the Changing Face of Rural America*, Indiana University Press, Bloomington, 1964.

Gartman, David, *Auto Slavery: the Labor Process in the American Automobile Industry, 1897–1950*, Rutgers University Press, New Brunswick, NJ, 1896.

Ghent, William J., *Our Benevolent Feudalism*, Macmillan, New York, 1902.

Giedion, Siegfried, *Space, Time and Architecture: the Growth of a New Tradition*, Harvard University Press, Cambridge, Mass., 1949.

Gillette, John M., *Rural Sociology*, Macmillan, New York, 1923.

Ginger, Ray, *Age of Excess: the United States from 1877 to 1914*, Macmillan, New York, 1965.

Goldman, Eric F., *Rendezvous with Destiny: a History of Modern American Reform*, Vintage Books, New York, 1977.

Goodwyn, Lawrence, *The Populist Moment – a Short History of the Agrarian Revolt in America*, Oxford University Press, Oxford, 1978.

Graham, George Adams, *Special Assessments in Detroit*, University of Illinois Studies in the Social Sciences, XVII, Sept.–Dec. 1929, Nos 3 and 4, University of Illinois, Urbana, 1929.

Greenleaf, William, *Monopoly on Wheels, Henry Ford and the Selden Patent Case*, Wayne State University Press, Detroit, 1961.

Groves, Grant, *The Rural Mind and Social Welfare*, University of Chicago Press, Chicago, 1922.

Gustin, Lawrence R., *Billy Durant: Creator of General Motors*. William Eerdmans, Grand Rapids, Mich., 1973.

Haber, Samuel, *Efficiency and Uplift: Scientific Management in the Progressive Era*, Chicago University Press, Chicago, 1964.

Hahn, Steven, *The Roots of Southern Populism: Yeoman Farmers and the Transformation of the Georgia Upcountry 1850–1890*, Oxford University Press, New York, 1983.

Hammond, John W., *Men and Volts, The Story of General Electric*, J.P. Lippincott, Philadelphia, 1941.

Handy, Moses P., *The Official Directory of the World's Columbian Exposition*, W.B. Conkey, Chicago, 1893.

Handy, Moses P., *World's Columbian Exposition Official Catalogue*, W.B. Conkey, Chicago, 1893.

Hartz, Louis, *The Liberal Tradition in America*, Harcourt Brace Jovanovich, New York, 1955.

Harvey, David, *The Urbanization of Capital*, Studies in the History and Theory of Capitalist Urbanization 2, Basil Blackwell, Oxford, 1985.

Havens, A. Eugene *et al.*, (eds), *Studies in the Transformation of US Agriculture*, Westview Press, Boulder, Colo., 1986.

Haynes, George E., *Negro Newcomers in Detroit, Michigan: a Challenge to Christian Statesmanship, A Preliminary Survey* (reprint), Arno Press, New York, 1969.

Hays, Samuel P., *Conservation and the Gospel of Efficiency, The Progressive Conservation Movement 1890–1920*, Harvard University Press, Cambridge, Mass., 1959.

Hays, Samuel P., *The Response to Industrialism, 1885–1914*, Chicago University Press, Chicago, 1959.

Henri, Florette, *Black Migration: Movement North 1900–1920: the Road from Myth to Man*, Anchor Books, Doubleday, Garden City, NY, 1976.

Herschberg, Theodore (ed.), *Work, Space, Family and Group Experience in the Nineteenth Century*, Oxford University Press, New York, 1981.

Hertzler, Arthhur E., *The Horse and Buggy Doctor*, Harper & Brothers, New York, 1938.

Hicks, John D., *The Populist Revolt: a History of the Farmers' Alliance and the People's Party*, University of Minnesota Press, Minneapolis, 1931.

Higham, John, *Strangers in the Land*, Rutgers University Press, Brunswick, NJ, 1955.

Higham, John and Conkin, Paul (eds), *New Directions in American Intellectual History*, Johns Hopkins Press, Baltimore, 1980.

Hindle, Brook (ed.), *America's Wooden Age*, Sleepy Hollow Restorations, Tarrytown, NY, 1975.

Hines, Thomas S., *Burnham of Chicago: Architect and Planner*, Oxford University Press, New York, 1974.

Hofstadter, Richard, *The Age of Reform: from Bryan to F.D.R.*, Vintage Books, New York, 1955.

Holli, Melvin, *Reform in Detroit*, Oxford University Press, New York, 1969.

Holt, W. Stull, *The Bureau of Public Records: its History, Activities and Organizations*, Service Monographs of the US Government No. 26, Institute for Governmental Research, Brookings Institution, Johns Hopkins Press, Baltimore, 1923.

Hounshell, David A., *From the American System to Mass Production*, John Hopkins University Press, Baltimore, 1984.

Howard, Robert W., *The Horse in America*, Pollett, Chicago, 1965.

Howe, Frederic, *The City: the Hope of Democracy*, University of Washington Press, Seattle, 1967 (first publ. 1907).

Howells, William Dean, *The Altrurian Romances*, Indiana University Press, Bloomington, 1968.

Hubbard, Elbert, *The Story of the Steinways*, Roycrofters, East Aurora, NY, 1926.

Hulbert, Archer B. (ed.), *The Future of Road Making in America: a Symposium*, Arthur H. Clark, Cleveland, 1905.

Huxley, Aldous, *Brave New World*, Chatto, London, 1932.

Jackson, Anthony, *A Place Called Home: a History of Low-Cost Housing in Manhattan*, MIT Press, Cambridge, Mass., 1976.

Jackson, Kenneth T., *Crabgrass Frontier: the Suburbanization of the United States*, Oxford University Press, Oxford, 1985.

Jackson, Kenneth T. and Schultz, Stanley (eds), *Cities in American History*, Alfred A. Knopf, New York, 1972.

Jackson Lears, T.J., *No Place of Grace: Anti-Modernism and the Transformation of American Culture, 1880–1920*, Pantheon, New York, 1981.

Jardim, Anne, *The First Henry Ford: a Study in Personality and Business Leadership*, MIT Press, Cambridge, Mass., 1970.

Johnson, Paul, *A History of the Modern World from 1917 to the 1980s*, Weidenfeld & Nicolson, London, 1983.

Johnson, Tom, *My Story*, B. Huebsch, Cleveland, 1911.

Joint Committee on Ceremonies, *The Dedicatory and Opening Ceremonies of the World's Columbian Exposition: a Memorial Volume*, Stone, Kastler & Painter, Chicago, 1893.

Kasson, John F., *Amusing the Millions, Coney Island at the Turn of the Century*, McGraw-Hill, New York, 1978.

BIBLIOGRAPHY

Kasson, John F., *Civilising the Machine: Technology and Republican Values in America 1776–1900*, Arno Press, New York, 1977.

Katz, Harold, *The Decline of Competition in the Automobile Industry, 1920–1940*, Arno Press, New York, 1977.

Katznelson, Ira, *City Trenches: Urban Politics and the Patterning of Class in the United States*, Pantheon, New York, 1981.

Kettering, Charles and Orth, Allen, *The New Necessity*, Williams & Wilkins, Baltimore, 1932.

Kolb, John H. and Brunner, Edmund De S., *A Study of Rural Society: its Organization and Changes*, Houghton Mifflin, Boston, 1935.

Kolko, Gabriel, *The Triumph of Conservatism; a Re-interpretation of American History, 1900–1916*, Quadrangle, Chicago, 1967.

Korman, Gerd, *Industrialization, Immigration and Americanizers: the View from Milwaukee 1866–1921*, State Historical Society of Wisconsin, Madison, 1967.

Kuznets, Simon, *National Income: a Summary of Findings*, National Bureau of Economic Research Inc., New York, 1946.

Laux, James M., *In First Gear: the French Automobile Industry to 1914*, McGill-Queens University Press, Montreal, 1976.

Layton, Edwin T., *Revolt of the Engineers: Social Responsibility and the American Engineering Profession*, The Press of Case Western Reserve University, Cleveland, 1971.

Le Corbusier, *The City of Tomorrow* (trans. by Frederick Etchells), MIT Press, Cambridge, Mass., 1971.

Leonard, Jonathan, *The Tragedy of Henry Ford*, Putnam's, New York, 1932.

Levine, David, *Internal Combustion: the Races in Detroit 1915–1926*, Greenwood Press, Westport, Conn., 1976.

Lewchuk, Wayne, *American Technology and the British Vehicle Industry*, Cambridge University Press, Cambridge, 1987.

Lewis, David L., *The Public Image of Henry Ford*, Wayne State University Press, Detroit, 1976.

Lincoln Highway Association, *The Lincoln Highway: the Story of a Crusade that Made Transportation History*, Dodd, Mead & Co., New York, 1935.

Lindsey, Almont, *The Pullman Strike: the Story of a Unique Experiment and a Great Labor Upheaval*, University of Chicago Press, Chicago, 1943.

Lubove, Roy, *The Progressives and the Slums*, University of Pittsburgh Press, Pittsburgh, 1962.

Lynd, Robert S. and Helen M., *Middletown: a Study in Modern American Culture*, Harcourt Brace, New York, 1929.

Macdonald, Austin F., *Federal Aid: a Study of the American Subsidy System*, Thomas Y. Crowell, New York, 1928.

McDonald, Forrest, *Let there Be Light. The Electric Utility Industry in Wisconsin 1881–1955*, American Historical Research Center, Madison, Wisconsin, 1957.

McKelvey, Blake, *American Urbanization – a Comparative History*, Scott Foreman & Co., Glen View, Ill., 1973.

McKenzie, Roderick D., *The Metropolitan Community*, McGraw-Hill, New York, 1933.

McLaughlin, Virginia Yans, *Family and Community: Italian Immigrants in Buffalo, 1880–1930*, Cornell University Press, Ithaca, NY, 1977.

McShane, Clay, *Technology and Reform: Street Railways and the Growth of Milwaukee, 1887–1900*, University of Wisconsin Press, Madison, 1974.

Mandelbaum, Seymour, *Boss Tweed's New York*, Wiley, New York, 1965.

Marquis, Dean S. S., *Henry Ford: an Interpretation*, Little, Brown, Boston, 1923.

Marx, Leo, *The Machine in the Garden: Technology and the Pastoral Ideal*, Oxford University Press, New York, 1964.

Maxim, Hiram P., *Horseless Carriage Days*, Harper Brothers, New York, 1937.

May, George S., *A Most Unique Machine – the Michigan Origins of the American Automobile Industry*, Eerdmans, Grand Rapids, Mich., 1975.

May, George S., *R. E. Olds: Auto Industry Pioneer*, Eerdmans, Grand Rapids, Mich., 1977.

May, George W., *Charles E. Duryea: Automaker*, Edward Brothers, Ann Arbor, Mich., 1973.

May, Henry F., *The End of American Innocence: a Study of the First Years of Our Own Time, 1912–1917*, Oxford University Press, New York, 1979.

Mayers, Lewis and Harrison, Leonard V., *The Distribution of Physicians in the United States*, General Education Board, New York, 1924.

Melosi, Martin (ed.), *Pollution and Reform in American Cities 1870–1930*, University of Texas Press, Austin, 1980.

Meyer, Stephen, *The Five Dollar Day: Labor, Management and Social Control in the Ford Company, 1908–1921*, State University of New York Press, Albany, 1981.

Miller, Zane L., *Boss Cos's Cincinnatti*, Oxford University Press, New York, 1968.

Moline, Norman T., *Mobility and the Small Town, 1900–1930 – Transportation Change in Oregon, Illinois*, University of Chicago Press, Chicago, 1971.

Montgomery, David, *Workers' Control in America*, Cambridge University Press, Cambridge, 1979.

Moore, Harry H., *American Medicine and the People's Health: an Outline with Statistical Data on the Organization of Medicine in the United States with Special Reference to the Adjustment of the Medical Services to Social and Economic Change*, Appleton, New York, 1927.

Morris, Lloyd, *Incredible New York: High Life and Low Life of the Last One Hundred Years*, Random House, New York, 1951.

Mowry, George E., *The Era of Theodore Roosevelt and the Birth of Modern America 1900–1912*, Harper & Row, New York, 1958.

Murray, Robert, *Red Scare: a Study in National Hysteria 1919– 1920*, University of Minnesota, Minneapolis, 1955.

Nelson, Daniel, *Managers and Workers: the Origins of the New Factory System in the United States 1880–1920*, University of Wisconsin Press, Madison, 1975.

Nevins, Allan and Hill, Frank, *Ford: Expansion and Challenge*, Scribner's, New York, 1957.

Nevins, Allan and Hill, Frank, *Ford: the Times, the Man and the Company*, Scribner's, New York, 1954.

Noble, David F., *America by Design: Science, Technology and the Rise of Corporate Capitalism*, Oxford University Press, New York, 1979.

Norwood, Edwin P., *Ford Men and Methods*, Doubleday, Garden City, NY, 1931.

Nye, David E., *Henry Ford – Ignorant Idealist*, National University Publications Series in American Studies, Kennikat Press, Port Washington, NY, 1979.

O'Geran, Graeme, *A History of Detroit's Street Railways*, Conover Press, Detroit, 1931.

Palmer, Bruce, *Man over Money: Southern Populist Critique of American Capitalism*, University of North Carolina Press, Chapel Hill, 1980.

Parsons, Stanley B., *The Populist Context: Rural versus Urban Power on a Great Plains Frontier*, Greenwood Press, Westport, Conn., 1973.

Passer, Harold C., *The Electrical Manufacturers 1875–1900: a Study in Competition Entrepreneurship, Technical Change and Economic Growth*, Harvard University Press, Cambridge, Mass., 1953.

Patten, Simon N., *The New Basis of Civilization*, John Harvard Library, Cambridge, Mass., 1968 (first publ. 1907).

Perot, Benoit, *Panhard, La Doyenne D'Avant Garde*, Editions Practiques Automobiles, Paris, 1979.

Philpott, Thomas L., *The Slum and the Ghetto: Neighborhood Deterioration and Middle Class Reform, Chicago, 1880–1930*, Oxford University Press, New York, 1978.

Potter, David, *People of Plenty: Economic Abundance and the American Character*, University of Chicago Press, Chicago, 1954.

Pound, Arthur, *The Turning Wheel*, Doubleday Doran, Garden City, NY, 1934.

Presbrey, Frank, *The History and Development of Advertising*, Doubleday, Garden City, NY, 1929.

Preston, Howard L., *Automobile Age Atlanta: the Making of a Southern Metropolis, 1900–1935*, University of Georgia Press, Athens, Ga., 1979.

Rae, John B., *American Automobile Manufacturers: the First Forty Years*, Chilton Company, Philadelphia, 1959.

Rae, John B. (ed.), *Henry Ford*, Prentice Hall, Englewood Cliffs, NJ, 1969.

Rae, John B., *The Road and the Car in American Life*, MIT Press, Cambridge, Mass., 1971.

Riis, Jacob, *How the Other Half Lives* (reprint), Dover, New York, 1971.

Ritterhouse, Jack D., *American Horse Drawn Vehicles*, Floyd Clymer Press, Los Angeles, 1948.

Roberts, Peter, *English for Coming Americans*, YMCA Press, New York, 1909.

Rogers, Frank, *A History of the Michigan State Highway Department, 1905–1933*, Frank DeKleine, Lansing, Mich., 1933.

Rosenburg, Nathan (ed.), *The American System of Manufactures*, University of Edinburgh Press, Edinburgh, 1969.

Rothschild, Emma, *Paradise Lost: the Decline of the Auto Industrial Age*, Vintage Books, New York, 1973.

Saloutos, Theodore and Hicks, John D., *Agricultural Discontent in the Middle West, 1900–1939*, University of Wisconsin Press, Madison, 1957.

Sanderson, Dwight, *The Farmer and His Community*, Harcourt, Brace & Com., New York, 1922.

Schmitt, Peter, *Back to Nature: Arcadian Myth in America*, Oxford University Press, New York, 1969.

Schram, Jack E. and Henning, William H., *Detroit's Street Railways: Volume I: City Lines, 1863–1923*, Central Electric Railfans Association, Chicago, 1978.

Schwantes, Carlos A., *Coxey's Army: an American Odyssey*, University of Nebraska Press, Lincoln, 1985.

Sennett, Richard, *Families against the City: Middle Class Homes of Industrial Chicago 1872–1910*, Harvard University Press, Cambridge, Mass., 1970.

Shannon, Fred A., *The Farmer's Last Frontier: Agriculture 1860–1897*, Farrar & Rinehart, New York, 1945.

Shaw, Barton C., *The Wool Hat Boys: Georgia's Populist Party*, Louisiana State University Press, Baton Rouge, 1984.

Sheldon, W. D. B., *Populism in the Old Dominion: Virginia Farm Politics, 1885–1900*, Peter Smith, Gloucester, Mass., 1967.

Shideler, James H., *Farm Crisis, 1919–1923*, University of California Press, Berkeley, Calif., 1957.

Siegfried, André, *America Comes of Age*, Harcourt Brace, New York, 1927.

Sims, Newell, *A Hoosier Village*, Columbia University Press, New York, 1912.

Slichter, Samuel, *The Turnover of Factory Labor*, Appleton, New York, 1919.

Sloan, Alfred P., *My Years with General Motors*, Pan, London, 1967 (1st edn, 1963).

Smith, Merritt Roe, *Harpers Ferry Armory and the New Technology*, Cornell University Press, Ithaca, NY, 1977.

Smith, Robert, *A Social History of the Bicycle – its Early Life and Times in America*, American Heritage Press, New York, 1972.

Sorensen, Charles (with Williamson, Samuel T.), *My Forty Years with Ford*, W. W. Norton, New York, 1956.

Spear, Allan H., *Black Chicago: the Making of a Negro Ghetto*, University of Chicago Press, Chicago, 1967.

Steinbeck, John, *The Grapes of Wrath*, Heinemann, London, 1975 (first publ. 1939).

Steinway, Theodore E., *People and Pianos: a Century of Service to Music*, Steinway & Sons, New York, 1953.

Stine, Jeffery K., *Nelson P. Lewis and the City Efficient: The Municipal Engineer in City Planning During the Progressive Era* (Essays in Public Works History, April 1981, No. 11), Public Works Historical Association, Chicago, 1981.

Strong, Josiah, *Our Country: its Possible Future and Present Crisis*, Baker & Taylor, New York, 1885.

Sullivan, Louis, *The Autobiography of an Idea*, Press of the American Institute of Architects, New York, 1926.

Sullivan, Louis, *Kindergarten Chats and Other Writings*, Nittenborn, Schultz, New York, 1947.

Sward, Keith, *The Legend of Henry Ford*, Rinehart, New York, 1948.

Tarr, Joel A., *Transportation Innovation and Changing Spatial Patterns in Pittsburgh, 1850–1934* (Essays in Public Works History, No. 6), Public Works History Society, Chicago, 1978.

Taylor, Carl C., *Rural Sociology in its Economic, Historical and Psychological Aspects* (revised edition), Harper Brothers, New York, 1933.

Thernstrom, Stephen, *Poverty and Progress: Social Mobility in a Nineteenth Century City*, Harvard University Press, Cambridge, Mass., 1964.

Thompson, J. A., *Progressivism*, British Association for American Studies Pamphlet Series no. 2, Peterson, South Shields, 1979.

Trachtenberg, Alan, *The Incorporation of America: Culture and Society in the Gilded Age*, Hill & Wang, New York, 1982.

Turner, Frederick Jackson, *The Significance of the Frontier in American History*, edited by Harold P. Simonson, Ungar Publishing, New York, 1963 (first publ. 1893).

Tuttle, Martin, *Automotive Statistics*, Motor List Company, Des Moines, Iowa, 1921.

Veblen, Thorstein, *The Theory of the Leisure Class: An Economic Study of Institutions*, Unwin, London, 1970 (first publ. 1899).

Ward, David, *Cities and Immigrants: a Geography of Change in Nineteenth Century America*, Oxford University Press, New York, 1971.

Warner, Sam B., *The Private City: Philapdelphia in Three Stages of its Growth*, University of Pennsylvania Press, Philadelphia, 1968.

Warner, Sam B., *Streetcar Suburbs: the Process of Growth in Boston, 1870–1900*, Harvard University Press, Cambridge, Mass., 1962.

Weber, Adna F., *The Growth of Cities in the Nineteenth Century*, Cornell University Press, Ithaca, NY, 1967 (first publ. 1899).

Weinstein, James, *The Corporate Ideal in the Liberal State 1900–1918*, Beacon Press, Boston, 1968.

Wiebe, Robert, *Businessmen and Reform*, Harvard University Press, Cambridge, Mass., 1962.

Wiebe, Robert H., *The Search for Order, 1877–1920*, American Century Series, Hill & Wang, New York, 1967.

Wik, Reynold, *Henry Ford and Grass Roots America*, University of Michigan Press, Ann Arbor, 1972.

Wilcox, Delos E., *Municipal Franchises: a Description of the Terms and Conditions upon which Private Companies Enjoy Special Privileges in the Streets of American Cities*, University of Chicago Press, Chicago, 1911.

Williams, James M., *The Expansion of Rural Life: the Social Psychology of Rural Development*, F.S. Crofts & Co., New York, 1931.

Williams, Lee E. and Williams, Lee E. II, *Anatomy of Four Race Riots: Racial Conflict in Knoxville, Elaine (Arkansas), Tulsa and Chicago 1919–1921*, University & College Press of Mississipi, Hattiesberg, Miss., 1972.

Wilson, Warren H., *The Evolution of the Country Community*, Pilgrim Press, Boston, 1923.

Winner, Langdon, *Autonomous Technology: Technics – Out-of-Control as a Theme In Political Thought*, MIT Press, Cambridge, Mass. (1977).

World's Columbian Exposition, Joint Committee on Ceremonies, *The Dedications and Opening Ceremonies of the World's Columbian Exposition: A Memorial Volume*. Stone, Kastler and Painter, Chicago, 1893.

Wright, Gwendolyn, *Moralism and the Model Home, Domestic Architecture and the Cultural Conflict in Chicago 1873–1973*, University of Chicago Press, Chicago, 1980.

Youngquist, W. G. and Fleischer, H. O., *Wood in American Life: 1776–2076*, Forest Products Research, Madison, Wis., 1977.

Zunz, Olivier, *The Changing Face of Inequality: Urbanization, Industrial Development and Immigrants in Detroit, 1880–1920*, University of Chicago Press, Chicago, 1982.

Secondary articles*

Barrett, Paul, 'Public policy and private choice: mass transit and the automobile in Chicago between the wars', *Business History Review*, XLIX, Winter 1975, pp. 473–97.

Boas, Charles W. 'Locational patterns of American automobile assembly plants, 1895–1959', *Economic Geography*, XXXVII, July 1961, pp. 218–30.

Brownell, Blaine, 'A symbol of modernity: attitudes towards the automobile in Southern cities in the 1920s', *American Quarterly*, XXIV, March 1972, pp. 20–44.

Burnham, John C., 'The Gasoline Tax and the Automobile Revolution', *Mississippi Valley Historical Review*, XLVIII, December 1961, pp. 435–59.

Corbin Sies, Mary, 'The city transformed: nature, technology and the suburban ideal, 1877–1917', *Journal of Urban History*, XIV, November 1987, pp. 81–111.

Davis, Donald F., 'The price of conspicuous consumption: the Detroit elite and the automobile industry 1900–1930', *Journal of Social History*, XVI, Fall 1982, pp. 21–46.

Duryea, M. J., 'America's first automobile controversy', *Antique Automobile*, December, 1953, pp. 25–48.

Franks, Carl D., 'Marker to first mile of concrete road', *Michigan History*, XLIII, March 1959, 99. pp. 109–14.

Heilbron, J. L. and Kevles, D. J., 'Science and technology in US textbooks: what's there – and what ought to be there', *Reviews in American History*, XVI, June 1988, pp. 173–85.

Interrante, Joseph, 'The road to autopia: the automobile and the spatial transmission of American culture', *Michigan Quarterly Review*, (double issue) XIX–XX, Fall/Winter 1980–81, pp. 502–17.

Kaplan, Stanley, 'Social engineers as saviours: effects of World War I on some American liberals', *Journal of the History of Ideas*, XVII, June 1956, pp. 347–69.

Kennedy, Charles E., 'Commuter services in the Boston area', *Business History Review*, XXXVI, Summer 1962, pp. 153–70.

BIBLIOGRAPHY

Leloudis, James L., II 'School reform in the New South: the Woman's Association for the Betterment of Public Schoolhouses in North Carolina, 1902–1919', *Journal of American History*, LXIX, March 1983, pp. 886–909.

McCormick, Richard L., 'The discovery that business corrupts politics: a re-appraisal of the origins of Progressivism', *American Historical Review*, LXXXVI, April 1981, pp. 247–74.

Madison, James H., 'Reformers and the rural church, 1900–1950', *Journal of American History*, LXXIII, December 1986, pp. 645–68.

Mason, Philip P., 'Horatio S. Earle and the Good Roads Movement in Michigan', *Papers of the Michigan Academy of Science, Arts and Letters*, XLIII, 1958, pp. 269–79.

May, George S., 'The Thanksgiving Day Race of 1895', *Chicago History*, XI, Fall 1982, pp. 175–183.

May, Martha, 'The historical problem of the family wage: the Ford Motor Company and the Five Dollar Day', *Feminist Studies*, VIII, Summer 1982, pp. 401–19.

Meyer, Stephen, 'Adapting the immigrant to the line: Americanization in the Ford factory, 1914–1921', *Journal of Social History*, XIV, Fall 1980, pp. 67–80.

Moses, L. and Williamson, Harold F., 'The location of economic activity in cities', *American Economic Review*, LVII, May 1967, pp. 211–22.

Parsons, Stanley B., Toombs Parsons, Karen, Killalee, Walter and Borgers, Beverly, 'The role of co-operatives in the development culture of populism', *Journal of American History*, LXIX, March 1983, pp. 866–85.

Preteceille, Edmond, 'Urban planning: the contradictions of capitalist urbanization', *Antipode*, VIII, March 1976, pp. 69–76.

Rae, John B., 'Coleman duPont and his road', *Delaware History*, XVI, Spring–Summer 1975, pp. 171–83.

Rae, John B., 'The Electric Vehicle Company: a monopoly that missed', *Business History Review*, XXIX, December 1955, pp. 298–311.

Roberts, Sidney I., 'Portrait of a robber baron: Charles T. Yerkes', *Business History Review*, Autumn 1961, pp. 341–71.

Russell, J., 'The coming of the line: the Ford Highland Park plant, 1910–1914', *Radical America*, 12, May–June 1978, pp. 30–45.

Schildberger, Frederick, 'Seventy-five years of Mercedes-Benz ties with the USA', *Horseless Carriage Gazette*, September–October 1964.

Schulz, Stanley and McShane, Clay, 'To engineer the metropolis: sewers, sanitation and city-planning in late-nineteenth century American cities', *Journal of Urban History*, LXV, September 1978, pp. 389–411.

Wachs, Martin, 'Autos, transit, and the sprawl of Los Angeles: the 1920s', *Journal of the American Planning Association*, L, Summer 1984, pp. 297–310.

Wilson, Leonard S., 'Functional areas of Detroit, 1890–1933, *Papers of the Michigan Academy of Science, Arts and Letters*, XXII, 1939, pp. 397–409.

Wise, David O. and Dupree, Marguerite, 'The choice of the automobile for urban passenger transportation: Baltimore in the 1920s', *South Atlantic Urban Studies*, II, 1978, pp. 153–79.

* References to contemporary periodical literature are provided in the footnotes.

Unpublished material

Barrett, Paul, 'Mass transit, the automobile and public policy in Chicago, 1900–1930', unpublished PhD, University of Illinois, Chicago, 1976.

Chavis, John M. T., 'James Couzens, Mayor of Detroit, 1919–1922', unpublished PhD, Michigan State University, 1970.

Edsforth, Ronald W., 'A second industrial revolution: the transformation of class, culture and society in twentieth century Flint', unpublished PhD, Michigan State University, 1982.

Hounshell, David A., 'From the American system to mass production: the development of manufacturing technology in the United States, 1850–1920', unpublished PhD, University of Delaware, 1978.

Huddleston, John D., 'Good Roads for Texas: a history of the Texas Highway Department, 1917–1947', unpublished PhD, Texas A. & M. University, 1981.

McShane, Clay, 'American cities and the coming of the automobile, 1870–1910', – unpublished PhD, University of Wisconsin, Madison, 1975.

Peters, Kenneth E., 'The Good Roads Movement and the Michigan State Highway Department, 1905–1917', unpublished PhD, University of Michigan, 1972.

Seely, Bruce E., 'Highway engineers as policy makers: the Bureau of Public Roads, 1893–1944', 2 vols., unpublished PhD, University of Delaware, 1982.

Ticknor, Thomas J., 'Motor City: the impact of the automobile industry upon Detroit 1900–1975', unpublished PhD, University of Michigan, 1978.

Index

INDEX

INDEX

INDEX